To Martin
lots & lots love
Mum. xxx
July 2001

REPRESENTATIONS OF AUSCHWITZ

This catalogue and the exhibition it accompanies were produced in the framework of the activities of 'Civil Society and Social Change in Europe After Auschwitz', a Tempus Joint European Project (03621) founded by the Commission of the European Union, Brussels. This three–year collaborative project (1992–95) focuses on the significance of ethnicity and genocide in twentieth–century European history and culture, and how they are understood and represented today.

The financial support of the following institutions
in contributing to special costs associated with the exhibition
is gratefully acknowledged

Alfried Krupp von Bohlen und Halbach Foundation, Essen
Auswärtiges Amt, Bonn
British Embassy, Warsaw
Österreichisches Generalkonsulat, Krakau
Stifterverband für die Deutsche Wissenschaft, Essen

A particular debt of gratitude is owned to
Dr Gerhard Sprenger, Bielefeld, and Mr Heinz Westphal, Bonn

When you drink of the water
remember the spring

REPRESENTATIONS OF

AUSCHWITZ

50 Years of Photographs, Paintings, and Graphics
50 lat w fotografii, malarstwie i grafice
50 Jahre Fotografie, Malerei und Grafik

YASMIN DOOSRY
Editor / Redakcja / Herausgeberin

Published for the Department
of European Studies
Jagiellonian University, Kraków

with the support of the Tempus Project
'Civil Society and Social Change
in Europe after Auschwitz'

Auschwitz–Birkenau State Museum
Oświęcim 1995

Published on the occasion of the exhibition 'Representations of Auschwitz: 50 Years of Photographs, Paintings, and Graphics', held at Pałac Sztuki, Kraków, 11 July–20 August 1995.

Design: Joachim Seinfeld

The exhibition is an initiative of the Tempus project 'Civil Society and Social Change in Europe after Auschwitz' funded by the Commission of the European Union, Brussels.

Participating institutions: Carl von Ossietzky University (Oldenburg), Jagellonian University (Kraków), Oxford Centre for Hebrew and Jewish Studies (Oxford), and the Auschwitz–Birkenau State Museum (Oświęcim)

Coordinators: Jonathan Webber (chairman, Oxford), Detlef Hoffmann (Oldenburg), Zdzisław Mach (Kraków), Krystyna Oleksy (Oświęcim)

Administration: Annette Winkelmann (project administrator, Oxford), Katharina Engeln (Oldenburg), Wojciech Marchwica (Kraków), Teresa Miłoń (Oświęcim)

Exhibition Committee

Concept: Detlef Hoffmann

Design: Joachim Seinfeld and exhibition team

Exhibition and research team: Yasmin Doosry, Bartek Lessaer, Ruth Levin, Stefanie Peter, Elke Preul, Bärbel Schmidt, Joachim Seinfeld, Dan Stone, Maren Ullrich, Ute Wrocklage

Translations: Yasmin Doosry, Rafael Czunikin von Krasowicki, Ruth Levin, Teresa Miłoń, Bärbel Schmidt

Administrative and editorial support: Oliver Freeman, Łucja Kapralska, Connie Webber

Unless otherwise stated, all photographs are the property of the Auschwitz–Birkenau State Museum.

ISBN 83–85047–50–6

Contents
Spis treści
Inhaltsverzeichnis

Foreword

I

'Civil Society and Social Change in Europe after Auschwitz', the Tempus project that has sponsored and organized the exhibition 'Representations of Auschwitz', is one of several hundred projects being conducted under the European Commission's Tempus Programme (Trans–European Co-operation Scheme for Higher Education). The purpose of the Tempus programme as a whole is to offer intellectual and scholarly opportunities for east European universities to attain specific objectives through collaboration with specific west European partners; Tempus itself forms part of the overall European Community assistance programme, known as the Phare programme, for the social and economic restructuring of countries in central and eastern Europe.

The 'Europe after Auschwitz' project (to refer to it by its shorter name), which has been in operation since September 1992 and will terminate in August 1995, has as its main intellectual focus the significance of genocide in recent European history and culture, and how it is remembered and represented today. The project's partners are the Oxford Centre for Hebrew and Jewish Studies/University of Oxford, the Carl von Ossietzky University in Oldenburg, and the Jagiellonian University in Cracow. Since the unquestioned symbol of genocide in Europe is Auschwitz, the Auschwitz (or Auschwitz–Birkenau) State Museum that was established in 1947 by the Polish government at the site of the former murder camp also figures formally as one of the project's four partner institutions.

'Europe after Auschwitz' is unusual in the Tempus Programme in that whereas most Tempus projects support collaborative activities in the experimental sciences, engineering, or business management, the objectives of this project are scholarly and educational in the broad sense. One of the central aims of the project is thus to support the Jagiellonian University in Cracow in its quest to consolidate its teaching and research resources in areas relevant to the project's intellectual focus. At the same time, a vital additional component of the project is the collaboration with the Auschwitz State Museum in developing its intellectual and museological resources in a way that will enable it to play a key commemorative and educational role for visitors well into the twenty–first century, even when all those who survived Auschwitz are long since dead.

Justification for the 'Europe after Auschwitz' project exists on many levels. Quite simply, however, twentieth–century European history and society cannot be properly understood without an understanding of the realities of ethnic conflict, genocide, and the Holocaust, of which Auschwitz universally remains the key European symbol. Given the recent evidence from Bosnia, a pessimistic view of the future of Europe in the twenty–first century would be that ethnic conflicts may well become more common across the continent. Just as the nationalism of the nineteenth century reflected itself in the nationalistic wars of the twentieth century, so too the rediscovery by many of their ethnic identity in our own times, even if initially relatively innocent and harmless, may well assert itself in bitter ethnic conflict in the next century. It follows that teaching and research in the fields of ethnicity and identity ought to take very seriously the genocide experience that Europe has had, which is, after all, still within living memory. Poland is a good area on which to focus such studies since most of the genocidal activities of the Nazi period took place in Poland and in neighbouring countries, and much of the documentary evidence and witnesses, as well as relics of the disappeared populations, are still to be found there.

Against this background, the 'Europe after Auschwitz' project has two principal educational objectives. At the scholarly level it aims to broaden the study of the Holocaust and place it firmly within the wider context of the ethnic conflicts and acts of genocide that have taken place in Europe in the twentieth century, and that indeed continue to this day. The key underlying emphasis has been on the symbolizing role of Auschwitz. At the popular level it aims to increase public awareness and understanding of the subject as a whole, in particular by helping to improve the exhibitions and educational programmes of the Auschwitz State Museum. Inasmuch as museums generally express (or are intended to express) the most important values of a given society, the way in which the subject is dealt with at the Auschwitz State Museum — a museum that attracts half a million visitors each year, from Poland, Germany, and the rest of Europe, the United States, Israel, and elsewhere — is clearly of great importance. The Museum is in the process now of completely restructuring its exhibitions and objectives, in the light of the new political circumstances in Poland since 1989, and seeks coherent and well–considered intellectual and scholarly collaboration in this venture.

These broad objectives of the project have been translated into more specific goals. For the Jagiellonian University, the goal has been the consolidation of teaching and research in relevant areas, including the publication of appropriate teaching texts. For the Auschwitz State Museum, the goal has been the development of intellectual and museological resources, with a view to developing its long–term role as a museum of the ethnic conflict, war, and genocide of twentieth–century Europe. For the universities of Oldenburg and Oxford, the goal has been to enable students and scholars to visit Poland so as to acquaint themselves with the subject at first hand and to build up local contacts as the basis for long–term collaboration.

In keeping with these goals, a major on–going component of project activity has been a series of staff and student exchange visits. In 1992/3, the first year of the project, 26 travel scholarships were awarded for visits by students and teaching staff to and from Poland, for long and short stays; in 1993/4 the number of exchanges increased to 34, and in 1994/5 to 74. Two intensive field–courses have also been organized to enable students to study the topography of genocide in southern Poland in the context of the pre–war cultures of ethnic minorities and to follow this with an in–depth study of Auschwitz, based on a week of guided visits, lectures, discussions, and independent work in the Auschwitz State Museum. These courses were held in summer 1993 and summer 1994, each year with the participation of 50 students and teaching staff drawn from all the participating institutions. In 1994 the field trip was preceded by an intensive two–week preparatory course, 'Jewish Culture, Polish–Jewish Relations, and the Holocaust: A Sociological Introduction to the Study of Ethnicity and the Topography of Genocide in Southern Poland'.

The project has also attempted to bring an awareness of its central themes to a wider academic audience through the organization of scholarly conferences. In the summer of 1993, a four–day conference on 'Auschwitz: Should the Relics be Conserved?' was held, in Auschwitz itself, on the moral, philosophical, and museological issues involved in the conservation of the Auschwitz site. The subject of the present publication, 'Representations of Auschwitz', is the focus also of an international conference that the project is organizing at the Jagiellonian University, in collaboration with the Historical Consciousness Research Group of the ZiF Interdisciplinary Research Centre at the University of Bielefeld in Germany, to mark the opening of the exhibition on the same theme under the project's auspices.

II

The intention of the 'Representations of Auschwitz' conference and exhibition, and indeed of this catalogue, is to foster discussion of the scope and limits of representation. Only in recent years have historians begun seriously to acknowledge that our understanding of history is mediated by how it is represented to us — that the past, in other words, is how we represent it. This is true of all representations of history, but in the case of Auschwitz the gap is particularly evident and provocative.

Neither the enormity of the atrocities committed in Auschwitz nor the suffering endured there, and certainly not the continuing consequences of the mass murder, are readily accessible to us today. What we have are only representations of what happened, not of course the reality itself. But reality can be represented in different ways. In seeing a variety of different representations, we see that any representation can only by definition be partial (no representation can convey everything) — but that with each partial glimpse, each fractured and fragmentary representation, one can better grasp both the nature of the reality of Auschwitz and the difficulty of comprehending it.

There is a large range of media through which Auschwitz is conventionally described and represented: photography, painting, sculpture, museums, monuments, survivor testimonies, films, commemorative lectures, exhibitions, prayer meetings, study tours to the Auschwitz site — even, for that matter, the writings of professional historians. The very range itself testifies to the functional impossibility of any unified presentation of what the Holocaust was, and what it might mean; but, in addition, the re–presentation of the Holocaust in any of these forms raises a series of difficulties. If the Holocaust was historically unique, how then can it be adequately described, accounted for, or understood? If it was not historically unique, but rather the convergence of a series of individual factors that in themselves were not exceptional, how can one provide a coherent representation of it, say in a work of art or in a liturgy, that at the same time adequately conveys a proper sense of the extraordinary combination of the relatively commonplace factors that brought it about? How does one really depict the total abnormality of the Holocaust, whilst at the same time revealing the banality and normality it also consisted of? How is an artist supposed to produce something that represents total destruction?

Once the question is put in this way it becomes clear that the sheer scope of possible description and representation is immense. In practice, the range of representations of Auschwitz with which people are familiar has an enormous hold over them, providing them with a definition of what they should in effect be thinking of when trying to conceptualize what Auschwitz was, what it was like, or what it might mean. After all, there *is* no other way to get hold of the past, in any case, except through some form of representation, most commonly today either textual or visual. But not all of the past can be shown at once; on the contrary, all that can usually be managed is to show some element or aspect of it at any one time. Unfortunately, the consequence of doing that is to overload the particular aspects being portrayed or represented with more symbolic meaning (and emotion) than they may historically deserve. Most people are not aware that any representation usually shows only one aspect — but how can 'Schindler's List' really be *the* Holocaust movie, or indeed *the* representation of the Holocaust?

To take a concrete example: how does one show Auschwitz in a Holocaust exhibition? Very often this is done by showing a photograph of the famous gate at the entrance to the concentration camp at Auschwitz, with the inscription 'Arbeit macht frei' — but there are problems with doing it this way. Visitors to such an exhibition would be tempted to reduce down their image of Auschwitz to just this entry–gate, thereby substituting a part for the whole. The comparative normality of the appearance of this entry–gate may in effect be shielding them from the horrific realities of what went on beyond. During my own fieldwork in the Auschwitz Museum I have in fact regularly encountered visitors who turn out to be somewhat confused just because of the widespread use of this image of the entry–gate: why, they ask, does the inscription refer to work or forced labour when everyone knows that what really was important at Auschwitz were the gas–chambers?[1]

To put it another way, the visual images that have informed our understanding of Auschwitz, such as drawings and photographs, purport to record reality, and in consequence we are persuaded to understand them as reality itself — the event as it really happened. But what we see is merely a reproduction of parts or aspects of an event, and therefore only a representation. Consider for example the photographs taken in the camp by the SS Bauleitung (the camp building site supervision staff). These pictures document the building process in a way that was perfectly standard in Germany at the period. But this very normality is itself deceptive. The ordinary nature of the photos makes Auschwitz look at first glance just like any other building site; the 'documentation' offered by these photographs in fact falsifies the extraordinary nature of what was being constructed. The same is true of the photographs of the Jews deported from Hungary arriving at Auschwitz–Birkenau: while purporting to record what was happening, they conceal the murderous consequences of the very process they document. Then, after the liberation, the wartime photographs of Auschwitz were put into entirely different contexts from that for which they had originally been intended: they were in effect instrumentalized, albeit in different ways. Photographs taken by the SS for bureaucratic purposes (such as the photographs of the arriving deportees) later came to be used in a humanitarian context, i.e. to document the atrocities committed at Auschwitz. A similar process of instrumentalization stands behind the use of photographs taken at the time of the liberation, and again for pictures taken in more recent years. What these various instrumentalizations have in common is that they all use the photographs within their own traditions and contexts, their

1. I should like here to acknowledge a personal research grant from the Economic and Social Research Council of the UK, which enabled me to conduct anthropological fieldwork in the Auschwitz Museum during the period 1992-95. I am grateful also to the Oxford Centre for Hebrew and Jewish Studies, which granted me special leave to take up two successive fellowships in Germany where I was able to continue this research interest: at the Kulturwissenschaftliches Institut, Essen, and the Zentrum für Interdisziplinäre Forschung (ZiF) of the University of Bielefeld. I am deeply indebted to Professors Detlef Hoffmann and Jörn Rüsen respectively for these latter two invitations. None of my work at the Auschwitz Museum could have been properly undertaken, however, had it not been for the unfailing courtesy and kindness of Krystyna Oleksy, deputy director of the Auschwitz Museum, and of Teresa Świebocka, director of the Museum's publications department. There are also three colleagues at the Jagiellonian University, Cracow, without whom I would never have been able to undertake this research at all, let alone lead a major Tempus project: Prof. Andrzej Paluch, who first invited me to Poland in 1987 and with whom I then made my first attempts at probing the hitherto uncharted terrain of contemporary Auschwitz studies in a Polish setting; Prof. Zdzisław Mach, whose friendship and wise counsel, as well as professional collaboration over a number of years, have been much valued; and Dr. Wojciech Marchwica, whose devotion to the project, and willingness constantly to take on new challenges far beyond the range of his more usual musicological interests, have been quite remarkable. Detlef Hoffmann, my German collaborator in the project, was from the beginning an irreplacable source of intellectual energy; during the last two years of the project, when we worked together in the same institute, his help and advice have been indispensable — always convivial and genial, a true friend and colleague. Last but not least, it is a pleasure to acknowledge the logistic support that I continuously received from Halina and Marian Pawelski, managers of the Sienkiewiczówka guest–house in Piłsudski Street in Cracow: these two good people ensured that even at the most unsocial hours I was never without a telephone or fax during my visits to Poland, and they faithfully recorded even the most complicated Tempus messages delivered in a variety of languages. I am glad that I have been very fortunate in having been able to enjoy the support and encouragement of such a broad range of fine friends and colleagues — chief amongst them my own wife Connie, who agreed to marry me in mid–project, despite it all.

own framework of understanding. There is a whole range of reasons — humanist, criminological, political, and economic — for their existence. These later photographs depict the camp site and its remaining buildings and relics in terms of a new context of meaning. The objects never only speak for themselves or about the topic they seemingly depict. 'Documentation' is never the sole agenda: documentation of what, and by whom, one must constantly ask.

Maybe there are makeshift solutions to all these epistemological and other museological difficulties; but the truth is that however well–educated about the Holocaust the public may theoretically become, there will inevitably be a gap that separates the representation of the Holocaust from the realities of the Holocaust — or, to put it more crudely, it may be that representing the Holocaust properly cannot really be done at all. 'The logic of representation', as Dan Stone has written in an article that appears in this volume, 'includes its own impossibility, [i.e.] the desire to give presence to what is not present'. I am sure he is right; but in the meantime artists as well as organizations of different kinds are still furiously producing more and more exhibitions and monuments as they struggle with the conceptual problems. I think one can now expect to see even more imaginative types of Holocaust representation coming up in the future; in Germany in particular, the range of new types of memorials being constructed — for example, to mark the sense of the loss or absence of the Jews of a specific town — is recently becoming very extended. The signs are that it is just *because* of the awareness of these difficulties of representation that the range of expression of these markers of the historical memory is steadily increasing nowadays.

The past becomes present, then, only through representation. We cannot know the past in any other way. But all too often we ignore the medium of representation and assume that it gives us immediate and unmediated access to the past. We forget that written texts impose order and structure in events that were chaotic; they even define the 'events' themselves. Photographs focus only on the visual, providing icons too one–dimensional to convey the reality properly: so–called 'documentary' photos document only part of reality. But these images are what people remember: they know the photos, and they think they know everything. In a sense, photos really do represent the past, for they are remnants of light captured from another time. But even so, they never show more than part of an event, from a certain angle or perspective: things outside the range of the viewfinder were also part of history. The difficulty of understanding Auschwitz through representations remains a major intellectual challenge of the new Europe. Auschwitz was part of European civilization — even a *product* of European civilization. Each year, hundreds of thousands of visitors visit the historical museum at Auschwitz, look at the displays and the ruins and the relics and try to put meaning into it all. Many more people seek to understand Auschwitz through books and films. Some, mistakenly, think they have understood; most think they never can, and perhaps abandon the effort. The exhibition 'Representations of Auschwitz: 50 Years of Photographs, Paintings, and Graphics' tries to tackle the subject by highlighting the diverse nature of the changing representations of Auschwitz, in drawings and photographs, over the past fifty years. By showing how certain representations of Auschwitz have come to dominate the discourse, and how representing them in different ways has affected our understanding, we hope to demonstrate how our understanding of history as a whole is shaped, and to alert people to the problems inherent in representation.

III

This exhibition was originally conceived by Detlef Hoffmann, professor of art history at the University of Oldenburg and coordinator of the project's activities there. Scholarly work on the idea, which was built in to the overall plan of the Tempus project from the beginning, started in earnest in May 1993, when Professor Hoffmann convened a meeting at the Kulturwissenschaftliches Institut in Essen, at which a series of preliminary studies were presented by three of his students — Katharina Menzel, Ines Rensinghoff, and Ute Wrocklage — and an Oxford student, Sonia Misak. But to acknowledge the origins of the concept far from represents the complex and painstaking task of actually bringing it to fruition. In 1994, Yasmin Doosry and Joachim Seinfeld spent many months sifting through materials in the archives of the Auschwitz State Museum in order to come up with a detailed prototype. Krystyna Oleksy, deputy director of the Museum, proved herself most amenable to the idea of this exhibition, which is quite different in concept from anything the Museum has been associated with before; without her commitment, her help, and her constant encouragement the whole venture would of course not have been possible. Professor Hoffmann put together an international team to take responsibility for all the detailed labours, including instructing Jagiellonian University students in various aspects of the work. An unexpectedly challenging assignment was the import of exhibition materials from Germany, past the exceptionally zealous eye of Polish customs officials — whose interest in what we were doing (or lack of interest, as some might prefer to represent it) was on occasion quite remarkable. Joachim Seinfeld took on the task of designing the exhibition, and Yasmin Doosry the similarly prodigious task of putting this multilingual catalogue together. As the reader will observe, the contributors' articles appear here in the language in which they were written but are accompanied by summaries that have been translated into the two other official languages of the project. Not the ideal way to communicate, perhaps —

but a fair representation, none the less, of the sometimes tortuous manner in which our trilingual project has had to function, i.e. without unnecessarily favouring one language or approach over the other two.

Elsewhere in this volume there appear the lists of people whose participation in the project requires and deserves formal acknowledgement — in particular, the members of the exhibition team: Stefanie Peter, Bärbel Schmidt, Ruth Levin, Dan Stone, Elke Preul, Maren Ullrich, Ute Wrocklage; and Yasmin Doosry and Joachim Seinfeld. We have indeed been fortunate in benefiting from the goodwill of these and many other people who contributed their toils; we could not have done without them. But I do wish to make special mention of Annette Winkelmann, who originally came to Oxford from Germany to be my research assistant but sportingly took on instead the administration of the whole Tempus project and all the headaches that went with looking after an international, multilingual venture with a total budget over three years of a figure not far short of 1 million German marks, with payments to be accounted for in ecu and three other currencies — and all this with a peripatetic and demanding boss. I owe her an enormous debt for her patience and constant devotion to what has been a very exhausting three years of hard work. Annette was ably assisted throughout by Katharina Engeln in Oldenburg, Wojciech Marchwica in Cracow (who, in addition to dealing with the ongoing administration of the project's activities at the Jagiellonian University, took the greatest load in organizing the opening of the exhibition, assisted by Łucja Kapralska), and Teresa Miłoń at the Auschwitz State Museum. Oliver Freeman and Connie Webber have also given most valued help and advice. Andrea Genest and Ewa Nowak, who helped to get the project off the ground in Poland in the first year of its existence, are not forgotten either — but they have since gone on to greater things.

I write this foreword on behalf of my three colleagues representing the partner institutions in the project — Detlef Hoffmann, Zdzisław Mach, and Krystyna Oleksy — whose collegiality and indeed friendship were of course indispensable for the proper functioning, and indeed existance, of the entire collaboration. I have learnt a great deal from them, both severally and jointly — and to say that there has been an exchange of ideas is an understatement. The partnership has at times been so close that I no longer remember how to attribute certain of the ideas I have acquired: they emerged through our mutual interaction. I think we all regret that our collaboration within the Tempus programme is now coming to an end. It was due in the first place to the foresight of Zdzisław Mach, who from the beginning displayed a most hospitable nature and willingly agreed to the Oldenburg–Oxford collaboration with the Jagiellonian University. During the period of the project Professor Mach rose to the deanship of the Faculty of Philosophy and became head of the new Department of European Studies; these developments bode well for the stature of Auschwitz–related studies at his university.

It is not for me but for others to judge what long–term effects the project has brought about. However, from amongst the exchanges of well over a hundred staff and students over the past three years (for periods of anything between one week and nine months) I know of quite a number of people who as a consequence of their participation in the project have redefined their doctoral programmes, decided to learn Polish, or otherwise devoted themselves to its intellectual goals. One Tempus beneficiary has even opened his own Holocaust museum. I think the project can be particularly proud of the fact that, for the first time, staff of the Auschwitz Museum were enabled to travel abroad in order to take full–length courses in Jewish studies; one such person spent a full academic year at the Oxford Centre for Hebrew and Jewish Studies. About these people, and many others happily too numerous to mention individually, I can only express the hope that the exchanges, interchanges, and interactions that they experienced during the life of the project will bring them many blessings, impossible to predict, over the coming years.

IV

And what of the future, indeed? During 1995, and the associated fiftieth anniversary commemorative events, much has been said about what happened in the past and how to understand and come to terms with it. All that, however, can be taken as a mode of thinking about what will happen to the Auschwitz memory in the future. My own view, particularly in the light of the experience I have gained after coordinating what has essentially been an interdisciplinary project, is that it will continue to diversify as time goes by. The articles in this volume, largely representing work in progress, can be taken collectively as confirming the ever–widening range of studies in Auschwitz representations, notably in the field of art history; and as such these articles provide good evidence for the future disciplinary spread of the subject.

By contrast, however, many people in Europe still think of Auschwitz and the Holocaust as belonging for example only to historians, or only to Jewish studies, but there is no good reason for this. In the United States, for instance, chairs in Holocaust Studies in some of the great universities exist in departments of religion or general education. In Poland, as elsewhere in eastern Europe, the intellectual focus regarding the Holocaust was for a long time relatively restricted, but following the collapse of Communist rule in 1989, Polish scholars and intellectuals are now seeking new ways to structure teaching and research on the Holocaust that would be sensitive also to Poland's own special historical relationship with the subject.

The opportunities for research are legion. We are all still very far from a clear understanding of precisely why the Jews and Gypsies in particular were singled out so successfully for genocide. We need to develop more of an intellectual infrastructure of questioning — for example, as regards the amoral nature of modern bureaucratic society which according to some scholars is the key social feature that made the Holocaust possible. Other scholars have stressed the need to reevaluate theologies that have rendered these victim populations the subject of contempt for centuries; and, as is now well known, the Catholic Church in particular has been spending much energy in totally reconsidering its position as regards its relations with the Jews and its position on antisemitism. In many ways these developments represent important energies directed towards a safer and happier Europe of the future.

The articles in this volume certainly point the way forward in a number of directions. As a social anthropologist, I would point to another group of topics (sadly under–researched hitherto within the context of my own discipline), which could be broadly classed as the sociology of military occupation: this would include such themes as the sociology of the family in crisis, the responses of religious and other forms of leadership, the demographic implications, the nature of public morality or natural law during a time of crisis, the nature of friendship, the sociology of food, the reorientation of public culture by the occupier. Similarly, the sociology and ethnosociology of genocide offers many important perspectives. For example, more work needs to be done on how populations were marked out at the local level for deportation prior to killing; the sociology of the concentration camp, including the sociology of labour and the urban sociology of very large labour camps, with their own leadership patterns, hierarchies, etc.; the development of folk histories to describe and account for the events; stereotypes of the murderers and of their victims; the sociology of betrayal, intercommunal love and sexual relations, acts of heroism and spiritual resistance; the sociology of fear; how and under what circumstances victim populations develop survival strategies or otherwise; the day–to–day behaviour of bystander populations; modes of representation of genocide in the local and foreign press at the time; and how genocide is subsequently treated in the cinema, in popular and scientific literature, in monuments — and in museums.

Each of these topics can of course be treated in different ways — for example, with reference to ethnic Poles, Polish Jews, to the Holocaust in general, or in a comparative perspective (with the 'ethnic cleansing' in former Yugoslavia, for example). The subject is exceptionally broad and can offer a great deal of scope for all kinds of scholarly work, in each case raising ethical and philosophical issues of great complexity.

Narrowly defined, the former concentration and murder camp at Auschwitz is now a Polish state museum and so has to be seen in museological terms, including the sociology of tourism and the aesthetics of a memorial site. But the sociology of today's Auschwitz memory also raises far wider moral, political, cultural, and educational issues of human concern — given the fact that Auschwitz is a key European symbol of war, intolerance, nationalism, and antisemitism, and represents the consequences of state policies that aimed to obliterate minorities. The subject thus leads directly into an interdisciplinary treatment of contemporary European civilization, notably as regards ethnic issues. Perhaps the most sensitive intellectual challenge today is to track down and expose the way in which Auschwitz remains surrounded by mythologies, taboos, and alternative ethnohistories. In this context the exhibition on 'Representations of Auschwitz' can best be seen as a modest contribution to the comparative sociology of knowledge.

Thus far some personal comments: doubtless an art historian, or a psychologist, would have presented the representations of Auschwitz rather differently. But perhaps there is nothing that can truly summon up our homage to all those who suffered in Auschwitz — those who died, and those who survived — men and women, children and infants, from many countries and nations, the overwhelming majority of them Jews.

Jonathan Webber
Tempus Project Coordinator
Bielefeld, April 1995

Przedmowa

Intencją wystawy 'Representations of Auschwitz: 50 lat w fotografii, malarstwie i grafice' jest uaktywnienie dyskusji na temat możliwości ekspozycyjnych. Chodzi o to, aby wyostrzyć świadomość i intelektualną wrażliwość na fakt, że przy tworzeniu się historii sam proces powstawania zostaje często przeoczony; istnieje zawsze przepaść między prezentowaniem a tym, co ma być prezentowane. Sytuacja taka dotyczy przedstawiania wszystkich historycznych zdarzeń, ale w przypadku Oświęcimia przepaść ta jest szczególnie widoczna i prowokacyjna. Z tego względu konferencję, mającą się odbyć na Uniwersytecie Jagiellońskim w Krakowie, poświęconą temu tematowi, włączono do programu badawczego grupy badawczej "Symbolika historii", Ośrodka Badań Międzywydziałowych Uniwersytetu w Bielefeld (ZiF).

Trudności *zrozumienia* Oświęcimia nie da się zatuszować. W pewnym sensie jednak trudność ta stanowi intelektualne wyzwanie dla nowej Europy. Oświęcim był częścią, a nawet *tworem* europejskiej cywilizacji. Co roku setki tysięcy ludzi odwiedzają Muzeum w Oświęcimiu. Zwiedzający oglądają wystawy, ruiny i relikty i usiłują w tym wszystkim co widzą, znaleźć jakiś sens. Znacznie więcej ludzi próbuje zrozumieć Oświęcim czytając książki i oglądając filmy. Niektórzy sądzą błędnie, że wszystko zrozumieli; większość myśli, że nigdy tych spraw nie zrozumie i z tego względu być może rezygnuje z dalszych wysiłków. Wystawa 'Representations of Auschwitz — 50 lat w fotografii, malarstwie i grafice' próbuje zgłębić tę zagadkę, eksponując zmiany uprzedmiotowienia Oświęcimia w rysunkach i fotografiach w ciągu ostatnich 50 lat. Dąży do uwydatnienia tego, co kształtuje naszą ogólną wiedzę historyczną, poprzez ukazanie, w jaki sposób określone formy reprezentacji Auschwitz zdominowały dyskurs oraz jak pewne sposoby przedstawiania wpłynęły na rozumienie tematu Auschwitz. Jednocześnie uwaga zwiedzających ma być zwrócona na problemy, które niosą z sobą różne formy przedstawiania historii. Wystawa oraz konferencja 'Representations of Auschwitz' powstały z inicjatywy projektu Tempus 'Civil Society and Social Change in Europe after Auschwitz', finansowanego przez Komisję Unii Europejskiej w Brukseli. Instytucjami partnerskimi są: Carl von Ossietzky Universität (Oldenburg), Uniwersytet Jagielloński (Kraków), Oxford Centre for Hebrew and Jewish Studies (Oxford) oraz Państwowe Muzeum Oświęcim–Brzezinka (Oświęcim).

Vorwort

Die Absicht der Ausstellung 'Representations of Auschwitz: 50 Jahre Fotografie, Malerei und Grafik' (und der angegliederten wissenschaftlichen Konferenz desselben Themas) ist es, die Diskussion über die Grenzen der Darstellung voranzutreiben. Es geht darum, das intellektuelle Bewußtsein dafür zu schärfen, daß beim Erzeugen eines Geschichtsbildes die Tatsache des Erzeugens oft übersehen wird: Es gibt immer eine Kluft zwischen dem Dargestellten und dem, was dargestellt werden soll. Dies trifft auf alle Geschichtsdarstellungen zu, aber im Falle von Auschwitz ist diese Kluft besonders offenkundig und provokativ.

Die Schwierigkeit, Auschwitz zu *verstehen*, kann nicht geleugnet werden. Aber in einem gewissen Sinne bedeutet sie auch die zentrale intellektuelle Herausforderung für das neue Europa. Auschwitz war ein Teil, ja sogar ein *Produkt* der europäischen Zivilisation. Jedes Jahr besuchen Hunderttausende das historische Museum in Auschwitz. Sie besichtigen die Ausstellungen, die Ruinen und die Relikte und versuchen, einen Sinn in all dem zu finden, was sie sehen. Noch sehr viel mehr Menschen wollen Auschwitz durch Bücher und Filme verstehen. Einige denken irrtümlich, sie hätten alles verstanden; die meisten denken, sie werden es niemals verstehen und verzichten deshalb vielleicht auf weitere Bemühungen. Die Ausstellung 'Representations of Auschwitz' versucht das Rätsel zu ergründen, indem sie die Veränderungen der Vergegenständlichung von Auschwitz in Zeichnungen und Fotografien der letzten 50 Jahre herausstellt. Indem sie vorführt, wie bestimmte Darstellungen von Auschwitz den Diskurs zu dominieren begannen und wie die unterschiedlichen Methoden sie einzusetzen, unser Verständnis von Auschwitz geprägt haben. Wir wollen deutlich machen, wodurch unser allgemeines Geschichtsverständnis geformt wird. Zugleich hoffen wir, in den Menschen Aufmerksamkeit für die Probleme zu wecken, die in den verschiedenen Formen der Darstellung enthalten sind.

Bei der Ausstellung und Konferenz 'Representations of Auschwitz' handelt es sich um eine Initiative des Tempus–Projektes 'Civil Society and Social Change in Europe after Auschwitz', die von der Kommission der Europäischen Union, Brüssel, finanziert wird. Partnerinstitutionen des Projektes sind: Carl von Ossietzky Universität (Oldenburg), Jagiellonische Universität (Krakau), Oxford Centre for Hebrew and Jewish Studies (Oxford) und das Staatliche Museum Auschwitz–Birkenau (Oświęcim).

Zdzisław Mach

Czym jest Auschwitz dla Polaków?

Pozostałości obozu koncentracyjnego Auschwitz, od chwili kiedy zostały przekształcone w muzeum państwowe, były dla Polaków istotnym symbolem skupiającym wiele wątków współczesnej polskiej kultury narodowej i organizującym społeczną świadomość przeszłości i historycznych związków z innymi narodami. W chwili obecnej, w związku z dekompozycją różnych aspektów społecznej tożsamości Polaków i przemianami kultury narodowej, symbol Auschwitz nabiera nowych znaczeń. Pięćdziesiąta rocznica wyzwolenia obozu przypadła na okres gruntownego przemyślenia roli Auschwitz we współczesnej historii i kulturze Polski.

Podobnie jak wiele innych historycznych pomników w Polsce, Auschwitz został przez władze komunistyczne przywłaszczony i przekształcony w element symbolicznej konstrukcji ideologicznej legitymizującej polityczne status quo. Państwowe Muzeum w Oświęcimiu stało się symbolem "państwowego nacjonalizmu", reprezentującym polskie męczeństwo narodowe, oficjalną interpretację historycznych relacji polsko–niemieckich i miejsce Polski w świecie. Najbardziej widocznym tego przejawem było podporządkowanie ekspozycji muzealnej politycznej wizji świata skonstruowanej według powojennych podziałów politycznych i eksponujących kryteria narodowo–państwowe kosztem innych, religijnych czy etnicznych, co stało się między innymi powodem rozmycia i przytłumienia fundamentalnej kwestii żydowskiej obecności w Auschwitz. Obecnie, w postkomunistycznej Polsce, dokonuje się reinterpretacja zarówno symbolu Auschwitz, jak i wizji świata, którą symbol ten reprezentował.

Każda reprezentacja wydarzeń historycznych jest interpretacją. Iluzją jest przekonanie, że przeszłość można przedstawić obiektywnie, bez żadnych uprzedzeń i zniekształceń. Przeszłość nie istnieje inaczej jak tylko w ludzkiej pamięci, której nośnikami są różnorakie teksty kulturowe. Każda opowieść o przeszłości, każda reprezentacja literacka czy artystyczna jest subiektywna, przynajmniej o tyle, że odzwierciedla system wartości autora, nawet jeśli stara się on być bezstronnym narratorem. Także naukowe opisanie dziejów jest ich interpretacją, choćby w tym sensie, że autor dokonuje wyboru faktów i koncentruje uwagę na procesach, które jego zdaniem są szczególnie istotne, gdyż pasują do jego wizji dziejów.

Nigdy nie można opisać jednocześnie wszystkich zdarzeń i procesów, a sam ich wybór jest już subiektywną interpretacją. Również reprezentacja przeszłości w postaci ekspozycji muzealnej jest z konieczności częściowa i subiektywna. Nie oznacza to jednak koniecznie zubożenia. Subiektywna interpretacja może być twórcza, nasycająca minione wydarzenia sensem, nakazująca faktom mówić o ideach i wartościach. Fakty, zdarzenia i procesy stają się w twórczej interpretacji symbolami organizującymi ludzkie myśli i uczucia i reprezentującymi idee składające się na obrazy świata i modele tożsamości grup społecznych. W ten sposób teraźniejszość określa przeszłość, gdyż nasza współczesna interpretacja minionych zdarzeń zdeterminowana jest w znacznej mierze współczesnymi problemami, systemami wartości, ideami i interesami. Współczesna interpretacja dziejów jest więc z jednej strony ich mistyfikacją, a z drugiej ich twórczym interpretowaniem i przekształceniem w teksty symboliczne komunikujące współcześnie ważne treści.

Dla współczesnych Polaków Auschwitz jest nasycony różnorodnymi znaczeniami. Jest ważną kartą dziejów Polski, ale równocześnie symbolem oznaczającym wiele idei: męczeństwo Polaków, ich narodową i polityczną tożsamość, stosunki łączące ich z innymi narodami. Dla wielu, mniej podatnych na nacjonalistyczną indoktrynację i bardziej otwartych, jest to też symbol męczeństwa Żydów i w ogóle ludobójstwa. Przez wiele powojennych lat Auschwitz był odwiedzany przez gości zagranicznych, wywożących stamtąd swoje własne wrażenia, którymi komunistyczne władze Polski, jak się zdaje, specjalnie się nie interesowały. Cudzoziemcy, w tym Żydzi, nie mieli też żadnej możliwości, a pewnie też aspiracji, wpływania na to, czym Muzeum było. Dla Polaków, którzy wszyscy w wieku szkolnym musieli obowiązkowo odwiedzić Auschwitz, był on jednym z wielu miejsc męczeństwa ich rodaków, którzy zginęli z rąk Niemców. Taka była ogólna wymowa Muzeum i taka jego ideologiczna i polityczna funkcja. Z punktu widzenia władz politycznych ważne było, aby Polacy, szczególnie młodzi, zaakceptowali wizję dziejów, zgodnie z którą Polska zawsze była w konflikcie z Niemcami, ze strony Niemiec przychodziły same nieszczęścia, czego kulminacyjnym momentem była druga wojna światowa. Ta oficjalna wizja historii propagowała powojenne granice państwa polskiego jako jedyne historycznie słuszne i z punktu widzenia Polaków korzystne. Podręcznikowa historia Polski kazała wierzyć, że ilekroć Polacy zaniedbywali swoje tereny zachodnie i zwracali się ku wschodowi, zawsze wynikały z tego katastrofalne skutki. Natomiast jeśli koncentrowali swoją uwagę i aktywność na zachodzie i na granicy z Niemcami, kraj ich rozkwitał. Granice państwa polskiego po drugiej wojnie światowej były z tego punktu widzenia najwłaściwsze, historycznie uzasadnione, sprawiedliwe i korzystne. Powojenne terytorium Polski było czyste etnicznie, a oficjalna ideologia głoszona przez władze komunistyczne wskazywała na jednolitość etniczną jako na wartość będącą warunkiem sukcesu historycznego. Wiązało się to z koncepcją, według której Polska Jagiellonów, wieloetniczna i daleko wysunięta na wschód, na ziemie etnicznie litewskie, ukraińskie i białoruskie, była Polską imperialną i społecznie niesprawiedliwą, a przy tym przyniosła Polsce zgubę. Naturalnie, taka wizja historii miała na celu legitymizację powojennej zmiany granic i utraty na rzecz Związku Radzieckiego ziem wschodnich, ale jej skutkiem była też negacja wartości jaką jest kulturowy i etniczny pluralizm.

Auschwitz w szczególny sposób reprezentował tę wizję historii, posługując się współczesnymi granicami terytorialnymi jako "naturalnymi" granicami Polski i operując kryterium politycznym raczej, niż etnicznym przy wyznaczaniu domen narodowych. Stąd na pierwszy plan wysunął się problem stosunków polsko–niemieckich, a kwestia żydowska została sprowadzona do stosunkowo skromnych wymiarów. Żydzi pojawiali się bowiem w ekspozycji jako obywatele poszczególnych krajów, w tym Polski, a nie jako jednolita etnicznie kategoria i jako taka skazana przez nazistów na zagładę. Problem męczeństwa Żydów zepchnięty był na dalszy plan, zgodnie z interesami władz komunistycznych, dla których ważne było ukazanie dziejowego konfliktu polsko–niemieckiego, a nie tragedii Żydów.

Polacy przeżywają obecnie kryzys tożsamości w wielu jej aspektach. Zniknął dominujący dawniej dychotomiczny podział na "władzę" i "naród", a powszechne upolitycznienie zbiorowej świadomości ustąpiło na rzecz innych, różnorodnych form przynależności, jak na przykład tożsamość regionalna, etniczna, zawodowa. Świadomość narodowa również ulega przemianom. Pytanie o to kim jesteśmy zadają sobie Polacy w związku z budową własnego, niezależnego państwa, podstaw społeczeństwa obywatelskiego, staraniami o przyjęcie do wspólnot europejskich. Tożsamość narodowa jest konstrukcją świadomościową określającą przynależność do kulturowo–politycznej wspólnoty i zarazem odrębność od innych narodów, od "obcych", których naród ma za sąsiadów i od których oddziela się symbolicznymi barierami (często mającymi bardzo widoczne fizyczne komponenty), konstruując jednocześnie wzory stosunków sąsiedzkich. Polacy żyli przez blisko pół wieku w sztucznie izolowanym kraju, którego władze budowały obraz sąsiadów, szczególnie Niemców (obraz jednoznacznie negatywny) i Rosjan (obraz całkowicie pozytywny). Niezależnie od tego w jakim stopniu Polacy zaakceptowali ten model świata, ich świadomość zbiorowa została znacznie zniekształcona. Z pamięci historycznej, stanowiącej ważny składnik narodowej tożsamości, zniknęli ludzie i wydarzenia, które mogłyby zaburzyć czysty obraz ideologiczny. Między innymi zniknęli Żydzi, których obecność w polskiej kulturze stałaby w sprzeczności z oficjalnym antysemityzmem polskich władz komunistycznych i z interpretacją dziejów, według której czystość etniczna jest czynnikiem postępu.

Polacy poszukują nowej interpretacji swojej przeszości i konstruują swoją narodową tożsamość na nowo. Proces ten polega między innymi na zbudowaniu na nowo wizji stosunków z innymi narodami, wśród których Rosjanie, Niemcy i Żydzi grają pierwszoplanową rolę. Rosjanie i Niemcy to dwaj potężni sąsiedzi, z którymi Polacy muszą nauczyć się żyć, rozmawiać i współpracować. Żydzi byli dawniej mniejszością w Polsce tak liczną i tak wszystkim Polakom znaną, że stali się stereotypowym "obcym", wobec którego Polacy określali swą tożsamość. Dzisiaj Polacy, szczególnie młodzi, próbują na nowo przemyśleć swoje dzieje w aspekcie stosunków polsko–żydowskich i chcą jak najwięcej o Żydach wiedzieć, nie tylko dla zaspokojenia ciekawości, ale też dlatego, że ten aspekt ich własnej historii pozwoli im lepiej zrozumieć kim sami są i jakie jest ich miejsce wśród innych narodów.

Auschwitz jest dla Polaków symbolem ich własnej przeszłości w relacji z tymi trzema najważnieszymi partnerami w historycznym rozwoju tożsamości narodowej. Dekompozycja zdominowanej przez ideologię komunistyczną i konflikt ideologiczny z komunistami tożsamości narodowej i proces tworzenia nowej tożsamości wymaga przebudowania kluczowych symboli, które tożsamość reprezentują. Dlatego Auschwitz stał się przedmiotem dyskusji i kontrowersji, a jednocześnie trwa proces jego przekształcenia. Przemyśleć trzeba na nowo ekspozycje narodowe, miejsce tragedii Żydów w całości Muzeum, rolę Polski jako państwa i narodu w całym historycznym kontekście Auschwitz. Miejsce to nie jest i nie może być dla Polaków obojętne, gdyż ogniskuje podstawowe problemy ich własnej tożsamości. Nerwowe i zdecydowane reakcje na próby przejęcia Auschwitz jako wyłącznej domeny przez radykalne grupy żydowskie są jeszcze jednym przejawem znaczenia Auschwitz dla Polaków, którzy nie chcą się zgodzić, aby ktoś inny dyktował im co mają robić we własnym kraju, tym bardziej, że rzecz dotyczy tak delikatnych i ideologicznie obciążonych kwestii. Polacy mają świadomość oskarżeń kierowanych w ich stronę o współudział w zbrodni ludobójstwa i nie mogą zgodzić się, aby Auschwitz stał się nośnikiem takiej konstrukcji dziejów, która na ten współudział wskazuje. Z kolei usiłowania kościoła katolickiego dobitnego zamanifestowania swojej obecności w Auschwitz są przejawem prób zdominowania życia ideologicznego we współczesnej Polsce. W tym również przejawia się rola Auschwitz jako jednego z dominujących symboli w polskiej kulturze.

Symbol nie tylko reprezentuje i przekazuje idee i wartości. Ma również właściwość generowania i organizowania myśli i uczuć, mobilizowania świadomości społecznej. Auschwitz jest dla Polaków kluczowym symbolem w procesie przekształcania ich tożsamości narodowej. Jest też symbolem zagrożeń, jakie niesie ze sobą wynaturzenie cywilizacji europejskiej, nietolerancji, nienawiści do innych, ludobójstwa, obłąkanych destrukcyjnych ideologii totalitarnych. Dlatego w procesie znajdywania dla Polski nowego miejsca w Europie Auschwitz odgrywa i będzie odgrywał znaczącą rolę.

What does Auschwitz Mean to Polish People?

During communist rule the State Museum of Auschwitz–Birkenau was considered a symbol of 'state nationalism'. In its exhibitions it therefore emphasized the martyrdom of the Poles above all else, and gave the impression that throughout history Polish misfortune had always originated with the Germans. Religious and ethnic aspects, especially the sufferings of the Jews, were forced into the background. The Jews were present as representatives of different nations, but not as a people condemned to extermination by the Nazis. The 50th anniversary of the liberation of the concentration– and deathcamp Auschwitz–Birkenau occurs at a time when Poles are endeavouring to find a new interpretation of their history on the one hand and a new national identity on the other. This gives the Polish–Jewish relation a particular significance. That is why the Museum Auschwitz–Birkenau is the subject of intense discussions and controversies: for example, against the background of the 50th anniversary of the concentration– and deathcamp liberation radical Jewish groups as well as representatives of the Catholic Church claimed Auschwitz as their symbol. This shows the necessity of broadening the historical framework of the museum's exhibitions in order to represent the Jewish tragedy and the role played by the Polish state and people. For the Polish people Auschwitz serves not only as a key symbol in their present search for a new national identity, but also, and in particular, as a symbol of threat, intolerance, xenophobia, genocide and dreadful, destructive, totalitarian ideologies.

Was bedeutet Auschwitz für die Polen?

Während der Herrschaft des Kommunismus galt das Staatliche Museum Auschwitz–Birkenau als Symbol des 'staatlichen Nationalismus'. Aus diesem Grunde betonte es in seinen Ausstellungen vor allem das Märtyrertum der Polen und vermittelte ein Geschichtsbild, nach der alles Unglück der Polen seit eh und je von den Deutschen herrührte. Religiöse und ethnische Aspekte, insbesondere das Leiden der Juden traten demgegenüber zurück: Letztere waren als Vertreter verschiedener Nationen, jedoch nicht als ein Volk präsent, das die Nazis zur Ausrottung verurteilt hatten. Der fünfzigste Jahrestag der Befreiung des Konzentrations– und Vernichtungslagers Auschwitz–Birkenau fällt in eine Zeit, in der sich Polen zum einen um eine neue Deutung ihrer Vergangenheit, zum anderen um eine neue nationale Identität bemüht. Hierbei wird den polnisch–jüdischen Beziehungen eine besondere Bedeutung zugemessen. Dies macht die Gedenkstätte Auschwitz–Birkenau zum Gegenstand heftiger

Diskussionen und Kontroversen: So wollten zum Beispiel vor dem Hintergrund des fünfzigsten Jahrestages der Befreiung des Konzentrations- und Vernichtungslagers Auschwitz-Birkenau sowohl radikale jüdische Gruppen als auch Vertreter der katholischen Kirche das Symbol Auschwitz für sich vereinnahmen. Dies zeigt, daß es notwendig ist, die Darstellung der Tragödie der Juden und die Rolle des polnischen Staates und Volkes in der Auschwitz-Frage in den Ausstellungen des Museums in einen weiteren historischen Rahmen zu stellen. Auschwitz dient den Polen nicht nur als Schlüsselsymbol bei ihrer gegenwärtigen Suche nach einer neuen Identität, sondern ist für sie auch und vor allem das Symbol der Bedrohung, der Intoleranz, des Fremdenhasses, des Völkermordes und wahnwitziger, destruktiver, totalitärer Ideologien.

Dan Stone

Chaos and Continuity: Representations of Auschwitz

* I should like to thank Ruth Harris, Sherman Sam, and Simon Sparks for their help in preparing this article.

> [Historical writing] creates these narratives of the past which are the equivalent of cemetries within cities; it exorcises and confesses a presence of death amidst the living. (Michel de Certeau 1988:87).

Seeing nothing in between the past itself and the past today has long been the goal of museum curators and historians. According to James Young, failure to pay attention to this gap, the gap which is the medium of representation, means that "in the subsequent fetishization of artifacts by curators, and of ruins by the 'memory–tourist', however, we risk mistaking the piece for the whole, the implied whole for unmediated history" (Young 1993:127). The intention of the exhibition 'Representations of Auschwitz' is to stress the organization of artifacts of the past, and, most importantly, to emphasize the fact that *representation* is of fundamental importance for our understanding of the past. For it is *how* we represent the past that determines how we feel its nearness, that is to say, how we make its absence into a presence. The past is how we represent it (Ankersmit 1988:222; 1989:26). This is as much true for photography, art, and journalism as it is for museum artifacts and historical texts.

All too often, however, we have *looked through* the medium by which we make the past present, assuming the text or the photograph to be merely tools which allow us immediate and unmediated access to the past. I hope in this paper to do two things. Firstly, to propose as axiomatic the fact that we never have the past itself, but only different ways of showing it. And secondly, to show that history — our written or visual portrayals of the past, not History understood in the speculative sense of the unfolding of a meaningful historical schema — is only ever the presentation of the past within its absence. The nature of representation helps decide how we give meaning to the past, for the past itself does not divulge its meaning to us. As a result the past remains always infinitely ungraspable, infinitely other.

Here the words of Jean–Luc Nancy are worth bearing in mind, for he attempts to show that it is not *being absent* but *absence* itself that facilitates the possibility of imagination, and hence the representational act. The status of this absence, the nature of the gap, allows for differing representations, and for the fact that representation is a perpetual coming to presence, but never presence as such: "And when the other comes/is present, what presents itself is precisely this: that it's the other, always infinitely improbable, unattainable" (Nancy 1993:357). This is not therefore a problem of empirical evidence, but of "understanding what it is that is presented in the present as history [...]. The question does not therefore concern the 'that' of history — its content — but history itself" (Benjamin 1991:84 n.3). And yet since the need to represent remains, I will claim that an awareness of this gap as Nancy articulates it can facilitate an affirmative reappraisal of our understanding of what it means to commemorate the past.

In the case of Auschwitz, the issues of representation are raised even more urgently, precisely because commemoration has very definite moral purposes. This does not imply that the past did not occur, nor even that there is something suspicious about the human desire to tell stories about the past. It is to recognize, however, that the way that those stories are told is itself constitutive of our understanding of the past. This necessary mediation is the realm of representation.

Such an argument does not mean that one way of representing the past is as acceptable as another; it does mean that any representation of the past is always so *for a purpose*. It is obvious that, as Lionel Gossman points out, "the disagreement of historians [...] cannot be resolved by confronting their testimonies with the real past" (Gossman 1990:300). If it could, then there would be no need for each generation or each culture to write history differently. However, Gossman does not see this as a result of the fact that the past only has the meanings that our representations of it provide. He tries to prove his point by citing the fact that "the historian does not normally confront such a chaos of events; the latter are almost always encountered in more or less intelligible patterns and relations (narratives), which the historian may wish to challenge, reject, or alter. He does not work alone, without precedent" (Gossman 1990:392 n.25). Yet his argument is self–contradictory: the precedent that Gossman is here talking about is the precedent of other historical works, not that of the past itself. Certainly the narratives of earlier historians may be questioned; not, however, on the basis of the past itself, but only on the basis of the traces of that past which remain. The past itself remains inaccessible as a reference point on the level of meaning, and is so only on the level of chronicle, of "individual statements" (Ankersmit 1990:277) — though the construction of the chronicle is by no means an innocent enterprise. Gossman in no way proves that the past itself is not chaotic; indeed, his footnote inadvertently reinforces the fact that the coherence of the past is always constructed by later representations, and that where the historian encounters 'intelligible patterns and relations' s/he does so by virtue of prior historical productions.

The historian Georg Iggers has written recently that, "not only the meaning of history, but also the possibility of historiographical [*geschichtswissenschaftlicher*] knowledge, indeed scientific knowledge generally has become problematic" (Iggers 1993:11). The implications for representation have long gone unnoticed in the area where the issue is raised most pressingly: the Holocaust. Only recently have critics pointed out that there may be "a paradox in the coherent narration of events which involve the dissolution of coherence" (Davis 1991:292). If the occurrence of Auschwitz in the midst of the great European traditions and civilization points to the fundamentally chaotic nature of the past (and not, as Gossman would have us believe, part of an inherently intelligible narrative of the historical scheme), then an explanation is necessary for the fact that only recently have traditional modes of representation been challenged. In historiography in particular, it is striking that in the years in which history was opened up to the discourses of sociology, anthropology, and the resulting 'new cultural history', from the 1960s until the present day, historical narratives of the Holocaust have followed very conventional guidelines. Linear chronology, strong empirical evidence at the expense of analysis, and the closure of the events within the stories of redemption, American/Soviet liberation, or the founding of the state of Israel (and thus of a return to progress), were the tools used for writing about the Holocaust. No doubt the reason for this is simple. The horrific nature of the events meant that there was an obligation to record them swiftly for posterity. Furthermore, the horror and the chaos demanded a coherent narration, if the events were to be mastered; only this would allow for continuity in history.

The events of Auschwitz, however, do not present themselves to the historian or to the photographer in the form of a ready–made plot that can simply be re–presented for easy (or even difficult) consumption. Nevertheless, the "realist fallacy" has ignored what Kellner (1989) calls the "other sources" of history, those of language, rhetoric, and moral choice, or in photography the question of exclusion from the frame of vision. All are as equally relevant in providing historical understanding as are the traces of the past that constitute historical evidence. The language the historian uses, the tropes and metaphors employed, the ordering scheme, all contribute to the meaning of the past that s/he generates.

The work of scholars such as Ankersmit and Kellner is so valuable because it shows how in the making of history the *making* element has been overlooked, obscuring the fact that there is a gap between any representation and what it represents. An excess of meaning always escapes us. As Claude Lanzmann, the maker of the film *Shoah* reminds us, "genocide cannot be brought to life and to attempt this is in some ways to deny the reality of it, to ignore the surge of violence" (Lanzmann 1986:11). In other words, those representations, such as realist photographs or historical texts, which appear to show us the past as it really was, actually protect us from its impact. A desire for continuity in historical existence lies behind such realist representations. If it is correct to state that "those living reality often find its representation inadequate" (Braun 1994:174) then how much more true this disjunction must be for our representations of the past.

Is there something about Auschwitz in particular that is unrepresentable? Such a belief has led Dan Diner to assert that "Auschwitz is a no–man's land of understanding, a black box of explanation, a vacuum of extrahistorical significance which sucks in attempts at historiographic interpretation" (Diner 1990:144). Similarly, Saul Friedländer claims that "the Shoah carries an *excess*, and this excess cannot be defined except by some sort of general statement about something 'which must be able to be put into phrases [but] cannot yet be' " (Friedländer 1992:19–20). In this reference to the work of Jean–François Lyotard, Friedländer is somewhat disingenuous about Lyotard's insistence on the existence of the unpresentable. When Lyotard asks us to imagine an earthquake so great that it destroys all the instruments for measuring (Lyotard 1988:56), and explicitly refers in this context to Auschwitz, he does not mean to say that Auschwitz is unique. For such a conclusion would leave it as an aberration outside of the range of human experience. Whilst the Holocaust can hardly be said to be an everyday occurence, those involved in it certainly were normal human beings, who led otherwise normal lives. The importance of the Holocaust from this perspective is that it makes us aware of general problems of representation which are normally passed by with ease.

But what does such a recognition of the long–neglected importance of representation actually tell us? In believing that a text or photograph reveals the past as it actually was, we give a meaning to the past that it did not necessarily have. This need not be a positive meaning; history as catastrophe has obvious attractions in the light of this century's disasters. But it would be too easy, indeed too comforting, simply to agree with E.M. Cioran when he speaks of "Universal history: history of Evil [...]. If you have not contributed to a catastrophe you will vanish without a trace" (Cioran 1990:102). Whether a positive or negative meaning is imputed to history, it is so through choice, and not because the past itself reveals such a meaning. When an event is represented according to certain cultural norms which demand order, causality and coherence, a certain desire is in evidence. In Kellner's words, "the desire to represent the Holocaust, however, is not the desire to repeat it as an event [...] it is a desire to repeat the Holocaust in a suitably altered form to meet complex, often contradictory, sets of present needs" (Kellner 1994:128). Essentially, the narratives that historians have employed, and the techniques that photographers have used in representing Auschwitz during and since the war are evidence of a strong desire not to surrender to the chaos of events. Thus Jörn Rüsen is wrong to believe that paying attention to the construction of coherency will lead historians to "reach for the greasepaint of irrational meanings as a cover for meaninglessness" (cited in Gossman 1990:290). Rather, it will allow for greater diversity of representation, since there is no one single meaning to history: "Until the lonely hour arrives in which the philosophical proof of the truth of history is produced, then history will inevitably continue as representation and interpretation of the past" (Young 1990:22).

These discourses of coherence have endured for so long thanks to their being discourses of power. When even the most horrific of occurrences can be mastered, then those who order them, whether by text or photograph, are in a privileged position. Those who represent the Holocaust in such a way imply that they enjoy a position of transcendence which gives them an unparalleled view over the past. A historian of the prestige of Raul Hilberg undoubtedly has immense knowledge about the events of the Holocaust on the level of chronicle, what Kellner (1989:331) calls the "subhistorical" level. When this is then transformed into a representation of the past, it lends the past a coherence that it clearly lacked. Hilberg is particularly apposite here, for there is no doubt that he has played a greater role than any other historian in bringing the facts of the Nazi genocide to the public, yet he has himself often been criticized for producing a narrative of events (*The Destruction of the European Jews*, 1961) that replicated the Nazi obsession with bureaucracy, portraying the events of the Holocaust as the unfolding of a strictly rational sequence.

The same is true of photography. It is striking that the same images have been used over and over again to represent Auschwitz. With photography, the language of representation is more obviously relevant than in historiography, for the photo (the positive of a negative of a positive) is clearly acting as a substitute for the missing object. Yet ever since the first photos of Auschwitz, the meaning imputed to it has been encompassed in the symbolic framework of the barbed wire, the ramp, or the famous entrance gate. These things were of course important parts of the camp, yet they are not the camp but only how we wish to keep seeing it. For the fifty years since the liberation of the camp the continuity in representing chaos is testimony to the enduring desire for order and the power of coherent narrative in providing it; proof therefore of the fact that, as Robert Braun notes, "problems of historical representation are politically and socially significant in the individual and communal search for legitimation — the past, it seems, is granted its own legitimation by the authority of the present" (Braun 1994:194).

It is of course neither possible nor desirable to replace this continuity of representation with a new representation which would be closer to the thing itself. In photography, however, the continuity in iconology can perhaps be explained without having to resort to talk of power, and/or the human desire for coherent stories. For in a sense, a photo really does represent the past in a way that a text can never do, for it is a remnant of light captured from another time. Thus, the photos in the so–called Lili Jacob Album really are manifestations of reality, they do show us the people who were among the first to arrive at the new ramp at Birkenau (Auschwitz II). Nevertheless, it should be borne in mind that we are only looking at part of an event, from a certain angle or perspective, and that these representations only allow us to recapture the event imaginatively, through the symbolic order provided by the iconology of the photo. The same photos in the album that we now view as evidence of the murders were used earlier to illustrate the different types of prisoners — those who were *noch einsatzfähig* (still capable of work) and those who were *nicht mehr einsatzfähig* (incapable of work and therefore to be killed immediately).

Photos taken after the war (especially those taken recently) of such elements as the gate at Auschwitz I, the watchtower at Birkenau, and the mountains of relics never simply provide documentary evidence. They also provide ways of giving meaning to what is no longer accessible. This multiple role is made abundantly clear by the recurrence of these images for 'plain' documentary and propaganda purposes immediately after the war (in particular in the Soviet films of the liberation of the camp), and their later reappearance in manifold forms including illustrating books on the challenge of the Holocaust to Christian theology (e.g. Cargas 1990), the sensational fetishization of the same images in popular war accounts (e.g. Russell 1976), and the romanticized postcards that one can purchase at the Auschwitz museum. The fact that the same photos are frequently used in different contexts shows how the very context of the photo changes its meaning. The juxtaposition in the exhibition of these recurrent images in their various manifestations not only reminds us that the past itself is ungraspable, but that even in the use of certain key images, the context of meaning which informs each photo is subtly (or not so subtly) shifted, according to how the photographer intends the aesthetic presentation of the photo to influence our understanding of the past.

This inescapable instrumentalization of the past is made more clear in the contrast between 'traditional' forms of representation and the contemporary, the kitsch, the abstract. In comics, for example, the most tasteless representations of Auschwitz with the most revolting attitudes (in particular a massive belittling of the events) sit easily with the most well known images of the camps (the piles of corpses, the 'zebra').[1]

Similarly, the work of artists often challenges our perception of events as necessarily having to be portrayed through realistic depiction. This is a result of the confusion between depiction and representation; as David Batchelor has written, abstract art "is an image of *something*, but not an image of some *thing*" (Batchelor 1991:55). Although it can be argued that abstract art refers inherently to its own history, or that an abstract piece by one artist can refer to that of another artist, the absence of obvious iconic reference is for our purposes a powerful reminder of the difficulty, indeed the necessary falsity, of all forms of representation; while they provide us with a framework for comprehending the past, they do not provide us with the past itself. In this regard, the inclusion of non–realistic artworks in the exhibition is a reminder that events such as took place at Auschwitz can be represented as powerfully in their non–depiction as in their realistic re–presentation. It is not that a 'better' or more authentic form of representation should be found; rather the logic of representation includes its own impossibility (the desire to give presence to what is not present), and the recognition of this condition should become the starting point for renewed thought.

Here we reach the crux of the argument. The contrast between the chaos of the Holocaust and the continuity in the representation of it has endured *precisely because* the Holocaust, more than any other occurrence, impugns traditional representation. In other words, with the Holocaust, the desire for continuity has required a forceful imposition upon forms of representation that even hint at the underlaying chaos. This imposition does not mean that historians have been unable to talk about the fact that chaos did characterize the Holocaust; rather it means that they have done so in a framework which implicitly brings that chaos under control, one which reinstates the power of 'pre–Auschwitz' ways of representing history. Thus the dearth of efforts to open the Holocaust up to representations provided by new historical approaches such as microhistories.

Representations of the Holocaust as they have been conceived by historians (and this explains the necessary contrast with art or comics) are actually no closer to presenting the past to us than are other forms of representation. Only cultural

1. The use of the notions of kitsch and tastelessness are not intended as indictments on those categories, as they are normally conceived. Rather, I wish to suggest that the line between 'kitsch' and 'high art', or between 'tasteful' and 'tasteless' is a shifting one, and one which is dictated not by formal, objective criteria (as Clement Greenberg famously believed) but by notions of what is or is not ethically acceptable in any given case. The exhibition blurs these categories in order to show how they can all play a role in forming one's symbolic understanding of Auschwitz.

imperatives dictate that a realistic representation of the past gives it more meaning than, say, a non–linear, ironic representation. Indeed, it is part of the modernist fallacy to suggest that "even though the signifier and the signified can never be the same, there is, none the less, a boundary which when transgressed would render the relationship inauthentic" (Benjamin 1991:62). The existence of such boundaries betrays the limits of desire or moral norms, not of representation. It is not that with Auschwitz one encounters special problems of representation, but rather that Auschwitz makes clearer than ever *the* problem of representation: the fact that there always exists a lacuna between the representation and what is represented, no matter how that representation is conceived. The possibility of representation is also its impossibility.

It is of course possible to argue that the realistic representation at least makes the lacuna as small as possible, and that to attempt other representations is deliberately to widen it. But this view perpetuates the 'modernist fallacy' by suggesting that it is possible to put forward one's sources in a way that allows the facts to 'speak for themselves'. This ignores the nature of sources mentioned earlier: that they too are only traces of the past and not the past itself, and that in the case of written sources they "in no way imitate the lived, experienced, 'real' form of the past itself, if we may speak of such a thing, for the form of the past depends on the text of written history" (Kellner 1989:28). The historian does not encounter a different problem from the anthropologist who wishes to tell us how a certain group of people represent the past to themselves not through narrative stories but through "embodied knowledge" or through everyday experience and tradition (Okely 1994). The fact of authorship still maintains a fundamental mediation between the past itself and its representation, whether the 'past itself' comes to the author in the shape of documentary evidence or bodily practices.

If the modernist conception of representation has ignored this split between the signifier (the representation) and the signified (what is represented) then the recognition of this split can be said to be "the crisis of modernity" (Benjamin 1991:62). This is what Lyotard means when he states that " 'Auschwitz' can be taken as a paradigmatic name for the tragic 'incompletion' of modernity" (Lyotard 1992:30). The split was always there, but only now does it come to be acknowledged.

And yet of course the irony is that all too often the split has not been acknowledged. Instead, traditional conceptions of representation have dominated the field of Holocaust studies, thus inadvertently perpetuating methods of thought which are themselves implicated in the downfall of the modernist 'project'. This perpetuation of the conventional is no doubt a result of what Saul Friedländer calls a "moral imperative" to talk of the Holocaust within "certain accepted norms of aesthetic collaboration or intellectual discourse" (Friedländer 1989:3097), a kind of remorse for the widespread silence that characterized the war years and the first fifteen years after the war where the Holocaust was concerned. But it is the gap between what is represented and the representation that provides the possibility for thinking anew the Holocaust: not to rewrite the events of the Holocaust, but to emphasize the way that those events are understood. Once we begin to attest to the existence of the split then the representation of the past can be formulated as testimony to it, thus ensuring that the presence of the past is never assumed, and instead stressing the fact that in its perpetual coming to presence, it is radically unattainable. Thus the commonplace that is attributed to Holocaust survivors — that we should know what happened even though we shall never know — can become the condition of an affirmative representation, one which bears witness to the split and acknowledges the *unpresentable* as a call for diversity in *representations*. Once the continuity in representation of the Holocaust has been shown to exist despite the impossibility of the logic of representation having been revealed, the possibility of a new tradition founded on the hiatus of representation is opened up. Rather than become melancholy because of the split it is possible to think the split as positive, bringing representation into a new sphere.

Chaos i kontynuacja: możliwości przedstawienia tematu Auschwitz

Dopiero w ostatnim czasie naukowcy zaczęli stawiać sobie pytania dotyczące możliwości przedstawiania historii Holocaustu. Problem wiąże się z faktem, iż nie tylko Holocaustu, ale i innych zdarzeń historycznych nie da się odtworzyć we właściwy sposób. Trudności występujące przy podejmowaniu próby przedstawienia tematu Holocaustu w ogólności, a Auschwitz szczególnie, dowodzą, że cel, dla którego uwspółcześnia się techniki, strategie wystawiennicze jest nieosiągalny. Nigdy nie będziemy w stanie posługiwać się rzeczywistym obrazem przeszłości, a jedyne co możemy, to za pomocą różych metod na nią wskazywać. Ponieważ przeszłość znamy wyłącznie z przedstawienia, chroni się więc zawsze przed naszą bezpośrednią ingerencją. Jeżeli wierzymy, że jakiś tekst względnie fotografia ukazują nam przeszłość taką, jaką była rzeczywiście, wówczas być może interpretujemy ją niewłaściwie. Ujmując przeszłość poprzez eksponowanie jej w określonych ramach, być może nadajemy jej wyraz, jakiego prawdopodobnie nigdy nie posiadała; jeżeli zastosujemy tradycyjne wzorce do przedstawienia historii Holocaustu, wówczas unikniemy interpretowania go jako kryzysu moderny. Kontrast między chaosem jakim był Holocaust, a upartym dążeniem do odnalezienia metody wystawienniczej dla zobrazowania tego faktu trwa do dzisiaj właśnie dlatego, że Holocaust przeciwstawia się przedstawianiu go tradycyjnymi metodami. To, na czym polega problem przedstawienia, wyraźniej niż gdziekolwiek uwidacznia się w Auschwitz. Między przedstawieniem a przedstawianym przedmiotem istnieje ciągle jakieś niedopełnienie, stwarzające możliwość przemyślenia Holocaustu na nowo: nie chodzi przy tym o ponowną relację zdarzeń Holocaustu, ale o takie ich wyeksponowanie, by zdarzenia te zostały zrozumiane. Zrozumienie to ułatwić może zastosowanie możliwie wielu sposobów relacjonowania tych zdarzeń.

Chaos und Kontinuität: Die Darstellbarkeit von Auschwitz

Erst seit kurzem stellen Wissenschaftler die Frage nach den Grenzen der Darstellbarkeit des Holocaust. Das Problem liegt darin, daß nicht nur der Holocaust, sondern Geschichte an sich nicht angemessen wiedergegeben werden kann. Die Schwierigkeiten, die bei dem Versuch auftreten, den Holocaust im allgemeinen und Auschwitz im besonderen darzustellen, erweisen das Ziel der Vergegenwärtigung als unerreichbar: Wir können niemals über die Vergangenheit selbst verfügen, sondern nur mit Hilfe verschiedener Methoden auf sie hinweisen. Da wir sie nur aus Darstellungen kennen, entzieht sich die Vergangenheit immer unserem unmittelbaren Zugriff. Wenn wir glauben, daß ein Text oder eine Fotografie uns die Vergangenheit zeigt, wie sie wirklich war, interpretieren wir sie möglicherweise unzutreffend. Indem wir der Vergangenheit durch ihre Darstellung Struktur auferlegen, verleihen wir ihr eine Kohärenz, die sie offenkundig nicht besaß; wenn wir traditionelle Paradigmen auf den Holocaust anwenden, verhindern wir sein Verständnis als eine Krise der Moderne. Das Spannungsverhältnis zwischen dem Chaos des Holocaust und den fortdauernden Versuchen ihn darzustellen hält bis heute an, gerade weil der Holocaust sich traditionellen Darstellungsformen widersetzt. Deutlicher als irgendwo sonst zeigt sich an Auschwitz, worin das Problem der Darstellung besteht. Es gibt immer eine Lücke zwischen Darstellung und Darstellungsgegenstand, die die Möglichkeit eröffnet, den Holocaust neu zu überdenken: Nicht nochmals über die Ereignisse des Holocaust zu berichten, sondern hervorzuheben, wie diese Ereignisse verstanden werden. Gefördert werden kann dieses Verständnis durch eine möglichst große Vielfalt der Darstellungsformen.

Ute Wrocklage

Majdanek und Auschwitz in der internationalen Bildpresse 1945

'Sich ein Bild machen', nicht nur von der eigenen Person, sondern vor allem von Personen des öffentlichen Lebens, von fernen Ereignissen, Sensationen und Naturkatastrophen, von fremden Orten der Geschichte, Schlachtfeldern, Städten, Häusern etc., ist ein uraltes Bedürfnis der Menschen. Das Bild — gemalt, gezeichnet, gedruckt, plastiziert oder fotografiert — versucht seit jeher, diesem Wunsch zu entsprechen.

Allerdings waren seiner Verbreitung bis zu einem geeigneten Druckverfahren enge Grenzen gesetzt, die zu Lasten der Aktualität gingen. Dem breiten, bild–ungshungrigen Lesepublikum konnte erst mit den in einem Holzstichverfahren, der Xylografie, hergestellten, bebilderten Magazinen ein für jedermann erschwingliches Blatt angeboten werden. In dieser Technik erschien 1842 in London das erste illustrierte Blatt, die "Illustrated London News", dem auf dem Kontinent bald andere und in Amerika unter anderem die "Saturday Evening Post" folgten.

Eine aktuelle bildliche Wiedergabe von Ereignissen und Personen wurde aber erst mit der Fotografie und vor allem ihrer Reproduzierbarkeit in den Printmedien möglich. Anfangs fügten die Herausgeber ihren Zeitungen eine wöchentliche Bildbeilage auf besserem Papier bei, wie "The New York Times Magazine" oder noch die Magazine der Nachkriegspresse 1945, z.B. die "Illustracja Polska" als Beilage zur Tageszeitung "Dziennik Polski". Auf normalem Zeitungspapier sind Fotografien erst seit 1926 publizierbar. Die Entwicklung zu den illustrierten Blättern vollzog sich im Anschluß sehr rasch und fand große Akzeptanz beim Publikum. Das 1936 erstmalig erscheinende "Life"–Magazin übernahm schnell die Führung auf dem internationalen Zeitschriftenmarkt. In Großbritannien setzt die 1938 edierte "Picture Post" Standards.

In der Sowjetunion entfaltet sich seit der Oktoberrevolution eine umfangreiche, obgleich ideologisch einseitig ausgerichtete Presselandschaft. Die Parteizeitungen "Prawda" und "Iswestija" nehmen hier neben der offiziellen Nachrichtenagentur "Tass" die wichtigste Bedeutung ein. Bebildert sind diese beiden Tageszeitungen äußerst sparsam, meistens mit kleinen, einspaltigen Aufnahmen, die im Sinne der Partei die marxistisch–leninistische Idee transportieren.

Fotografien bilden die vor ihr liegende Wirklichkeit nicht realistisch und wertneutral ab. Perspektive, Wahl des Ausschnitts — um nur einige Aspekte zu nennen — beeinflussen das fotografische Bild bereits bei der Herstellung. In den Printmedien wird den Abbildungen nicht nur durch den beigefügten Bericht und die Bildunterschriften eine zusätzliche bis hin zu einer völlig neuen Aussage unterlegt, sondern auch die Zusammenstellung der Illustrationen vermittelt eine Botschaft, eine Nachricht, eine Idee. Die Einzelaufnahmen ergänzen sich zu einer visuell erzählten Geschichte, auch wenn die Fotos Gegensätze thematisieren.

Hier sollen im Überblick die ersten Bildberichte über die Konzentrationslager Majdanek und Auschwitz auf ihre visuelle 'Representation' befragt werden.[1] Die Aussage der Bildgeschichte, die Wiederholung bestimmter Bildthemen stehen im Vordergrund.

Das erste Konzentrations– und Vernichtungslager, von dem ausführlich berichtet wird, ist Majdanek bei Lublin, das die 'Rote Armee' am 23. Juli 1944 befreite. Am 11. August erscheint in der "Prawda" ein ganzseitiger Artikel "Lager Majdanek" von Boris Gorbatow, den sechs Abbildungen des Fotokorrespondenten J. Rumkin illustrieren.[2] Unter dem Bildteil mit der Überschrift "Im Lubliner Vernichtungslager" fällt der Blick durch den in zwei Reihen und unter Strom gestellten Stacheldraht auf die Baracken. Es folgen die noch erhaltenen Verbrennungsöfen des gesprengten Krematoriums, das 'Leichenlager' — so die Bildunterschrift — mit unzähligen, im Vordergrund liegenden Skeletten, die hinter einer brusthohen Mauer von Zivilpersonen besichtigt werden. Unter den persönlichen Sachen der Ermordeten finden sich etliche private Fotografien, die die Opfer selbst oder ihre nächsten Angehörigen zeigen. Eine Aufnahme mit einer Vielzahl dieser Bilder schließt sich an. Auf der nächsten, gegenüberliegenden Seite sind ein endloser Berg Schuhe, auf dem Soldaten der Roten Armee stehen, und ein Foto der Pässe plaziert. Der Fotoredakteur der "Prawda" hat diese hochformatige Aufnahme aus einem Querformat herausgeschnitten. Es scheint, die Pässe fielen von oben herunter. Entscheidend für diesen Ausschnitt war aber offenbar nicht der noch zur Verfügung stehende Platz, sondern die Hervorhebung der Identitäten durch kyrillische Lettern. Die im Lager ermordeten Bürger der Sowjetunion werden so visuell in den Vordergrund gestellt, aber auch die anonyme Masse der Ermordeten, beschrieben in den vorherigen Bildern, wird damit zu Sowjetbürgern.

Die Bedeutung, die den Bildern eingeräumt wird, ist dem großzügig bemessenen Platz und der Größe über drei Spalten zu entnehmen. Auch den Redakteuren der "Prawda" wird bekannt gewesen sein, daß mit der Größe der Fotos nicht nur die Leserschaft zunimmt — nach einer Untersuchung in den USA von 37% bei einspaltigen, bis zu 64% bei

1. Die englische Terminologie soll hier beibehalten werden, da keine angemessene Übersetzung im Deutschen vorhanden ist.

2. Leider war es nicht möglich bis zur Drucklegung, reproduzierfähige Vorlagen aus der "Prawda" zu erhalten, da aufgrund der Kriegswirren die Jahrgänge in den Bibliotheken sehr lückenhaft bzw. nur auf Microfilm erfaßt sind. Dieses Problem stellte sich auch in Polen. Für die Übersetzungen der Bildunterschriften aus dem Russischen danke ich T. Miłoń und A. Strzelecki.

vierspaltigen Bildern —, sondern auch der gefühlsmäßige Eindruck und die Einprägsamkeit eines Bildes zusammenhängt.[3] Mit dem fast eine ganze Seite einnehmenden Bildbericht der nur vierseitig erscheinenden Zeitung während des Krieges wird die Wichtigkeit des Fundes betont. Dem Textbericht wird — unterstützt durch die Bildunterschriften — ein sachlicher Bildbericht beigegeben.
Die Verleger der westlichen Verbündeten, die der Berichterstattung über Majdanek vergleichsweise breiten Raum zumessen[4], haben ebenfalls Fotomaterial von J. Rumkin erhalten, das offiziell über die Agentur "Sovfoto", die als Quelle in einigen Druckwerken angegeben ist, vertrieben wird.[5]

In dem nordamerikanischen, auflagenstarken "Life"–Magazin erscheint bereits am 28. August 1944 ein einseitiger Bildbericht mit sechs Aufnahmen unter dem Titel "Lublin Funeral. Russians honor Jews whom Nazis gassed and cremated in mass" (Abb. 1). Zwei Fotos der polnisch–russischen Trauerfeierlichkeiten eröffnen hier den Bericht. Ihnen folgt eine Ansicht der Krematoriumsöfen mit davor liegenden Skeletten und eine Sicht in einen geöffneten, mit Knochen gefüllten Ofen auf der linken Hälfte. Diesen Aufnahmen wird ein Massengrab und ein Berg mit unzähligen Schuhen vor einer Baracke gegenübergestellt. Durch das Layout der Seite mit einem durchgehenden schwarzen Hintergrund und einem weißen, schmalen Rand um die einzelnen Abbildungen, wird der Charakter einer Todesanzeige betont. Die Trauer um die im Bild anwesenden, noch nicht bestatteten Ermordeten steht im Mittelpunkt der Botschaft.

Zwei Monate später ediert am 14. Oktober 1944 die "Illustrated London News" einen Beitrag mit dem Titel "The Most Terrible Example of Organised Cruelty in the History of Civilisation. Mass Murder by the Germans in the Majdanek 'Camp of Annihilation' " (Abb. 2).

LUBLIN FUNERAL

① "LIFE", Vol. 17, No. 9, 28.8.1944

3. Vgl. hierzu K. Sanders: Photojournalism Research, in: Clifton C. Edom: Photojournalism. Principles and Practices, Dubuque, Iowa, 1980, S. 164-183.

4. Das neu gegründete Polnische Komitee der nationalen Befreiung hatte zu einem Pressetermin am 6. August 1944 die von Moskau aus berichtenden ca. 30 ausländischen Korrespondenten nach Majdanek eingeladen. Sie besichtigten das Lager und nahmen an der Befragung von Augenzeugen — Opfer wie Täter — durch die polnisch–russische Untersuchungskommission teil.

5. Die Rolle der Fotoagenturen bei der Vermittlung von Pressefotos ist ein nicht zu unterschätzender Faktor im Aufbau eines kollektiven Bildgedächtnisses. Aus den zahlreichen Aufnahmen der Fotografen wählt in erster Instanz die Agentur die ihrer Meinung nach aussage– und 'schlagkräftigsten' Fotografien aus, die an ihre Vertragspartner — Zeitungs– und Zeitschriftenverleger — oder weiteren Kunden auf Anfrage weitergegeben werden.

THE MOST TERRIBLE EXAMPLE OF ORGANISED CRUELTY IN THE HISTORY OF CIVILISATION.
MASS MURDER BY THE GERMANS IN MAJDANEK "CAMP OF ANNIHILATION."

② "Illustrated London News", 14.10.1994

Hier erscheint das in "Life" veröffentlichte Bild der Schuhe vor der Baracke. Die Krematoriumsöfen, von einer Aufsicht aufgenommen, wirken durch die Wahl der Perspektive kleiner, vor allem aber machen sie einen 'ordentlichen' Eindruck. Die Aufnahmen der Behälter von den verwendeten Gasen, Kohlenmonoxyd und Zyklon B, lassen an Produktaufnahmen im Stil des 'Neuen Sehens' der 1920er Jahren erinnern. Die Stätten der Vernichtung, Gaskammer und Galgen, werden in Innen- und Außenansicht vorgestellt. Spuren menschlicher Überreste sind hier im Bild nicht sichtbar. Die Londoner Redaktion hält derartige Fotografien für "too horrible to reproduce"[6] und wählt recht harmlos anmutende Bilder aus. Die britische Bevölkerung war an solche Bildthemen noch nicht gewöhnt. Nur so wird verständlich, daß die Redaktion den Abbildungen dennoch die Kraft zumißt, Berichten über die seit einiger Zeit in der Presse veröffentlichten Massenmorden und Vernichtungslagern den propagandistischen Charakter zu nehmen.[7] Mit dieser Bildauswahl eines aufgeräumten und sauberen Lagers, 'Produktaufnahmen', ohne Spuren menschlicher Überreste, wird dem beigefügten Text die Schärfe seiner Nachricht genommen. Lediglich die im Bild anwesenden Besucher sollen die Authentizität der Illustrationen garantieren.

6. Illustrated London News, 14. Oktober 1944, S. 442.

7. In Großbritannien und den USA stand man diesen Meldungen skeptisch gegenüber aufgrund ähnlicher Nachrichten während des Ersten Weltkriegs, die sich nach 1918 als Propaganda herausstellten. Nach dem deutschen Einmarsch in Belgien im August 1914 verbreiteten die Kriegsparteien Berichte über die "hunnischen Barbaren", die Frauen und Kinder schändeten. Die neutralen Staaten sollten damit zum Kriegseintritt gewonnen werden, zugleich wollte man der eigenen Bevölkerung eine Rechtfertigung für den Einsatz der Armee liefern.

Auch in der "Saturday Evening Post" vom 28. Oktober 1944 erscheinen zwei Aufnahmen, die in der "Prawda" gedruckt waren: Das der Privatfotos der Ermordeten und ein fast identisches Bild der Schuhberge (Abb. 3).

Here the Nazi Butchers Wasted Nothing

By EDGAR SNOW

From a Nazi murder factory in Poland, a Post editor gives you an audit on the war's most frightful crime.

This is Why There Must be No Soft Peace

③ "Saturday Evening Post", 28.10.1944

Die amerikanischen Fotoredakteure bevorzugen allerdings eine Ansicht möglichst ohne Soldaten der Roten Armee. Sie betonen damit eher die Masse der ermordeten Frauen, Männer und Kinder, während in der "Prawda" die Befreiung des Lagers durch die russischen Soldaten, die dem Massenmord ein Ende setzten, im Vordergrund steht.

Beim Vergleich beider Aufnahmen wird deutlich, daß das Original ein Querformat gewesen sein muß, wie das Bild in der "Illustrated London News" und in "Life", das von der gegenüberliegenden Seite entstanden ist. Allerdings liegt bei dem Foto in der "Saturday Evening Post" nach einem Vergleich des Vordergrundes die Vermutung nahe, daß die "Rot Armisten" nachträglich entfernt wurden. Die Möglichkeit, daß die "Prawda" die siegreichen Soldaten einkopierte, ist auch nicht gänzlich auszuschließen. Beide Techniken sind in der Presse häufig angewandt worden. Nur Originalvorlagen können diese Frage noch klären. Wichtig war den Fotoredakteuren der "Saturday Evening Post" vor allem der Schuhberg, mit dem die eindrückliche Beschreibung des Autors, Edgar Snow, auch visuelle Bestätigung findet. Hierzu wird der Hintergrund fast bis zur Unkenntlichkeit gebleicht. Zaun und Pfähle sowie eine Person im Hintergrund sind fast völlig verschwunden. Den Blick des Betrachters lenkt nichts mehr von den Schuhen ab. Die Anzahl der Ermordeten wird im Bild der Schuhe betont. Individualisiert wird diese Menschenmenge durch die Abbildung ihrer Besitzer, hier durch die Privataufnahmen. Auch die mit Knochen gefüllten Krematoriumsöfen sind visuell präsent. Diese Aufnahme wirkt jedoch stark inszeniert. Die beiden Männer neben dem linken Ofen sind so plaziert, daß sie ihren Blick in den Ofen, dem man folgen soll, nicht verdecken, eine Strategie der Werbebranche, den Blick des Käufers auf das Produkt zu lenken. Der Mann vor dem nächsten Ofen steht starr, Schrecken signalisierend. Vier Frauen im Hintergrund weisen durch ihre gestische und körperliche Haltung die sich vor ihnen offenbarenden Tatsachen verängstigt und trauernd zurück. Das Grauen ist für sie zu unerträglich, als daß sie es aus der Nähe betrachten könnten. Den Redakteuren der "Saturday Evening Post" geht es bei der visuellen Unterstreichung des Berichtes um die Herausstellung des Massenmordes, der grauenhaften, abstoßenden Verbrechen. Hierzu setzt die Redaktion Fotos ein, die erst durch die Bildunterschriften ihre Brisanz erhalten, was auch für die "Illustrated London News" gilt. Beide Illustrierten zielen auf die Familie als Käuferschicht, so daß aus Rücksichtnahme auf die kindlichen Leser Abbildungen wie in "Life" und der "Prawda" nicht ediert werden.

Der Grund für die recht späte Berichterstattung — fast drei Monate nach Befreiung des Lagers — liegt in der skeptischen Haltung gegenüber den Berichten über den systematischen Massenmord begründet. Erst als auch die Westalliierten Konzentrationslager an ihrer Front betreten, wird über Majdanek berichtet. Die "Illustrated London News" veröffentlicht unmittelbar auf der Seite vor der Majdanek–'Story' einen Bildbericht mit insgesamt sieben Fotos über die Bestattung der Opfer in Lublin und der Befreiung des KZ Breendonck in Belgien im August/September 1944. Auch sind den Lesern in der Zwischenzeit Berichte über weitere Konzentrations–, Internierungs– und Durchgangslager bekannt, z.B. über Gurs in Frankreich und Vught in Holland im Westen und von der Ostfront über Sobibor und dem KZ Klooga. Fast jeden dritten Tag sind neue Enthüllungen über die Massenmorde der Tages– und Wochenpresse zu entnehmen, in der Schweiz, Großbritannien und den USA wie auch in der sich seit August 1944 wieder neu aufbauenden französischen und polnischen Presse. Während "Le Monde" in dieser Zeit völlig ohne Bildmaterial herausgegeben wird, berichtet die polnische Wochenzeitung "Zwyciężymy" in vier Teilen (Nr. 168 –171) über das Lager Majdanek mit dem Abdruck des "Prawda"–Artikels von B. Gorbatow. Die insgesamt fünf Aufnahmen sind jedoch nicht mit der sowjetischen Vorlage identisch. Aufnahmen der Trauerfeierlichkeiten sind vorrangig. Nur in dem Aufmacher, dem ersten Teil des Artikels, erscheint neben dem Foto des Befehlshabers der polnischen Armee, General Aleksander Zwadzki, der zum Kampf und zur Rache für die begangenen Verbrechen der nationalsozialistischen Aggressoren — so der Untertitel — aufruft, das Bild halb verkohlter Skelette. Wofür und warum gekämpft werden muß, wird hier visuell erklärt.

Von den "Spuren ungeheuerlichster Verbrechen" (*Śladem Najpotworniejszej Zbrodni*) erfährt am 4. März 1945 die polnische Bevölkerung in der Wochenbeilage "Ilustracja Polska" (Nr. 3) zur Tageszeitung "Dziennik Polski". Die drei Fotos der verkohlten Skelette im Leichenlager, der Schuhe, hier als Innenaufnahme, und der Sicht in einen geöffneten, mit Knochenresten gefüllten Ofen haben die visuelle 'Representation' von Majdanek bereits auf die wesentlichen Sujets reduziert, die auch in allen früheren Berichten abgedruckt sind: Krematorien, Skelette und Schuhe. Sie symbolisieren das Vernichtungslager noch heute.

Während die Berichterstattung über das KZ Majdanek in West und Ost recht ausführlich ist, sind die Meldungen über die Befreiung von Auschwitz äußerst spärlich, das im November 1944 beispielsweise durch den Bericht der geflohenen Rudolf Vrba und Alfred Wetzler auch in der amerikanischen und britischen Presse bekannt wurde. Warum die russische Regierung Auschwitz nicht die Publizität zukommen ließ wie Majdanek, kann vermutlich erst ein Aktenstudium in den russischen Archiven beantworten.

Die "Prawda" meldet am 1. Februar 1945 nur kurz die Befreiung des Konzentrationslagers, am nächsten Tag folgt ein ausführlicherer Bericht. Auf diese Darstellung bezieht sich die Berichterstattung in der Westpresse, z.B. in "The New York Times" am 3.2. und "Le Monde" am 8.2. Zwei Wochen später erscheint ein erster Bericht der Untersuchungskommission in der "Prawda", dem in den Westmedien keine weitere Beachtung geschenkt wird. Alle diese Beiträge sind nicht illustriert.

Mit der Befreiung weiterer Lager durch die Westalliierten, wie Ohrdruf am 4.4., Nordhausen und Buchenwald am 11.4., Bergen–Belsen am 15.4., Dachau am 29.4., Mauthausen und Wöbbelin am 5.5., erfahren die Briten und Amerikaner von den in den Westen evakuierten Häftlingen von den Vorgängen in dem Vernichtungslager Auschwitz. Sie sind aber von den sich vor ihnen offenbarenden Zuständen so schockiert, daß keine Nachrichten über das Todeslager im Osten an die Weltöffentlichkeit der westlichen Verbündeten dringt. Auch die "Prawda" bringt keine weiteren Nachrichten.

Die neu in Krakau erscheinende Illustrierte "Przekrój" widmet dem KL Auschwitz gleich in der zweiten Nummer vom 23. April 1945 unter dem Titel "Komisja dla Badania Zbrodni Niemiecko–Hitlerowskich w Oświęcimiu już pracuje" (Die Kommission zur Untersuchung der deutschen nationalsozialistischen Verbrechen in Auschwitz arbeitet schon) einen ganzseitigen Bildbericht mit sieben Fotografien des Ateliers Rosner (Abb. 4). Neben einer ersten Aufnahme der Kommissionsmitglieder wird der Galgen und im Hintergrund die Todeswand (noch ohne den schwarzen Kugelfang) gezeigt, Gefangene in gestreiften Anzügen vor Block 21, der Chirurgischen Abteilung des Häftlingskrankenbaus im Stammlager, der Stacheldrahtzaun, perspektivisch auf einen in der Ferne stehenden Wachturm ausgerichtet, das Tor "Arbeit macht frei", die mit Haaren gefüllten Säcke und die Lagerstätten einer Unterkunftsbaracke in Birkenau. Die Bildunterschriften geben überwiegend kurze, knappe Informationen über das Abgebildete wieder. Nur das Bild der Haare wird mit Zusatzinformationen über die Herkunft und Bestimmung ausgestattet. Das Objekt der sachlich arbeitenden, Fakten erschliessenden Untersuchungskommission wird hier visuell vorgestellt.

KOMISJA DLA BADANIA ZBRODNI
niemiecko-hitlerowskich w Oświęcimiu już pracuje

④ "Przekrój", Nr. 2, 23.4.1945

Am 7. Mai 1945 veröffentlicht die "Prawda" in einer Sondermeldung über drei Seiten das Ergebnis der staatlichen Untersuchungskommission "Über die ungeheuerlichen Verbrechen der deutschen Regierung in Auschwitz", die mit zwei Fotografien illustriert ist. Es ist eine Nahaufnahme von bis auf das Skelett abgemagerten Leichen, die Kopf an Kopf, mit geöffneten Mündern und Augen auf dem Körper eines anderen Mannes liegen. Die zweite Ansicht ist in dem Lagerraum der für den Transport nach Deutschland verpackten menschlichen Haare entstanden. Der Bürgermeister von Oświęcim, auf einem Berg von Haaren stehend, hält anderen Delegierten die 'Ware' zur näheren Begutachtung hin. Diese Aufnahme ist als Standbild dem von einem sowjetischen Kamerateam von Mitte Februar bis Herbst 1945 gedrehten Film "Chronik der Befreiung" entnommen.[8] Da die Haare erst am 7. März in der Gerberei außerhalb des Lagergeländes gefunden wurden, konnte es den frühen Artikeln im Februar nicht beigefügt werden.[9] Sie sind die letzten Beweise menschlicher Existenz im allgemeinen und seiner Individualität im besonderen, die den Häftlingen aus rein ökonomischer Berechnung geraubt wurden. Die Haare als Symbol für den

8. Viele Einzelaufnahmen aus diesem Film sind in das Bildgedächtnis über Auschwitz eingegangen. Inwieweit die in der britischen und amerikanischen Zone veröffentlichten Fotos und Filme in der Ikonographie dieses Films 'Pate gestanden' haben, kann hier nicht geklärt werden. Für die Szene 'Menschen hinter Stacheldraht' beispielsweise, die erst im Herbst 1945 gedreht wurde, ist eine visuelle Rezeption des viel publizierten Fotos von Margaret Bourke–White aus Buchenwald vom April 1945 nicht auszuschließen.

9. Dokument 008–USSR: Bericht der sowjetischen Kriegsverbrecher–Kommission vom 6. Mai 1945, in: Der Prozeß gegen die Hauptkriegsverbrecher vor dem Internationalen Militärgerichtshof, Bd. 39, Nürnberg 1949, S. 260.

industriellen Massenmord und die industrielle Verwertung der ermordeten Individuen in Auschwitz ist hier ebenfalls enthalten. Die im Bild anwesenden Kommissionsmitglieder garantieren einerseits für den Wahrheitsgehalt des unglaublichen Fundes von 7 000 kg der 140 000 Frauen — so der Untertitel —, unterstreichen andererseits aber auch das Bild des Siegers, wie die Soldaten der Roten Armee auf dem Schuhberg.

In den Printmedien der westlichen Verbündeten ist kein Foto von Auschwitz zu finden. Überhaupt geht diese Nachricht in den Meldungen und dem Freudentaumel über das Kriegsende in Europa völlig unter. So erscheint beispielsweise in der "New York Times" vom 8. Mai 1945 erst auf Seite 12 ein auf eine knappe Spalte gekürzter Bericht. Den von Briten und Amerikanern seit April befreiten Lagern wird dagegen mehr Aufmerksamkeit gewidmet, auch der visuellen Berichterstattung. Bergen–Belsen und Buchenwald werden hier zu Synonymen für die industrielle Massenvernichtung. Die Fotos und Wochenschauen treffen inzwischen auf ein Publikum, das psychisch durch die schriftlichen Berichte gut vorbereitet ist und geradezu auf eine visuelle Bestätigung wartet. Es erwartet eine Rechtfertigung für den Krieg und einen Beweis, daß man es mit dem Teufel zu tun hatte. So entspricht das "Inferno" der ersten Bildberichte in der "Picture Post" vom 5. Mai und im "Life"–Magazin vom 7. Mai 1945, die zum ersten Mal Fotos von völlig abgemagerten Menschen und Leichenbergen drucken, den Erwartungen der Leser, übertreffen sie möglicherweise. Die Reaktionen über den Abdruck dieser Bilder sind durchweg zustimmend.[10]

10. Vgl. hierzu die Leserbriefe in "Life" vom 28. Mai 1945.

Erschienen war in "Life" eine sechsseitige Fotoreportage mit zwölf Aufnahmen von George Rodger aus Bergen–Belsen (4), Margaret Bourke–White aus Buchenwald (2), William Vandivert aus Gardelgen (5) und Johnny Florea aus Nordhausen (1), (Abb. 5). Es sind Aufnahmen von überwiegend toten und verbrannten Menschen, die sich in ihrer äußeren Erscheinung kaum von den Lebenden unterscheiden.

ATROCITIES

CAPTURE OF THE GERMAN CONCENTRATION CAMPS PILES UP EVIDENCE OF BARBARISM THAT REACHES THE LOW POINT OF HUMAN DEGRADATION

⑤ "LIFE", Vol. 17. No. 19, 7.5.1945

In der "Prawda"–Ausgabe vom 7. Mai 1945 erhielt das Foto der Leichen die Bildunterschrift "Die von Deutschen ermordeten Märtyrer". Mit diesem Bildtitel wird sogleich der heldenhafte Opfertod der in den Konzentrationslagern Ermordeten thematisiert. Dem Bild wird damit eine gewisse Schockwirkung genommen, da die Toten in einen positiven Sinnzusammenhang gebracht werden.

Im polnischen "Przekrój" vom 21. Juli 1945 werden erstmals Fotos von Leichenbergen veröffentlicht, und zwar zwei der im Juni 1944 von einem Mitglied des Sonderkommandos heimlich fotografierten Bilder von der Verbrennung der Leichen und den zu der Gaskammer gehenden Frauen. Sie erscheinen als formatfüllende Aufnahmen. Das Original der Leichenverbrennung macht deutlich, daß es aus der schützenden Tiefe eines Raumes durch die offene Tür aufgenommen wurde.[11] Die veröffentlichte Aufnahme eliminiert den Schutz bietenden Raum, schaltet jede Heimlichkeit aus und thematisiert so direkten, offenen Widerstand.

11. Vgl. hierzu die Abbildung auf der Bildtafel zur Sektion 'Comics' in diesem Katalog.

Bilder der Leichenberge erscheinen in der illustrierten Presse West– und Osteuropas, wie auch auf dem amerikanischen Kontinent gleichermaßen, obgleich die Fotos jeweils andere sind. Die Bilder der Leichenberge sind so weltweit zum Symbol des Holocaust geworden. Für die Häftlinge ist es ein Zitat des Lageralltags, für die alliierten Befreier das Bild der vorgefundenen infernalischen Zustände.[12] Der Weltöffentlichkeit wird das Trauma mittels der Fotos der Leichenberge, Massengräber und Skelette weitergegeben, so daß jeder Augenzeuge der Zustände in den Konzentrationslagern wird.

12. Vgl. hierzu Z. Amishai Maisels: Depiction and Interpretation. The Influence of the Holocaust on the Visual Arts, Oxford, New York, Seoul, Tokyo 1993.

Bekannt ist das Bild der Leichenberge in der Kunst allerdings schon seit Jahrhunderten, vor allem in Bildern zur Apokalypse. Was in diesen Bildern, wie z. B. in Pieter Bruegels "Triumpf des Todes" (von 1562–1564) und auch in den Holocaust–Fotos so irritiert, ist der respektlose Umgang mit den Toten. Größtenteils nackt, mit in letzter Agonie erstarrten, geöffneten Mündern und Augen, in einem völligen Durcheinander über– und nebeneinandergestapelt, die Füße des einen auf dem Kopf oder der Brust des anderen liegend, zeugen sie von einer menschen– und todesverachtenden Haltung, die jeden moralischen und religiösen Umgang mit dem Tod und den Toten verhöhnt. Für die Holocaust–Fotografien kommt ein weiteres Faktum hinzu: Im Gegensatz zu den apokalyptischen Bildern, auf denen größtenteils wohlgenährte Menschen in den Tod gehen, sind wir hier mit bis auf das Skelett abgemagerten Menschen konfrontiert. Die in Eugène Delacroix' "Die Freiheit auf den Barrikaden" (1830) oder in Franz von Stucks "Der Krieg" (1894) dargestellten Toten treten noch in ihrer Todeshaltung für einen siegreichen Kampf oder Rache ein. Die Toten sind kräftig genug, um die geballte Faust zum Kampf zu heben. Die bis auf das Skelett abgemagerten Menschen in den Holocaust–Aufnahmen thematisieren dagegen nur Schwäche, Hilflosigkeit und Hoffnungslosigkeit, deren letzte Station nur der Tod sein kann, deren körperlicher Zustand nicht durch eine Naturkatastrophe herbeigeführt wurde, sondern von Menschen, die einer rassistischen, menschenvernichtenden Ideologie anhingen und diese ausführten. Sind die Bilder zur Apokalypse immer auch mit der Erlösung und Zukunftserwartung verbunden, diese Fotos sind ohne jedes Hoffnungsmotiv.

Bilder wie die der Leichenberge lösen starke emotionale Reaktionen aus und prägen sich so besonders intensiv dem Gedächtnis ein. Nicht nur schockierende Fotos, sondern Illustrationen generell ziehen eine erhöhte Aufmerksamkeit auf sich, sie werden drei– bis viermal häufiger "gelesen" als der dazugehörige Text.[13] Gedruckte Fotos erreichen ein breites Publikum, so daß die Grundlage für ein kollektives Bildgedächtnis gelegt ist. Jeder Rückgriff in später erscheinenden Publikationen auf diese bekannten, publizierten Bilder erhöht nicht nur deren Popularität, sondern trägt zum Prozeß der Symbolisierung bei, z.B. zählen die Fotografien von Auschwitz im "Przekrój" zu den meist veröffentlichten Aufnahmen. Sie symbolisieren heute die Geschichte des Konzentrationslagers. Aber nicht nur die Bequemlichkeit der Fotoredakteure oder bereits erworbene Bildrechte der Verlage, sondern auch die ausdrucksstarken, in ihrem Bildaufbau klar strukturierten, somit leicht erinnerbaren Fotografien fördern die visuelle 'Representation' des Ortes und seiner Geschichte. Nichts lenkt von den wesentlichen Objekten ab. Mit den Bildern und den Inhalten der Erstveröffentlichungen, für Majdanek die Krematoriumsöfen, die Schuhe und Skelette, für Auschwitz die Haare, das Tor, die Todeswand und Stacheldraht, wird offenbar der Grundstein für die künftige 'Representation' gelegt.

13. Vgl. hierzu Sanders (s.o. Anm. 3).

Majdanek and Auschwitz in the International Illustrated Press in 1945

The news about the mass murder of people in the Third Reich's concentration camps was met with great scepticism in the Western Allied countries. The liberation of the Majdanek concentration camp found world wide interest and several illustrated reports came out. They emphasize different points of importance. In contrast with the rest of the world press "Prawda" sometimes showed photos depicting suffering and massacres. Two photos from Auschwitz accompanied an article from May 7th 1945. This went almost unnoticed in western countries because of the celebrations at the end of the war in Europe. In the western countries photographs and films were met with an audience who were already convinced of the dehumanizing conditions in concentration camps but were lacking the illustrations as final proof. Many of these published photographs have become icons of concentration camps in the world.

Majdanek i Auschwitz w międzynarodowej prasie ilustrowanej z 1945 roku

Wiadomości o eksterminacji ludzi w obozach koncentracyjnych Trzeciej Rzeszy przyjmowane były w krajach zachodnich sprzymierzeńców z dużą dozą sceptycyzmu. Oswobodzenie obozu koncentracyjnego na Majdanku odbiło się wielkim publicznym echem, ukazały się bowiem w tym czasie liczne ilustrowane reportaże. W przeciwieństwie do prasy zachodniej gazeta "Prawda" sporadycznie pokazywała fotografie zwłok i zbrodni. Dwa zdjęcia z Auschwitz ilustrowały artykuł prasowy z 7 maja 1945, jednakże w radosnym upojeniu z okazji zakończenia wojny, na Zachodzie nie zwrócono na nie niemal żadnej uwagi. Fotografie i filmy trafiają na Zachodzie do publiczności, która wiedziała już o nieludzkich stosunkach panujących w obozach koncentracyjnych, nie widziała jednak materiałów fotograficznych, które mogą stanowić ostateczny dowód. Wiele z tych, opublikowanych w kwietniu i maju 1945 roku, zdjęć urosło w zachodnim świecie do roli "ikon" obozów koncentracyjnych.

Henryk Świebocki

Dokumentacja nazistowskich zbrodni ukryta przez więźniów w KL Auschwitz

I. Społeczność więźniarska wobec zbrodni popełnionych w obozie.

Zamierzeniem SS było utrzymanie w całkowitej tajemnicy zbrodni popełnionych w KL Auschwitz. Służył temu stworzony i stale udoskonalany system zabezpieczenia obozu oraz jego izolacji od świata. Nad sprawnym funkcjonowaniem tego systemu czuwała zbrojna załoga SS. Od zewnątrz zaś niemieckie siły policyjne zamykały już i tak dość szczelny pierścień bezpieczeństwa otaczający obóz. Rozbudowany aparat represyjny tak wewnątrz KL Auschwitz, jak i poza jego drutami stanowił dodatkową barierę uniemożliwiającą przeciekanie informacji odsłaniających prawdziwe oblicze obozu.

Społeczność więźniarska podejmowała jednak nieustanne wysiłki, aby dokumentować zbrodnie popełnione w obozie. Chodziło jej o uzyskanie jak najwięcej dowodów o Holocauście Żydów, eksterminacji Polaków, Cyganów i innych narodowości, o warunkach życia za drutami oraz o metodach fizycznego i moralnego dręczenia więźniów. Równolegle czyniła wszystko, by prawda o tych zbrodniach przedostawała się na zewnątrz, ażeby świat dowiedział się o nich i zrozumiał, do czego prowadzi system nazistowski. Miała przy tym nadzieję, że ludzkość wstrząśnięta tymi okropnościami uruchomi siły skuteczne dla zahamowania procesu zagłady i wyniszczania w KL Auschwitz. Te zabiegi społeczności więźniarskiej znalazły zrozumienie i poparcie ze strony Polaków — tak mieszkających na terenie przyobozowym jak i działających w ruchu oporu — którzy podjęli się pośrednictwa w przekazywaniu z obozu wiadomości na zewnątrz.

Dokumentowanie zbrodni nazistowskich stało się szczególną troską konspiracji obozowej. Niemniej też i zabiegi w tym kierunku poszczególnych więźniów, działających w pojedynkę czy w grupach, odegrały swoją rolę.

Więźniowie z polecenia kierownictwa organizacji ruchu oporu bądź z własnej inicjatywy zbierali wszelkie dane o obozie i przeprowadzanym tam procesie eksterminacji. Sporządzali również kopie, odpisy i wyciągi z dokumentów SS, co było głównie zasługą tych, którzy pełnili różne funkcje w obozie i mieli dostęp do dokumentacji. W niektórych przypadkach więźniowie dokonywali nawet kradzieży dokumentów. Niebezpieczeństwo, na jakie się narażali przeprowadzając te akcje, było ogromne; na każdym kroku ryzykowali życiem.

Szczególną rolę w tych działaniach odgrywali więźniowie pracujący w takich placówkach obozowych, jak administracja, wydział polityczny, centralne biuro budowlane, biuro zatrudnienia, szpital. Wiele informacji, w tym także niektóre dokumenty, dostarczali członkowie Sonderkommando.

Więźniowie jako bezpośredni świadkowie wydarzeń w obozie starali się też potajemnie zapisywać własne spostrzeżenia, przeżycia i uczucia czy utrwalać je w postaci wierszy, grafiki, rysunków. Obraz panujących stosunków w KL Auschwitz uzupełniały również ich listy do rodzin i przyjaciół o treści nie tylko osobistej, wysyłane z obozu sekretnymi drogami.

Niektóre dokumenty i materiały ukrywali więźniowie na terenie obozu. Nie mieli bowiem możliwości, aby wysłać je na zewnątrz. Henryk Porębski, polski więzień zatrudniony jako elektryk, informuje po wojnie, że współdziałał w 1944 z członkami Sonderkommando w zakopywaniu w pobliżu krematoriów w obozie Birkenau dowodów zbrodni nazistowskich. Były to ukryte w puszkach różne dokumenty obozowe, dowody tożsamości bądź paszporty osób zabitych w komorach gazowych, stop z widocznymi jeszcze i nie stopionymi koronkami zębów, notatki i zapiski członków Sonderkommando. Inicjatorem tych działań był polski Żyd o imieniu Dawid.[1] Inny bezpośredni świadek zbrodni w KL Auschwitz Alter Fajnzylberg (w obozie Stanisław Jankowski) podaje: “my więźniowie Sonderkommando staraliśmy się pozostawić po sobie ślad tego, co robić musieliśmy, co przeżywaliśmy, co widzieliśmy (...) Robiłem więc po kryjomu różne notatki, które następnie zakopywałem na terenie przy krematorium V”[2].

1. APMO. Zespół Oświadczenia, t. 21 k.15–18, relacja byłego więźnia Henryka Porębskiego.

2. APMO. Zespół Oświadczenia, t.111 k.57, fragment relacji byłego więźnia, członka Sonderkommando.

Więźniowie ukrywając w obozie dokumenty mieli nadzieję, a nawet przekonanie, że kiedyś po wojnie zostaną one odnalezione i ujrzą światło dzienne. Dzięki temu odkryje się prawda o zbrodniach nazistowskich przeciwko ludzkości. Wśród zabezpieczonej dokumentacji przez więźniów są materiały sporządzone przez nich samych oraz dokumenty władz obozowych.

II. Zabezpieczanie dokumentacji

1. Materiały sporządzane przez więźniów

W latach 1945, 1952, 1962 i 1980 odkryto i wydobyto z ziemi w pobliżu krematoriów na terenie byłego KL Auschwitz II–Birkenau siedem rękopisów członków Sonderkommando. Pięć z nich sporządzonych było w języku jidysz, jeden w języku francuskim i jeden w języku greckim. Autorami rękopisów w jidysz byli Żydzi polscy: Lejb — prawdopodobnie Lajb Langfus; Załmen Gradowski, który napisał dwa z odnalezionych manuskryptów; Załmen Lewental i więzień nazwany Nieznanym Autorem. Rękopis francuski jest dziełem Żyda z Francji, Chaima Hermana, a grecki — Żyda z Grecji, Marcela Nadjary'ego. Tylko ten ostatni przeżył obozy i wojnę. Pozostali zginęli w KL Auschwitz.[3]

Lejb (Lajb Langfus), Załmen Gradowski i Załmen Lewental zostali przywiezieni do KL Auschwitz w grudniu 1942 roku. Wcieleni do Sonderkommando i zmuszeni do pracy w krematoriach, nie poddali się rezygnacji. Włączyli się do działań obozowego ruchu oporu; stali się członkami kierownictwa konspiracji w Sonderkommando, należeli też do organizatorów buntu 7 października 1944 roku.

Lejb (Lajb Langfus), Załmen Gradowski i Załmen Lewental przedstawili w zapiskach swój pobyt w gettach i obozach przejściowych, następnie transport do KL Auschwitz. Relacje z KL Auschwitz koncentrują na losie i zagładzie Żydów: selekcjach na rampie, scenach rozgrywających się przed wejściem ofiar do komory gazowej, przebiegu gazowania, widoku komory gazowej wypełnionej ciałami zamordowanych, paleniu zwłok w dołach na wolnym powietrzu.[4] Lewental przeprowadza ponadto analizę psychiki więźniów Sonderkommando, charakteryzuje niektórych jego członków, przedstawia przygotowania do buntu i jego przebieg 7 października 1944 roku, na koniec snuje refleksje o sytuacji po buncie. Daje on też wstrząsający i pełen grozy opis tragedii około 3000 wyselekcjonowanych w obozie w Brzezince żydowskich więźniarek i zamordowanych w komorze gazowej w 1944 roku oraz w sposób może jeszcze bardziej dramatyczny przedstawia podobny los około 600 żydowskich chłopców.[5]

Gradowski ukazuje również przejmujący i nie wolny od liryki obraz wymordowania w komorach gazowych KL Birkenau w marcu 1944 roku Żydów czeskich, podając przykłady ich postaw w obliczu nieuchronnej śmierci, pełnych bohaterstwa i patriotyzmu. On też analizuje psychikę członków Sonderkommando.[6]

Więzień nazwany Nieznanym Autorem — wiemy, że pochodził ze środowiska ortodoksyjnego i przywieziony został prawdopodobnie w 1943 roku — opisuje w swoich notatkach niektóre wydarzenia w komorach gazowych w KL Birkenau, postawy Żydów a także i Polaków wobec śmierci, pełne godności i pogardy wobec oprawców. Kreśli sylwetki niektórych esesmanów (wśród nich szefa krematoriów Otto Molla), informuje o rozbiórce krematoriów w jesieni 1944 roku i paleniu przez esesmanów dokumentów.[7]

Rękopis Chaima Hermana, przywiezionego do KL Auschwitz na początku marca 1943 roku z obozu w Drancy, jest listem pożegnalnym do rodziny, datowanym na 6 listopada 1944 roku. Herman opisuje w nim przybycie do obozu, śmierć współtowarzyszy w komorach gazowych, swoją pracę w Sonderkommando, podaje nazwiska znajomych, którzy zgi-

3. *Wśród koszmarnej zbrodni. Notatki więźniów Sonderkommando.* Oświęcim 1975, s. 66–68, 127–130, 166, 187–188, 245–247 (informacje o znalezionych rękopisach pióra Danuty Czech, Jadwigi Bezwińskiej, Bernarda Marka); APMO. Zespół Wspomnienia, t. 174 k. 6, tekst przetłumaczonej z jidysz na język polski książki *W sercu piekła. Dokument oświęcimskiego Sonderkommando 1944* wydanej w Jerozolimie w 1978 r. (przez Chaima Wolnermana) w oparciu o znalezione po wojnie na terenie byłego KL Auschwitz notatki członka Sonderkommando, Załmena Gradowskiego; APMO. Zespół Wspomnienia, t. 135 brak paginacji, protokół z 24. X. 1980 r. sporządzony na okoliczność odnalezienia rękopisu Marcela Nadjary'ego, protokół z 20. XII. 1980 r. z oględzin rękopisu Marcela Nadjary'ego, notatka służbowa z 19. XII. 1983 r. dotycząca korespondencji z żoną Marcela Nadjary'ego.

4. *Rękopis Lejba (Lajba Langfusa).* (w:) *Wśród koszmarnej zbrodni...*, s. 73, 123; *Rękopis Załmena Gradowskiego.* (w:) *Wśród koszmarnej zbrodni...*, s. 131–162; *Rękopis Załmena Lewentala.* (w:) *Wśród koszmarnej zbrodni...* s. 191–201.

5. *Rękopis Z. Lewentala*, op.cit., s. 201–241.

6. APMO. Zespół Wspomnienia, t. 174 k. 32–124, tłumaczenie z jidysz na język polski książki W sercu piekła... opartej na notatkach Z.Gradowskiego.

7. *Rękopis Nieznanego Autora.* (w:) *Wśród koszmarnej zbrodni...*, s. 166–175; Bernard Mark, *O rękopisie Nieznanego Autora.* (w:) *Wśród koszmarnej zbrodni...*, s. 165.

nęli. Zdając sobie sprawę, że i on wkrótce podzieli los zamordowanych, żegna się z rodziną.[8]

Marcel Nadjary, autor ostatniego ze znalezionych manuskryptów, został przywieziony do KL Auschwitz w kwietniu 1944 roku w transporcie z Aten. Opisuje on pracę Sonderkommando, zabijanie ludzi w komorach gazowych, zacieranie przez nazistów śladów zbrodni. Wymienia liczbę około 600 000 Żydów z Węgier, Francuzów, Polaków (tekst w tym miejscu uległ zniszczeniu), która prawdopodobnie dotyczy zamordowanych. Sądząc, że nie przeżyje, pragnie zemsty na nazistach. Odczuwa satysfakcję z faktu, że jego ojczyzna Grecja jest już wolna.[9]

Te rękopisy z uwagi na ich treść, stanowią kapitalne źródło do badań nad eksterminacją w KL Auschwitz, przede wszystkim Żydów. Jest to zapis unikalny, pochodzący od bezpośrednich świadków wydarzeń, pisany "na gorąco", w miarę jak rozwijała się sytuacja. Opublikowanie go w różnych wersjach językowych było cennym wkładem w rozwój historiografii.[10]

Inny rodzaj źródeł stanowią rysunki przedstawiające sceny z życia obozowego, wykonane tajnie przez więźniów. Niektóre przesyłano potajemnie na zewnątrz, inne ukrywano w obozie. W 1947 roku na terenie byłego szpitala męskiego w Brzezince znaleziono szkicownik zawierający 22 rysunki (ołówek, kredka) o wymiarach 13,5 x 19.5 cm. Znajdował się on w butelce ukrytej pod belką w fundamentach jednego ze zniszczonych baraków. Autor rysunków podpisujący się inicjałami "M M" jest nieznany.[11] Rysunki przedstawiają warunki życia w obozie, kary i znęcanie się nad więźniami, ciężką pracę, różne metody zabijania a także samobójstwa więźniów rzucających się na naelektryzowane druty ogrodzenia. Zagładę ilustrują sceny z przybycia transportu Żydów, selekcji na rampie i odprowadzenie ofiar do komór gazowych.[12] Rysunki były wielokrotnie prezentowane na organizowanych przez Państwowe Muzeum w Oświęcimiu wystawach w Polsce i za granicą. Publikowano je także w albumach.[13]

Do tej kategorii źródeł należą też napisy i ilustracje wykonane (wydrapane, wygrawerowane, wyryte) wtedy przez więźniów w różnych miejscach KL Auschwitz. Na strychu w blokach 6, 7, 13, 15, 17 a także na zewnątrz bloków 7 i 9 obozu macierzystego widnieją do dzisiaj nazwiska więźniów różnych narodowości, podobnie w Brzezince na zewnętrznej ścianie łaźni w obozie kobiecym i na cembrowinie studni na terenie tzw. Meksyku[14]. Na parterze "Bloku Śmierci" w obozie macierzystym znajdują się na ścianach w różnych pomieszczeniach prawie że niewidoczne, maleńkie napisy tej treści: "Wojciechowski M. z Porombki został stracony 30 paź. 44 r."; "Schumacher Julian z Trzebini, 31.10.44 ogłoszono wyrok, 1.11.44 jeszcze żyje"; "Dnia 1.11.1944 został zawyrokowany na śmierć Władysław Świerguła z żoną z Wilkowic, Nr 595",

8. *Rękopis Chaima Hermana.* (w:) *Wśród koszmarnej zbrodni...*, s. 248–258.

9. APMO. Zespół Wspomnienia, t. 135 brak paginacji, notatka służbowa z 19. XII. 1983 i fotokopie rękopisu Marcela Nadjary'ego wraz z tłumaczeniem na język polski.

10. Wydawnictwo Państwowego Muzeum w Oświęcimiu opublikowało rękopisy Załmena Gradowskiego, Nieznanego Autora, Załmena Lewentala i Chaima Hermana pod wspólnym tytułem w specjalnej serii "Zeszytów Oświęcimskich" — *Wśród koszmarnej zbrodni. Rękopisy członków Sonderkommando. Zeszyty Oświęcimskie 1971 nr specjalny (II)*; toż samo w wersji niemieckiej — *Inmitten des Grauenvollen Verbrechens. Handschriften von Mitgliedern des Sonderkommandos. Hefte von Auschwitz 1972, Sonderheft (II)* oraz angielskiej jako odrębną publikację — *Amidst a Nightmare of Crime. Manuscripts of members of Sonderkommando.* Oświęcim 1973. Rękopis Lejba (Lajba Langfusa) wydano w serii podstawowej "Zeszytów Oświęcimskich". Oświęcim 1972 nr 14 oraz w wersji niemieckiej "Hefte von Auschwitz" 1973 nr 14. Wydanie z 1971 roku nr specjalny (II) "Zeszytów Oświęcimskich" poszerzone o rękopis Lejba (Lajba Langfusa) wznowiono w postaci odrębnej publikacji *Wśród koszmarnej zbrodni. Notatki członków Sonderkommando.* Oświęcim 1975.

11. Zbiory Państwowego Muzeum w Oświęcimiu. Protokoły darów. Prot. nr 13 a / 47.

12. Zbiory Państwowego Muzeum w Oświęcimiu. Nr inw. PMO–I–2–417/1–22, rysunki.

13. Ibidem, zob. też Jerzy Dałek, Teresa Świebocka (oprac). *Cierpienie i nadzieja.* Katowice 1989.

14. APMO. Materiał ikonograficzny z bloków 6, 7, 13, 15, 17 byłego obozu macierzystego oraz z odcinka B III ("Meksyk") byłego KL Birkenau; *Last Traces. The Lost Art of Auschwitz. Photography and Text by Joseph P. Czarnecki.* New York 1989, s. 156–161.

"Cupiał Jan z Trzebini, Danzingerstr. 6 (...) został skazany na karę śmierci dnia 31/10.41, proszę powiadomić Rodzinę".[15]

W podziemiach tegoż bloku, w osławionych bunkrach widnieją na ścianach i drzwiach różne napisy, nazwiska, rysunki. W celach 17–21 i 26 wykonał je Polak Edward Galiński, który przebywał w nich w drugiej połowie 1944 roku po nieudanej ucieczce z obozu podjętej wraz z Żydówką Malą Zimetbaum. W każdej z tych cel pozostawił jakiś ślad: napis, nazwisko (bądź inicjały) swoje i Zimetbaum a także jej wizerunek. W celi 18 znajduje się napis w języku rosyjskim informujący, że przebywał w niej uciekinier z KL Auschwitz, Białorusin Michaił Antonow. W celi 8 jest na ścianie cytat nawiązujący do "Boskiej Komedii" Dantego: "Porzućcie nadzieję wchodzący wszyscy, 2.10.43".[16] W innych celach widnieją również tego rodzaju pamiątki. Pełniejszy obraz śladów pobytu więźniów i ich cierpień w obozie zawiera album Józefa P. Czarneckiego.[17]

Innym rodzajem materiałów są wykazy więźniów, powstałe tajnie w obozie. Polak Jan Olszewski, zatrudniony w izbie pisarskiej, sporządził wraz ze swoim rodakiem Izydorem Łuszczkiem wykaz więźniów pochodzących z Podhala, którzy zginęli w KL Auschwitz lub zostali przeniesieni do innych obozów. Wykaz zawiera blisko 100 nazwisk z numerami obozowymi, datami urodzenia, miejscami zamieszkania i datami zgonów w KL Auschwitz, względnie przeniesienia do innych obozów.[18] Łuszczek zabezpieczył ten wykaz w obozie i chronił go. W październiku 1944 roku został on wywieziony do KL Sachsenhausen. Zabrał wtedy wykaz ze sobą i przechowywał w tamtejszym obozie a potem strzegł go w czasie marszu ewakuacyjnego aż do oswobodzenia przez wojska amerykańskie na początku maja 1945 roku.[19]

W podobny sposób ocalał wykaz około 450 więźniarek czeskich, które zginęły w KL Auschwitz lub zostały przeniesione do innych obozów. Sporządziła go w czerwcu–lipcu 1943 roku Czeszka Vlasta Kladivová (w obozie Vlastimila Ruprychová), zatrudniona w izbie pisarskiej w obozie kobiecym w Brzezince. Uwzględniła ona w wykazie podobne dane (tylko bez miejsca zamieszkania) co dwaj wymienieni poprzednio Polacy. W sierpniu 1943 roku Kladivova została wywieziona do KL Ravensbrück, ale zdążyła przed tym przekazać wykaz innej więźniarce, Steficy Stibler z Jugosławii. Ta w 1945 roku, po ewakuacji KL Auschwitz, znalazła się również w obozie w Ravensbrück, spotkała tam Kladivovą i oddała jej ten dokument.[20]

15. APMO. Materiały t. 67 Blok nr 11, k. 14, 16, 19, 23.

16. Ibidem, k. 48–50, 57, 59, 68; *Last Traces...*, s. 81, 83, 85–87, 89, 95, 119, 122–123, 127, 131.

17. Joseph P. Czarnecki, *Last Traces. The Lost Art of Auschwitz.* New York 1989.

18. APMO. Mat. RO, t. XXXIII zamiast paginacji sygn. D–RO/223, wykaz więźniów z Podhala; APMO. Zespół Oświadczenia, t. 97 k. 154, relacja byłego więźnia Izydora Łuszczka.

19. APMO. Zespół Oświadczenia, t. 97 k. 161–162, relacja I. Łuszczka.

20. APMO. Mat. RO, t. XVII k. 69–81 d, wykaz więźniarek czeskich z załączonym protokołem z 20. IX. 1972 r. spisanym z Vlastą Kladivovą i uzupełniony dodatkowymi wyjaśnieniami 6. IV. 1995 r.

2. Dokumenty władz obozowych

Wśród dokumentów odnalezionych po wojnie znalazły się dwie księgi ewidencyjne z obozu familijnego dla Cyganów w Brzezince. Jedna obejmuje mężczyzn i chłopców, druga — kobiety i dziewczęta. Zawierają one blisko 21 000 nazwisk oraz takie dane jak: numer więźniarski, przynależność państwową, datę i miejsce urodzenia, zawód, datę przybycia do obozu a także dalsze losy w KL Auschwitz — zgon, skierowanie do karnej kompanii, przeniesienia itp. Informacje o zgonach wskazują na szczególnie wysoką śmiertelność wśród Cyganów, zwłaszcza u małych dzieci.[21] Księgi prowadzili oficjalnie pisarze więźniowie. Od lutego 1944 roku pisarzem raportowym w obozie dla Cyganów był Polak Tadeusz Joachimowski. Wobec zaplanowanej przez nazistów likwidacji obozu familijnego — tj. wywiezienia do innych obozów silnych i zdrowych Cyganów i Cyganek oraz wymordowania pozostałych, głównie kobiet, dzieci i starców, w komorach gazowych, co nastąpiło w nocy 2/3 sierpnia 1944 roku — Joachimowski oraz jeszcze dwaj Polacy, Ireneusz Pietrzyk i Henryk Porębski, już w lipcu wynieśli po kryjomu księgi ewidencyjne Cyganów i zawinięte w ubranie umieścili w wiadrze, uszczelnionym od góry drewnianą pokrywą. Następnie wiadro zakopali w ziemi na terenie obozu dla Cyganów. W 1949 roku pracownicy Państwowego Muzeum w Oświęcimiu w obecności Joachimowskiego, który wskazał miejsce ukrycia dokumentów, wydobyli wiadro wraz z księgami.[22] Były one uszkodzone na skutek wilgoci, stąd trzeba było je poddać zabiegom konserwatorskim. W 1993 roku zostały one w całości opublikowane.[23]

21. APMO. Syg. D–Au II–3/1–2, księgi ewidencyjne z obozu dla Cyganów.

22. Ibidem, protokół z 13. I. 1949 r. sporządzony na okoliczność odnalezienia i przejęcia ksiąg ewidencyjnych z byłego obozu dla Cyganów.

23. *Memorial Book. The Gypsies at Auschwitz–Birkenau. Księga Pamięci. Cyganie w obozie koncentracyjnym Auschwitz–Birkenau. Gedenkbuch. Die Sinti und Roma im Konzentrationslager Auschwitz–Birkenau.* (redakcja Jan Parcer) t. 1–2, München 1993.

Po wojnie odnaleziono również dwie księgi operacyjne oddziału chirurgicznego z bloku 21 obozu macierzystego. Ukryli je więźniowie w czasie ewakuacji KL Auschwitz w styczniu 1945 roku, wykorzystując towarzyszące jej zamieszanie i pośpiech. Najprawdopodobniej miejscem ukrycia był piec znajdujący się w pomieszczeniach łaźni obozowej.[24]

24. APMO. Zespół Oświadczenia, t. 119 k.17, relacja byłego więźnia Stanisława Kłodzińskiego; Tadeusz Orzeszko, *Relacja chirurga z obozu oświęcimskiego* "Przegląd Lekarski — Oświęcim" 1971, s. 47.

Księgi zawierają nazwiska i numery obozowe więźniów, daty, rozpoznanie i rodzaj zabiegów. Obejmują okres od 10 września 1942 roku do 23 lutego 1944 roku. Jak wynika z wpisów, dokonano w tym czasie 11 246 różnego rodzaju zabiegów.[25]

25. APMO. Sygn. D–Au I–5/1–2. Książka chirurgiczna Bl. 21, t. 1–2 oryg.

Wśród dokumentów ukrytych przez więźniów i odnalezionych po wojnie znajdują się fotografie wykonane przez esesmanów bądź na ich polecenie. Do nich należą 52 zdjęcia, których autorem jest esesman Dietrich Kamann, prowadzący sekcję fotograficzną przy Centralnym Zarządzie Budowlanym Waffen SS i Policji (Zentralbauleitung der Waffen SS und Polizei) w obozie. Fotografie sporządzone przez Kamanna, głównie w 1943 roku, przedstawiają więźniów i więźniarki przy pracach ziemnych, przy kopaniu kanałów, przy wydobywaniu żwiru, przy rozładunku wagonów, przy budowie baraków, budynków gospodarczych, krematoriów i innych obiektów. Widać na nich obóz, baraki, urządzenia zagłady, wnętrze krematoriów wraz z piecami.[26]

26. APMO. Proces Hössa, t. 15 k. 32–50, fotografie autorstwa Dietricha Kamanna.

Odbitki zdjęć wykonali potajemnie z filmów Kamanna dwaj polscy więźniowie, Ludwik Lawin i Tadeusz Kubiak, zatrudnieni w sekcji fotograficznej. Lawin włożył zdjęcia do butelki po lekarstwach, którą zakorkował i zalał świecą. Butelkę umieścił w puszcze po konserwach i zakopał w pobliżu jednego z baraków biura budowlanego. Miało to miejsce w lecie, prawdopodobnie w sierpniu 1944 roku.[27] Po wojnie w 1946 roku Lawin wskazał miejsce, gdzie ukrył fotografie. Zostały one odnalezione.[28] Służyły potem wielokrotnie jako materiał ilustracyjny w różnych publikacjach i na wystawach.[29]

W podobny sposób wykorzystywane były po wojnie fotografie obozowe więźniów, tzw styki. Wykonywano je oficjalnie w pracowni służby rozpoznawczej (Erkennungsdienst) wydziału politycznego w pierwszych latach istnienia obozu, stąd większość fotografowanych — to Polacy. Później fotografie obozowe sporządzano tylko sporadycznie. W zbiorach Archiwum Państwowego Muzeum w Oświęcimiu jest blisko 39 000 zdjęć — styków więźniarskich.[30] Zachowały się one dzięki panującemu chaosowi i rozgardiaszowi oraz pospiesznemu tempu ewakuacji w styczniu 1945 roku. Nie omieszkali tego wykorzystać więźniowie, którzy pragnęli ocalić chociaż część dokumentacji obozowej. O uratowaniu styków relacjonują Bronisław Jureczek i Wilhelm Brasse, więźniowie Polacy zatrudnieni w Erkennungsdienst, którzy z polecenia esesmanów mieli spalić dokumentację fotograficzną. Pierwszy z nich donosi: "W ostatniej niemal chwili polecono nam spalić wszelkie negatywy i fotografie znajdujące się w Erkennungsdienst. Do pieca kaflowego w pracowni wsadziliśmy wpierw zamoczony papier fotograficzny i fotografie a następnie masę zdjęć i negatywów. Wtłoczone do pieca duże ilości materiałów zatkały odpływ dymu. Kiedy zapaliliśmy w piecu byliśmy przekonani, że spłonie tylko część zdjęć i kliszy tuż przy drzwiczkach piecowych a potem z braku powietrza w piecu — ogień zgaśnie (...) Rozmyślnie (...) pewną ilość zdjęć i negatywów pod pozorem pospiechu rozrzuciłem w pokojach pracowni. Wiedziałem, że przy pospiesznej ewakuacji nikt nie będzie miał czasu wszystkiego zabrać i coś się ocali".[31] Relację tę zaś uzupełnia Brasse: "Gdy zaczęła się ewakuacja obozu, filmy robione przez Waltera i Hoffmana (esesmani z Erkennungsdienst — HŚ), zdjęcia dla dra Mengelego zostały wywiezione prawdopodobnie do KL Gross–Rosen. Natomiast negatywy zdjęć więźniarskich kazano mnie i Jureczkowi spalić w piecu. Robiliśmy to pod nadzorem Waltera. Gdy on wyszedł, przydusiliśmy ogień w piecu i wyjęliśmy resztki negatywów. Przed opuszczeniem obozu w dniu 18 stycznia 1945 roku negatywy zabezpieczyliśmy w pracowni, zabijając deskami wejście, aby nikt się tam nie dostał".[32]

Ukryte przez więźniów i odzyskane po wojnie materiały i dokumenty stanowią tylko część tych dowodów zbrodni nazistowskich, jakie zdołali oni zgromadzić. Nie wszystkie zostały odnalezione. Zapewne do dzisiaj tereny byłego KL Auschwitz kryją w sobie dokumentację, którą więźniowie zakopali bądź schowali w im tylko wiadomych miejscach.

Znaczna jednak część dowodów o KL Auschwitz i zbrodniach w nim popełnionych została przesłana poza obóz jeszcze w

27. Ibidem, k. 31 c, zeznanie byłego więźnia Ludwika Lawina; APMO. Zespół Oświadczenia, t. 114 k. 139–142, relacja byłego więźnia Ludwika Lawina; APMO. Nr inw. 46614. Ankieta byłego więźnia Tadeusza Kubiaka.

28. APMO. Proces Hössa, t. 15 k. 31a, protokół z 25. IX. 1946 r. sporządzony na okoliczność odnalezienia i przejęcia fotografii autorstwa Dietricha Kamanna; APMO, Zespół Oświadczenia, t. 114 k. 142, relacja L. Lawina.

29. Spośród publikacji na uwagę zasługuje album *Auschwitz — zbrodnia przeciwko ludzkości* (oprac. Kazimierz Smoleń, Teresa Świebocka przy współpracy z Renatą Bogusławską–Świebocką). Warszawa 1990 i jego powtórzenie w wersji angielskiej *Auschwitz. A History in Photographs (Auschwitz. Historia w fotografii)* Warszawa 1993. Wielokrotnie fotografie prezentowano jeszcze w innych publikacjach Państwowego Muzeum w Oświęcimiu, m.in. w "Zeszytach Oświęcimskich" oraz w innych wydawnictwach.
Jeśli chodzi o wystawy, które zawierały fotografie autorstwa Dietricha Kamanna, było ich bardzo wiele. Ostatnio prezentowana wystawa "Auschwitz — a Crime against Mankind" [Auschwitz — zbrodnia przeciwko ludzkości] była pokazana w USA (1985 r., 1986 r., 1987 r., 1992 r., 1993 r.), Austrii (1990 r.), Szwajcarii (1990 r.), na Węgrzech (1990 r.), we Włoszech (1991 r. i 1994 r.), w Niemczech (1993 r.), w Belgii (1995 r.).

30. Z opracowanych przez sekcję komputerową Państwowego Muzeum w Oświęcimiu danych wynika, że w zbiorach Archiwum jest 6 947 styków kobiet i 31 969 styków mężczyzn, w sumie 38 916 fotografii (Archiwum Państwowego Muzeum w Oświęcimiu. Fotografie więźniów z obozu Auschwitz–Birkenau 1993 tom I).

31. APMO. Zespół Oświadczenia. t. 19 k. 31, fragment relacji b. więźnia Bronisława Jureczka.

32. APMO. Zespół Oświadczenia, t. 125 k. 52, fragment relacji byłego więźnia Wilhelma Brasse.

trakcie jego istnienia. Zawierały one dane na temat całokształtu życia więźniów i przeprowadzanej eksterminacji. Przesłane na zewnątrz materiały sporządzone były głównie przez więźniów. Niemniej wśród nich znalazły się też kopie, odpisy i wyciągi z akt SS, a nawet oryginalne dokumenty obozowe.

Społeczność więźniarska przekazywała poza druty różnymi drogami dowody o zbrodniach SS. Szczególną rolę w tym odegrali więźniowie polscy, którzy nawiązali i utrzymywali stałą, tajną łączność z zewnątrz i dzięki temu był możliwy przerzut z KL Auschwitz wiadomości i danych. Informacje i meldunki z obozu przesyłane były też poprzez zwolnionych więźniów a także za pośrednictwem zbiegłych stamtąd. Zdarzały się również przypadki wykorzystania do tego członków załogi SS oraz cywilnego personelu niemieckiego, zatrudnionego w KL Auschwitz.

Documentary Records of Nazi Crimes Committed in Auschwitz Concentration Camp Hidden by Prisoners

The Nazis tried to hide the truth about the Auschwitz concentration camp. But with the aim of documenting the crimes committed by the SS, the prisoners passed on a multitude of evidence and written documents from inside the camp to the Polish resistance movement and they also hid evidence on the camp grounds. The following forms of evidence were found after the war: notes taken by members of the Sonderkommando about the genocide of the Jews, a sketch–book with drawings of life and death in the concentration camp, inscriptions and drawings found on the walls of blocks and barracks illustrating the fate of the prisoners, lists of prisoners who were killed and those who were transported to other camps. Furthermore, important documents written by camp officials [*Lagerleitung*] were hidden by Polish groups and found after the war. For example, two registers from the Gypsy camp with approximately 21 000 names and dates of death, plus approximately 39 000 photographs taken of prisoners. This material contains an extensive range of information on the Nazi crimes. It forms an important source for research on the camp's history.

Von Häftlingen versteckte Dokumente der Nazi–Verbrechen im KL Auschwitz

Die Nazis versuchten, die Wahrheit über Auschwitz zu verheimlichen. Doch die Gefangenengemeinschaft setzte sich das Ziel, die Verbrechen der SS zu dokumentieren, indem sie eine Vielzahl von Beweismaterialien und schriftlichen Unterlagen aus dem Lager der polnischen Widerstandsbewegung zuspielte oder auf dem Gelände des Konzentrationslagers versteckte. Zu den Beweisen, die nach dem Krieg entdeckt wurden, gehören u. a.: Aufzeichnungen von Mitgliedern des Sonderkommandos über die Auslöschung der Juden; ein Skizzenbuch mit Zeichnungen über Leben und Tod im Konzentrations– und Vernichtungslager Auschwitz–Birkenau; an den Mauern und Wänden der Blöcke und Wohnbaracken angebrachte Inschriften und Zeichnungen, die das Schicksal der Gefangenen veranschaulichen; Auflistungen der getöteten oder in andere Lager fortgeschafften Häftlinge. Weiterhin wurden nach dem Krieg wichtige Dokumente der Lagerleitung gefunden, die polnische Gruppen versteckt hatten: So z. B. zwei Register aus dem Zigeunerlager mit fast 21 000 Namen und dem jeweiligen Todesdatum, ferner etwa 39 000 Fotos von Gefangenen. Das genannte Material enthält zahlreiche und vielfältige Informationen über die Verbrechen der Nazis und bildet eine wichtige Quelle für die Erforschung der Lagergeschichte.

Krystyna Oleksy

Rzeczywistość obozu Auschwitz w utworach literackich

Właściwie już od początku swojego istnienia literatura przekazuje doświadczenia wojenne, a na ich tle przeżycia i portrety ludzi, którzy tworzyli historię. Wydarzenia wojenne opisuje wielokrotnie Biblia, wojna jest także inspiracją pierwszego wielkiego dzieła literackiego z kręgu kultury śródziemnomorskiej — "Iliady". Do dziś epopeja ta stanowi lekturę współczesnego inteligenta, przedstawia bowiem nie tyle opis działań wojennych, ile obraz postępowania ludzi, kształtowania się postaw i charakterów. Wojna jest szczególnym sprawdzianem zachowań — zarówno jednostek jak i społeczeństw.

Wiek XX poddany został szczególnym wstrząsom, jakimi były dwie wojny o zasięgu światowym. Ich areną była przede wszystkim Europa, stąd też pisarze zastanawiali się, czy nie nadszedł kres cywilizacji europejskiej, a świat nie stanął w obliczu zagłady. Poglądy te, głoszone już po zakończeniu I wojny światowej, odezwały się ze wzmożoną siłą po roku 1945. Druga wojna z obozami koncentracyjnymi, z obozami zagłady, zrodziła pesymizm i zwątpienie w uznane wartości. Wielu myślicieli zastanawiało się, dlaczego społeczeństwa nie potrafią przeciwstawiać się wybuchowi kataklizmu. Wojna nie jest przecież wyłącznie sprawą tylko garstki polityków. Odpowiedzialność spada zarówno na tych, którzy ją wywołali, jak i na tych, którzy nie chcieli, czy nie potrafili się jej przeciwstawić.

Dla byłych więźniów nazistowskich obozów koncentracyjnych i obozów zagłady tworzących po wyzwoleniu, najważniejszym przesłaniem było dać świadectwo prawdzie czym był obóz, pokazać bezmiar dokonanych w nim zbrodni, pokazać ogrom ludzkiego cierpienia. Niewiele można znaleźć w tym okresie utworów, które w swej warstwie treściowej wychodzą poza opis wydarzeń. Autorzy ich bowiem nade wszystko pragnęli, by wiedzę o tym, co działo się poza drutami obozów zapisać na zawsze w pamięci ludzkości. Większość utworów literackich powstałych już po wyzwoleniu poświęcona jest utraconym w obozie najbliższym — przyjaciołom, rodzicom, dzieciom. Dotyczy to zwłaszcza autorów żydowskich, których do obozu przywieziono z całymi rodzinami w ramach akcji "ostatecznego rozwiązania kwestii żydowskiej" — masowej zagłady europejskich Żydów. Dla Żydów Auschwitz utożsamia wszelkie cierpienia, jakich doznał ten naród w całej swojej historii. Zagłada narodu budzi bowiem uczucie bólu nie tylko po utracie bliskich, lecz także i tego, co dla istnienia każdego człowieka stanowi istotną wartość — utratę korzeni, poczucie głębokiego związku z tradycją stworzoną przez praojców, z kulturą materialną pokoleń, z ziemią. Auschwitz jest miejscem, gdzie wraz z pogrzebaniem setek tysięcy, czy jak często przeczytać można — "milionów", pogrzebano najwyższe wartości nadające sens naszemu istnieniu: miłość, braterstwo, wiarę w człowieka.

Na tle pierwszych powojennych utworów literackich o tematyce oświęcimskiej wyróżniają się zdecydowanie obozowe opowiadania Tadeusza Borowskiego. Napisane zostały zaraz po wyzwoleniu autora w Dachau i wydane wiosną przez polską oficynę wydawniczą w Monachium. Pisane są w pierwszej osobie — co nie jest wyjątkowe — a bohaterem uczynił autor człowieka całkowicie przystosowanego do obozowej rzeczywistości, akceptującego ją jako normalną i przez nią zdemoralizowanego. Borowski ukazał cały bezmiar obozowego terroru i okrucieństwa, totalnego zagrożenia śmiercią a na tym tle tragizm ofiary, która przez machinę obozową została wciągnięta w jej tryby. Tragedia tych, co przeżyli — zdaniem Borowskiego, to utrata niewinności, utrata spokoju sumienia, bo okoliczności nie zmieniają samego faktu, że uczestniczyło się w takim porządku. Tragizm Borowskiego rozumiany jest jako tragiczny przymus — więzień został pozbawiony możliwości wyboru, został w sytuacji bez wyjścia. Przedstawiając rzeczywistość obozową Borowski rezygnuje z patosu i długich opisów. Jednakże efekt jaki osiąga stosując lakoniczne stwierdzenia i definicje, np. głodu: "Głód jest wtedy dopiero prawdziwy, gdy człowiek patrzy na drugiego człowieka jako na obiekt do zjedzenia", jest bardziej wstrząsający niż rozwlekłe opisy drastycznych scen.
Masowość zagłady, śmierci jest motywem przewodnim, bez względu na to czy jej poświęcone jest całe opowiadanie ("Ludzie z rampy"), czy też opowiada ono o życiu w obozie. Krótkie stwierdzenia: "Między jednym a drugim kornerem za moimi plecami zagazowano trzy tysiące ludzi", czy też "Paru ludzi kierujących ruchem, żeby tłoku nie było, i ludzie płyną jak woda z kranu za odkręceniem kurka", ostrzej niż wielostronicowe opisy przestawiają okrutną machinę zbrodni. Tadeusz Borowski, który pierwszy przedstawił w swych utworach także zbrodnie jakich dokonano na psychice więźniów, ogrom spustoszenia wewnętrznego i demoralizacji, spotkał się z totalną krytyką i głębokim oburzeniem środowiska więźniarskiego.

W opisie okrucieństw obozowych, w utworach zarówno powstałych w obozie jak i w okresie bezpośrednio po wojnie, dominuje tendencja demonizacji dokonanego zła. Objawia się to także w warstwie językowej. Określenia — "piekło Auschwitzu", "bestie", "kaci", "oprawcy" powtarzają się stosunkowo często. W literaturze tego okresu jaskrawo jest widoczny podział całej społeczności obozowej w kategoriach czarno–białych, podział na ofiary i katów, podział według kategorii narodowościowych lub koloru obozowego winkla. Niemiec — symbol wszelkiego zła, Żyd, Polak — to szlachetna ofiara. Z drugiej strony więzień polityczny to człowiek skłonny do poświęceń nawet w tak skrajnych warunkach jak obóz, to jednostka walcząca o godność i zachowanie najwyższych wartości, w odróżnieniu od zbrodniarzy z kręgów aspołecznych czy kryminalnych. Taki sposób przedstawiania jednostki w obozie, przedstawiania opisywanego świata służyć miał intensywności protestu moralnego wymierzonego przeciwko złu i do dziś ciąży na sposobie rozumienia oświęcimskiej tragedii i oświęcimskiej zbrodni.

Literatura martyrologiczna jest swoistym dokumentem oporu z jakim świat przyjmował do wiadomości fakt, że zbrodni dokonali normalni ludzie, których nawet często z trudem można było nazwać złymi w tradycyjnym znaczeniu tego słowa, którzy w życiu pozaobozowym nie przejawiali żadnych skłonności przestępczych czy sadystycznych. Prawda ta godzi bowiem w całą ludzkość, stawia pod znakiem zapytania podstawowe wartości moralne i kulturowe, jakie wypracowane zostały przez stulecia.

Czy istnieje granica, która oddziela literaturę dokumentalną od tzw. literatury pięknej? Chyba stanowi ją jedynie fikcja literacka, a więc kreowanie rzeczywistości w przeciwieństwie do jej wiernego odtworzenia. Literatura pamiętnikarska, ciesząca się dużą popularnością i uznaniem czytelników, mająca walor dokumentu historycznego, spełnia ważną funkcję społeczną i kulturalną, jest łącznikiem między fikcją a opracowaniem naukowym. Jest ona niezwykle cenną gałęzią literatury ze względu na wielorakość omawianych zagadnień.

Autentyzm i prostota literatury pamiętnikarskiej, wspomnieniowej spowodowały, że do dziś kształtuje ona wyobraźnię społeczną. O tym, jak wielka była siła przeżyć wojennych, a zwłaszcza przeżyć obozowych, świadczy m.in. fakt, że do tematów tych nawiązują jeszcze dziś, po 50 latach, twórcy młodzi, urodzeni już wiele lat po zakończeniu tej dziejowej katastrofy. I w miarę upływu czasu coraz mniej literatura zajmuje się rejestrowaniem faktów, a coraz częściej — nawet w literaturze autorów starszego pokolenia, w literaturze wspomnieniowej — znaleźć można szeroki komentarz, którego celem jest pogłębienie naszej wiedzy historycznej, znalezienie odpowiedzi na pytanie, czy historia jest złożona z bezmyślnych i przypadkowych wydarzeń pozbawionych głębszego sensu, czy też przeciwnie — wynika logicznie ze świadomych działań podporządkowanych woli człowieka i czy można z niej wysnuwać wnioski na przyszłość, czy można z niej się uczyć ? Druga wojna światowa nabrała cech apokaliptycznych nie tylko dlatego, że objęła całą ziemię, lecz przede wszystkim ze względu na masową zagładę Żydów prowadzoną w systematyczny, uprzemysłowiony sposób, z jakim ludzkość nigdy się jeszcze nie zetknęła.

Literatura piękna odgrywała doniosłą rolę po wojnie jako jedno z podstawowych źródeł wiedzy o niedawnej przeszłości. Wiele z pierwszych utworów literackich przedstawiających rzeczywistość obozową traktowanych było jako dokumenty, jako odbicie wydarzeń historycznych, a nie jako literatura piękna. Jednocześnie literatura starała się wyjaśnić zjawiska, których autorzy byli świadkami i uczestnikami zarazem.

Czy możliwe było, aby w jednym dziele ujawnić wszelkie sprzeczności epoki — upadek i wielkość człowieka? Literatura stanęła wobec konieczności przekazania zjawisk i przeżyć zupełnie nowych, nie znanych dotąd, nie mieszczących się w obrębie dotychczasowych doświadczeń zarówno jednostki jak i całego społeczeństwa. Niebezpieczeństwo pisania o rzeczywistości obozowej polegało na widzeniu już gotowych schematów kompozycyjnych, na odtwarzaniu rzeczywistości w czarno–białych barwach. Pokusie tej uległo wielu twórców dostrzegających zaledwie zewnętrzne przejawy zjawisk. Jednym z problemów, które do dziś nie zostały do końca zanalizowane jest zagadnienie psychiki sprawców. Jedną z pierwszych książek na ten temat jest zbeletryzowana biografia Rudolfa Hößa autorstwa Roberta Merlé "Śmierć jest moim rzemiosłem" (La mort est mon metier). Autor oparł ją na wydanych w Polsce w 1951 roku autentycznych wspomnieniach komendanta obozu Auschwitz Rudolfa Hößa, napisanych w więzieniu podczas prowadzonego przeciwko niemu procesu. Merle winą za to, że życie Hößa ukierunkowane zostało tak, by mógł on skrupulatnie realizować nazistowski plan zagłady Żydów obarcza jego najbliższe środowisko — rodzinę. Taki sposób interpretacji wydaje się być nadmiernie uproszczony i powierzchowny. Zdecydowanie lepszą lekturę stanowi autentyczny zapis Hößa, dając przy tym znaczną ilość informacji o wydarzeniach historycznych.

Nowe spojrzenie na rzeczywistość obozową mogło pojawić się jednak dopiero w latach 60–tych, kiedy punkt widzenia ofiary przestał być jedynym i wyłącznym. Zaczęły jawić się nowe pytania podyktowane nie tylko osobistym, emocjonalnym stosunkiem do przeszłości. Ci, którzy wojnę przeżyli jako dzieci, problemy wojny widzieli w powiązaniu z własnym dojrzałym życiem przeżywanym 20 lat później.

Znany dotąd wizerunek zbrodniarza — sadysty zaczęły coraz intensywniej korygować procesy lat 60–tych, ukazując byłych oprawców Oświęcimia jako zwyczajnych obywateli. O ile stwierdzenie, że przed Oświęcimiem większość z nich prowadziła normalne, przeciętne życie, przyjmowane mogło być z niedowierzaniem i usuwane ze świadomości, to szokiem było stwierdzenie naoczne podczas procesu, że i po Oświęcimiu mogli oni nie odróżniać się niczym od innych.

Literatura wspomnieniowa w dużej mierze zapełnić może lukę poznawczą czytelnika, dać informacje o konkretnych wydarzeniach, mających miejsce w obozie. Jest to szczególnie ważne w procesie przygotowania młodzieży do odwiedzenia Auschwitz, ponieważ brak podstawowych informacji z zakresu wiedzy historycznej uniemożliwia zupełnie wyciągnięcie jakichkolwiek wniosków natury filozoficznej czy moralnej. Z biegiem lat zmienia się też forma wspomnień obozowych. Autorzy decydują się na formę bardziej literacką, unikając często pisania w pierwszej osobie, starają się beletryzować, dając liczne dialogi i opisy. W tematyce przeważa opis martyrologii i terroru, ale także autorzy coraz częściej podkreślają rolę ruchu oporu, organizowanie samopomocy, życia kulturalnego, próby stworzenia w obozie namiastki "normalności" poprzez podkreślanie roli uczuć i poświęcenie większej uwagi relacjom międzyludzkim. Zdarza się też, że autorzy nie ograniczają się wyłącznie do przedstawienia wzajemnych relacji pomiędzy więźniami, lecz piszą o relacjach więzień — esesman w kategoriach związków międzyludzkich, a nie wyłącznie w kategoriach ofiary i kata.

W całym 50–leciu powojennym we wszystkich krajach europejskich, a także w Ameryce i Australii, nie mówiąc już o Izraelu, ukazały się tysiące książek podejmujących tematykę oświęcimską. Nie mogę tutaj ograniczyć się do analizy dzieł polskich, nie jest także możliwa analiza całej twórczości poobozowej. Zatrzymam się więc trochę nad przykładowo wybranymi dziełami, które — znane w wielu językach — niewątpliwie znacznie przyczyniły się do kształtowania pojęć o tym, czym był Auschwitz.

W Polsce przeważa do dziś literatura wspomnieniowa — reportażowa. Szerokiemu czytelnikowi znane poza Borowskim są książki Seweryny Szmaglewskiej "Dymy nad Birkenau" czy Krystyny Żywulskiej "Przeżyłam Oświęcim", przedstawiające problemy życia w obozie kobiecym. Znana jest głośna książka Wiesława Kielara "Anus mundi". Autor — więzień z pierwszego transportu Polaków przywiezionych do Oświęcimia — przeżył w obozie ponad 4 lata. Przedstawia więc w niej różne etapy rozwoju obozu — od obozu koncentracyjnego, założonego w 1940 roku dla Polaków, poprzez jego umiędzynarodowienie, gdy rozpoczęto deportację radzieckich jeńcow wojennych i więźniów politycznych innych narodowości, aż do czasu, kiedy Auschwitz stał się gigantyczną machiną śmierci — po rozpoczęciu w 1942 roku. realizowania akcji masowego zabijania w komorach gazowych Brzezinki transportów Żydów, deportowanych z wszystkich krajów okupowanej Europy. Kielar nie cofa się w swojej książce przed ukazaniem skomplikowanych stosunków między więźniami i grupami więźniów, ukazuje jak zmieniał się człowiek w obozie, jak tworzył się system wartości moralnych.

Szeroko pojętą problematykę moralną Oświęcimia podejmował w swych książkach Hermann Langbein. Pozycje takie jak "Die Stärkeren", "Menschen in Auschwitz" czy "Der Auschwitz Prozess" należą już dzisiaj do klasyki literatury oświęcimskiej. Langbein — zwłaszcza w pozycji "Menschen in Auschwitz" — porusza wiele problemów życia obozowego, przy czym nie ogranicza się wyłącznie do omówienia problemów więźniów, lecz sporo uwagi poświęca sprawom sprawców. Jako materiał dydaktyczny przed i po wizycie w Auschwitz mogą być książki Langbeina bogatym źródłem infromacji, zarówno jeżeli chodzi o problemy historyczne jak i moralne.

Jeżeli literatura ma kształtować postawy moralne i uczyć, to nie powinna — moim zdaniem — ograniczać się wyłącznie do przekazywania przykładów negatywnych. W bezwzględnej walce o przeżycie, jaką był obóz udało się ocalić wartości najwyższe — przyjaźń, miłość, dobro. Przyjazny gest, dobre, życzliwe słowo ratowały czasem życie. Kiedy szukamy informacji o ruchu oporu, spotykamy przede wszystkim opór duchowy, wewnętrzny, niewyrażenie zgody na sytuację w jakiej więzień został postawiony. Nie udawało się to wielu, wielu załamywała rzeczywistość obozowa, twarda walka o przeżycie. Jak ważne jednak było znaleźć siłę na opór podkreśla w swych wspomnieniach wielu byłych więźniów. Mówią o tym także tak znani autorzy jak Elie Wiesel i Primo Levi.

Trudno mówić o literaturze obozu oświęcimskiego w oderwaniu od literatury Getta, przy czym najobszerniejsze odbicie w utworach literackich odnalazło getto warszawskie. Jest to w większości literatura dokumentalna, oparta na faktach, relacjonująca przeżycia własne lub cudze. Ze swobody beletrystycznej utwory te korzystają w stopniu bardzo nieznacznym. Dokument, pamiętnik, dziennik, literatura faktu zyskuje w sposób naturalny bardzo wysoką rangę. Najwybitniejsze z pamiętników na temat getta to pamiętniki Hirszfelda, Władysława Szpilmana, Noemi Szac–Wajkranc, a najbardziej znane — "Dziennik" Janusza Korczaka i Adama Czerniakowa "Dziennik getta warszawskiego". Szczególnie cenny jest pamiętnik Hirszfelda. Hirszfeld, tak jak w literaturze obozowej Tadeusz Borowski — potrafi zobaczyć i pokazać, że nazizm obalił dotychczasowy system stosunków międzyludzkich na linii kat — ofiara. Że niszczył ofiary łamiąc ich solidarność, dzieląc je i wydobywając z nich to, co nieludzkie. Hirszfeld pokazuje, że getto było rodzajem obozu koncentracyjnego, w którym tak zorganizowano system zakazów i nakazów, że ludzie chcąc żyć, musieli występować przeciwko sobie.

Oddzielny rozdział wspomnieniowy i pamiętnikarski literatury poświęconej gettu warszawskiemu stanowią wspomnienia związane bezpośrednio z przygotowaniem i przebiegiem powstania w kwietniu 1943 roku. Pokazano w nich patos samotnej, męczeńskiej walki i cierpienia. Pokazano los Żydów ocalałych z powstania, a także wiele odmian polskich reakcji na powstanie: od prób pomocy udzielanej walczącym poprzez postawy biernej życzliwości połączonej z przerażeniem, aż po zbrodniczą działalność kolaborantów.

Nasuwa się w tym miejscu ogólna refleksja, że utwory literackie dotyczące wojny, a więc i życia w obozie koncentracyjnym opowiadały początkowo o ludzkich zbiorowiskach, o bohaterstwie grup ludzi. W miarę upływu lat coraz więcej dzieł zmieniło główny przedmiot rozważań i kierunek wyobraźni. Ten nowy nurt, to potrzeba spojrzenia na zbiorowe okrucieństwo oczyma pojedynczego, szarego człowieka; przekonanie, że nie jest możliwe zrozumienie całego bezmiaru nieszczęścia spowodowanego zabiciem milionów ludzi, bez zrozumienia, czym jest śmierć jednostki. Do prawdy Oświęcimia, do wstrząsu sumienia jaki powinien on u nas budzić dojść można tylko poprzez odzyskanie wrażliwości na twarz ludzką, pojedynczą twarz. Coraz częściej w utworach literackich na temat Auschwitz dominuje pragnienie "ocalenia twarzy", tamtych twarzy, ale takich "jak ty i jak ja".

Fenomen "człowieka — ofiary", "człowieka — kata" długo jeszcze będzie frapował nie tylko pisarzy, ale i uczonych. W Polsce pojawiły się na ten temat książki nie–historyków, a na szczególną uwagę zasługują dwie z nich — "Rytm życia" Antoniego Kępińskiego — psychiatry oraz "Wartości i przemoc" Anny Pawełczyńskiej. Obaj autorzy rozpatrują problemy zachowania się jednostek zarówno z kręgu sprawców, jak i ofiar.

Obozy zagłady nie były efektem zmasowanego sadyzmu, lecz wynikiem całkowitego uprzedmiotowienia drugiego człowieka. Załamanie się podstawowej zasady stosunków międzyludzkich, zasady humanizmu, zdegradowanie drugiego człowieka do roli numeru doprowadziło do totalnej tragedii. To jednak co łączy obie grupy, to przynależność do wspólnego gatunku "Homo sapiens" i stwierdzenie to zmusza do postawienia podstawowego pytania — "jaki ja jestem?" Czy literatura współczesna znalazła odpowiedź na to pytanie? Myślę, że nie to jest najważniejsze. Najważniejsze jest, moim zdaniem, samo zadawanie pytań i poszukiwanie odpowiedzi. A to dokonuje się w literaturze do dziś.

The Reality of Auschwitz in Works of Literature

The central wish of former prisoners of Nazi concentration camps was to give truthful testimony about life in the camp. They wanted to highlight the monstrous dimensions of the crimes committed and the extreme nature of the suffering of the prisoners. One finds very few publications from the camp time that contains more than just details of events. The primary aim of the authors then was to engrave on collective memory knowledge of what happened behind barbed wire.

It was not until the sixties that a new way of looking at the camp reality became possible. From then on it was not only the prison camp inmates that were seen as victims. New questions were asked that did not only focus on personal and emotional experiences from the past. Those who had experienced war during their childhood began twenty years later to see the problems in connections with their lives as mature adults. The more the temporal distance grew the more a new attitude towards the Holocaust developed, the main tendency of which is to perceive the collective cruelty through the eyes of one directly concerned individual. This attitude is based on the notion that it is impossible to grasp the enormity of a disaster on the scale of millionfold murder, if the experience of individuals is not understood.

Die Wirklichkeit von Auschwitz in literarischen Werken

Den ehemaligen Häftlingen der unter den Nationalsozialisten entstandenen Konzentrations– und Vernichtungslager war es ein zentrales Anliegen, wahrheitsgemäß über das Lagerdasein Zeugnis abzulegen. Sie wollten die Maßlosigkeit der dort begangenen Verbrechen und die ungeheure Dimension des menschlichen Leidens aufzeigen. Es finden sich aus jener Zeit nur wenige Veröffentlichungen, die mehr anstreben als eine detaillierte Beschreibung der Geschehnisse. Den Autoren ging es vor allem darum, das Wissen darüber, was sich hinter dem Stacheldraht ereignet hatte, für immer dem Gedächtnis der Menschheit einzuschreiben. Eine neue Sehweise der Lagerrealität wurde erst in den sechziger Jahren möglich. Man kam davon ab, die Lagerinsassen ausschließlich als Opfer zu betrachten. Es wurden neue Fragen gestellt, deren Bezugspunkt nicht mehr allein persönliche Gefühlseindrücke aus der Vergangenheit waren. Diejenigen, die den Krieg als Kinder erlebt hatten, sahen seine Problematik nach nunmehr 20 Jahren in Verbindung mit ihrem Leben als gereifte Menschen. Mit der wachsenden zeitlichen Entfernung entwickelte sich eine neue Einstellung, deren Grundtendenz darin besteht, die kollektive Grausamkeit mit den Augen der einzelnen davon betroffenen Menschen zu sehen. Sie orientiert sich an dem Gedanken, daß es unmöglich ist, das gesamte Ausmaß des durch den millionenfachen Mord herbeigeführten Unglücks zu erfassen, wenn die individuelle Erfahrung des Todes nicht verstanden wird.

Stefanie Peter

Symbole Instandhalten

Außer in der Darstellung ihrer Vernichtung, kommen die Juden in den europäischen Museen kaum vor.[1]

1. J. Young: Beschreiben des Holocaust, Frankfurt a.M. 1992, S. 286.

Ausstellungsstücke

Das Staatliche Museum Auschwitz–Birkenau hat seine ständige Ausstellung in den Blöcken des ehemaligen Stammlagers, Auschwitz I, untergebracht. Dort enthält die Abteilung "Vernichtung" in Block 4 ein besonders umstrittenes Exponat: Einen Berg von Haaren, hauptsächlich von Frauen.

① Permanent exhibition — Block 4 / Wystawa stała — Blok 4 / Ständige Ausstellung Block 4
L. Foryciarz

Man betritt Saal 5 des Obergeschosses, dessen Eingang die Überschrift "Ausbeutung der Körper" trägt, und sieht zur Linken einen wandhohen Schaukasten, der ein Viertel des Raumes einnimmt. Hinter der Glasscheibe liegt eine mattgraue, staubige, verfilzte Masse, die dem Aussehen nach einem dicken Teppich gleicht (Abb. 1).

An der gegenüberliegenden Wand hängt eine große schwarz–weiß Fotografie, auf der Männer vor aufgestapelten weißen Säcken mit menschlichen Haaren stehen.[2] Unter dieser Fotografie befinden sich in einer Vitrine Dokumente der SS über die Verschickung von Skeletten, Zahngold und Haaren ins Reich, um dort industriell verwertet zu werden — so diente

2. Das Bild zeigt Mitglieder der sowjetischen Untersuchungskommission beim Inspizieren der Magazine. Es handelt sich hierbei um ein Standfoto aus dem Film "Chronik der Befreiung", der nach der Befreiung von einem russischen Filmteam gedreht wurde und eine Grundlage für die KZ–Ikonographie liefert. Eine fünfzehnminütige Fassung davon ist im Besucherkino des Museums Auschwitz zu sehen.

menschliches Haar als Rohmaterial für die Herstellung von Matratzenfüllungen, Geweben und Einlagen.[3] Diese Art der Verwertung von Menschenhaar führen die Exponate einer dritten Vitrine dem Besucher vor Augen: Er sieht einen Ballen hellbraunen Gewebes, das zum Teil ausgerollt ist. Darauf liegen einige lange, geflochtene Zöpfe, in unterschiedlichen Haarfarben und an den Enden mit inzwischen verschlissenen Stoffschleifen fixiert.
Der übrige Raum ist leer.

3. APMO, Akten des Nürnberger Prozesses, Dok. 511–USSR: Anordnung des SS–Obergruppenführers Pohl vom 6.8.1942.

Fundstücke

Wie den Quellen des Museumsarchivs zu entnehmen ist, wurden nach der Befreiung des Lagers 7 000 kg Haar in den Räumen der 'Bekleidungswerkstätten–Lederfabrik' entdeckt, einer ehemaligen Gerberei, in der sich ein Teil des Lagers 'Kanada'[4] befand.[5] Die Lagerleitung hatte das bereits in Säcke verpackte, zur industriellen Verwertung bestimmte Haar nicht mehr rechtzeitig vor der Evakuierung des Lagers abschicken können.

4. Lagerjargon für die Magazine, in denen die Habe der Deportierten aufbewahrt und sortiert wurde.

5. APMO, IZ–1–5: Protokoll des Besuchs der sowjetischen Untersuchungskommission.

Bei der Einrichtung des Museums 1947, brachte man zwei Tonnen des gefundenen Haares in den bereits erwähnten, raumhohen Schaukasten in Block 4 (Abb. 2), während etwa 16 kg im Magazin verblieben und auf Anfrage an andere Museen und Gedenkstätten verleihbar sind. Sowohl das Holocaust Memorial Museum in Washington, wie auch die Yad Vashem Martyrs' and Heroes' Remembrance Authority in Jerusalem, griffen auf diese Möglichkeit zurück, entschieden jedoch, die Haare nicht auszustellen.

② Permanent exhibition before 1955 — Block 4 / Wystawa stała przed 1955 r. — Blok 4 / Ständige Ausstellung vor 1955 — Block 4.

Konservierung

Wie jedes Museum, so besitzt auch die Gedenkstätte Auschwitz eine konservatorische Abteilung. Deren Arbeiten reichen von Hausmeistertätigkeiten über die Installation technischer Anlagen bis hin zur Restaurierung und Konservierung des Geländes mit seinen Gebäuden und den einzelnen Exponaten.

Die in den verschiedenen Blöcken ausgestellten Hinterlassenschaften der Ermordeten bedürfen mit der Zeit immer dringender einer Konservierungsmethode, die den natürlichen Verfallsprozeß aufhalten kann. Dazu gehören zum einen Schuhe, Koffer, Brillen, Gebetschals, Prothesen, Töpfe, Körbe, Bürsten oder Rasierpinsel, zum anderen aber auch die unmittelbaren Überreste ihrer Körper, wie z.B. Haare. Speziell die Haarkonservierung erweist sich als kompliziert und kostenaufwendig.[6] Um das Haar vor Insektenbefall zu schützen, sind besondere klimatische Bedingungen erforderlich, die in den sommers wie winters ungeheizten Blöcken derzeit nicht gegeben sind. Für die chemische Bearbeitung des Haares hat der Chefkonservator des Museum of Modern Art in New York, James Frantz, dem Museum Vorschläge

6. J. H. Frantz: Unveröffentlichtes Manuskript zum Symposion "The future of Auschwitz: should the relics be preserved?", Oświęcim, 23. bis 26.8.1993.

unterbreitet. Aber auch Wissenschaftler der entsprechenden Fakultäten der Universitäten Warschau und Thorn denken über Konservierungsmöglichkeiten nach.

Relikte als Beweise

Im aktuellen, leicht überarbeiteten Konzept für die ständige Ausstellung des Museums nehmen die Haare mit den bereits erwähnten Hinterlassenschaften der Deportierten nach wie vor einen zentralen Platz in der Abteilung "Verlauf der Massenvernichtung der Juden" ein.[7] Sie sollen dort in Zukunft mit Fotografien von der Selektion an der Rampe in Birkenau, mit schriftlichen Dokumenten, Bauplänen und Modellen von Krematorien und Gaskammern, neben leeren Zyklon B–Behältern, Prothesen und Brillen ausgestellt werden, um den Ablauf des Massenmordes zu illustrieren.

7. T. Świebocka und T. Zbrzeska: Concept of a permanent exhibition, unveröffentlichtes Manuskript PMO.

Desweiteren gelten die Haare als eindeutiges Beweisstück gegen die Thesen der Revisionisten. Wie verschiedene chemische Analysen — die letzte stammt aus dem Jahre 1990 — belegen, enthalten sie Rückstände von Zyklon B. Sie wurden den weiblichen Opfern in Birkenau, im Gegensatz zu Treblinka oder anderen Vernichtungslagern, erst nach ihrem Tod in der Gaskammer abgeschnitten.

Relikte als Symbole

Der Ort des ehemaligen Konzentrations– und Vernichtungslagers Auschwitz–Birkenau bildet eine Grundlage für den während, vor allem aber nach der Lagerzeit in Gang gekommenen Prozeß der Symbolisierung. Bilder und Metaphern, symbolische Formen durch die wir 'Auschwitz' darstellen, entstehen im Zusammenhang mit seiner heutigen Topographie, mit den Überresten seiner Architektur und mit den Exponaten seiner ständigen Ausstellung in den Blöcken des Stammlagers.

Die den Ermordeten geraubte Habe, die 'Effekten', wie auch die unmittelbaren Überreste ihrer Körper, die Haare, spielen in diesem Symbolisierungsprozeß eine besondere Rolle. Vor allem durch die Art und Weise ihrer musealen Präsentation hinterlassen sie beim Betrachter eine bleibende, emotionale Wirkung.

Basis der Gestaltung dieser Abteilung der ständigen Ausstellung waren erste Fotoaufnahmen, die nach der Befreiung des Lagers entstanden sind, sowie der bereits erwähnte Film "Chronik der Befreiung", in dem die überfließenden Magazine von 'Kanada' zu sehen sind: Aus den Lagerräumen quellende Kleidermassen, Berge von Schuhen und Brillen, stapelweise Koffer und andere persönliche Gegenstände, alles auf große Haufen geworfen.

In dieser Form sind sie zuerst zu Museumsstücken, dann zu Symbolen für Auschwitz geworden (Abb. 3, 4).

③ Still from the film "Chronicle" / Zdjęcie z filmu "Kronika" / Standfoto aus dem Film "Chronik"

Die Gegenwartskünstler, die ihre Arbeit explizit als Kunst nach dem Holocaust verstehen oder sich anderweitig darauf beziehen, verwenden fortwährend die 'Effekten' als Symbol: Kleidermassen in den Installationen von Christian Boltanski (z.B. "Réserve: Canada", 1988, Paris; "Réserve: Lac des morts", 1990, Japan) und Lily R. Markiewicz (z.B. "I don't celebrate Christmas", 1990, London), Koffer bei Fabio Mauri ("Western or Wailing Wall", 1993, Rom), Haare bei Ann Hamilton ("tropos", 1993, New York), um nur einige aktuelle Beispiele zu nennen.

Doch auch in der Lyrik 'nach Auschwitz', sind besonders die Haare ein immer wiederkehrendes Motiv, dem in erster Linie die museale Präsentation als Vorlage dient. Beispiele dafür finden sich in den Texten von Johannes R. Becher, Władysław Broniewski, Michael Etkind, Arno Reinfrank, Dmytro Pavlycko, Peter Pausch, Heinar Kipphardt[8] und Primo Levi.[9]

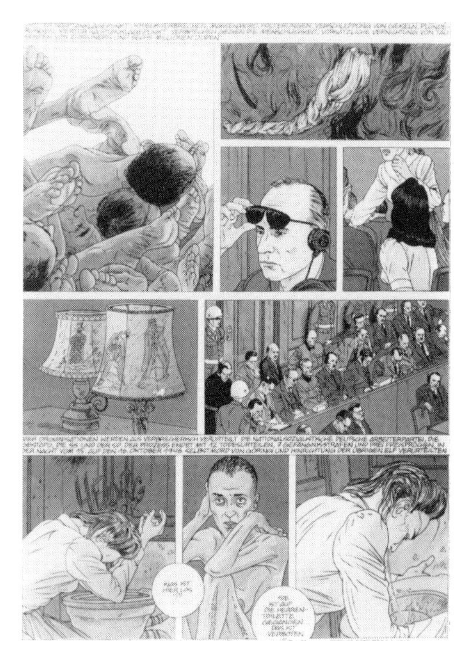

④ From the comic "Die Zerbrochene Zeit" / Z komiksu "Die Zerbrochene Zeit" / Aus dem Comic "Die Zerbrochene Zeit", Carlsen, Hamburg
1921

Der polnische Autor Tadeusz Różewicz, hat dem Thema sogar ein ganzes Gedicht, "Kleiner Zopf", gewidmet, das "das spröde haar der vergasten, unter den sauberen scheiben" beschreibt, in dem zwar noch "nadeln und hornkämme" stecken, das aber "kein wind zerzaust" und "kein licht durchleuchtet".[10]

Joanna Bielobradeks (Pseudonym Andrea Morro) Gedicht "Iphigenie aus Birkenau" spricht von der "Lawine der Haare hinter Glas," von "eine(m) Berg schreiender Haare".[11] Und in Fritz Depperts Gedicht "Vom Himmel zur Hölle", hängt "Saras Haar, zyanwasserstoffgetränkt grau und verglast in Block 4".[12]

Wie in vielen anderen Gedichten wird auch hier das Motiv aus Paul Celans "Todesfuge" verwendet, die er 1944 schrieb, und in der das Haar mit einem jüdischen Frauennamen verknüpft ist.

Aus der Menge isolierte, einzelne, abgeschnittene, meist geflochtene Zöpfe werden auf Bildern, Plakaten und im

8. s. Gedichtband: A. A. Zych und D. Müller-Ott: Auschwitz-Gedichte, Oświęcim, 1993.

9. P. Levi: Ist das ein Mensch, München 1992, S.9.

10. Zych (s.o. Anm. 8), S. 202.

11. Ebd., S. 13–14.

12. Ebd., S. 52.

Museum selbst verwendet, um eine emotionale, persönliche Verbindung zwischen dem Betrachter und dem Exponat herzustellen (Abb. 5). Man soll in dem anonymen Berg von Haaren das Haar seiner Geliebten, Frau, Mutter oder Schwester sehen und in der grauen Masse plötzlich ein Individuum erkennen.

⑤ Wiesław Szamocki
'KL Auschwitz–Birkenau 1940–1945'
1987; Poster / plakat

Diese Beobachtung wirft die wichtige Frage nach der Intention und den Folgen dieser musealen Ausstellungsstrategie auf. Zum einen, so die Verantwortlichen des Museums, sollen die Berge von Hinterlassenschaften und körperlichen Überresten hinter Glas einen Eindruck von den Menschenmassen vermitteln, die in Birkenau ermordet wurden. Desweiteren sollen sie "metonymisch an die Menschen erinnern, zu deren Leben sie einst gehörten"[13] und vor allem Emotionen hervorrufen: Trauer, Angst und Schrecken.

13. Young (s.o. Anm.1), S. 269.

Doch worin besteht die tatsächliche Wirkung des Exponates auf den Betrachter? Haben die ausgestellten Haare in ihrem gegenwärtigen Zustand als grauer staubiger Haufen — nach fast fünfzig Jahren hinter Glas — nicht vor allem einen Gruseleffekt? Ist es nicht purer Voyeurismus, so etwas in eine Museumsvitrine zu bringen, um über Auschwitz zu erzählen? Ist es nicht bloß eine nochmalige Zurschaustellung, Entwürdigung der Opfer? Wird damit das, was in Auschwitz passierte, verständlich oder haben solche Exponate eher zur Folge, daß man sich nach anfänglicher emotionaler Rührung von diesem absoluten Grauen lieber distanziert?

In diesem Fall hätte das Museum mit seiner Ausstellungsstrategie lediglich erreicht, sich selbst in einen "Begräbnisort für unbequeme uns beunruhigende historische Erzählungen zu verwandeln".[14] Der Museumsbesuch hat einen Horroreffekt, evoziert Emotionen, trägt aber nicht unbedingt zu einer weiteren Auseinandersetzung mit dem Thema Auschwitz bei, geschweige denn liefert er Informationen über den industriell geplanten Massenmord.

14. I. Rogoff: Von Ruinen zu Trümmern. Die Feminisierung von Faschismus in deutschen historischen Museen, in: S. Baumgart (Hrsg.): Denkräume zwischen Kunst und Wissenschaft. Kunsthistorikerinnentagung in Hamburg, Berlin 1993, S. 267.

Es gibt viel Kritik an der Ausstellung und speziell an den dort gezeigten Haaren. Vor allem gläubige Juden plädieren dafür, das Haar, als letztes übriggebliebenes Körperteil der in Auschwitz ermordeten Menschen, zu beerdigen. Wie bereits erwähnt, ist im aktuellen Konzept für die ständige Ausstellung jedoch keine Entfernung dieses Exponates vorgesehen.[15]

15. Świebocka/Zbrzeska (s.o. Amn.7).

Wirklichkeit der Symbole

Die Gefahr bei Gedenkstätten oder Museen, die sich auf dem Gelände früherer Konzentrations– und Vernichtungslager befinden, liegt darin, so James Young, daß die Denkmäler selbst für die Realität der Lager und das dort Erzählte für unvermittelte Geschichte gehalten wird.[16] Durch die konservatorische Arbeit der vergangenen Jahrzehnte sind in Auschwitz etliche Veränderungen, vor allem das Stammlager betreffend, vorgenommen worden, so daß die Gedenkstätte und ihre

16. Young (s.o. Anm.1), S. 270.

Umgebung schon rein architektonisch kaum noch etwas mit dem Vernichtungslager von damals zu tun haben.[17] Desweiteren hat der Massenmord an den Juden in Birkenau stattgefunden, wo heute außer den Lagerbaracken, den Krematoriums- und Gaskammerruinen und einem Denkmal nichts außer einer 1,9 ha weiten Fläche übriggeblieben ist.

17. Vgl. R. J. van Pelt et al. "Memorandum concerning the future of Auschwitz", unveröffentliches Manuskript zum Symposion 'The Future of Auschwitz: Should the relics be preserved', 23. bis 26.8.1993, Oświęcim.

Es ist ein Irrtum zu glauben, daß eine Gedenkstätte oder ein Holocaust-Mahnmal oder, wie in diesem Beispiel, ein Schaukasten mit zwei Tonnen Menschenhaar, wegen seines Dokumentencharakters, dem Betrachter das näherbringt, was in Auschwitz stattgefunden hat. Darüber hinaus bedarf es noch einer Reihe von historischen Informationen, Fakten, die durchaus zugänglich, jedoch immer im Hinblick auf die 'Politik der Erinnerung', kritisch zu betrachten sind. Das meint zum einen immer den kulturellen und historischen Kontext miteinzubeziehen, in dem das jeweilige Museum oder die Gedenkstätte stehen, denn keine historische Erzählung existiert jenseits davon. Zum anderen sollte man die Nicht-Identität dieser 'Dokumente' in den Vitrinen und Schaukästen mit der Realität dessen, was in Auschwitz stattgefunden hat, bedenken. Es gilt herauszufinden, wer die über Symbole vermittelte Sinngebung kontrolliert und definiert und mit welchen politischen Interessen das geschieht.

In den meisten Gedenkstätten ist ein Mangel an Informationen über das Leben derer zu erkennen, die von den Nazis ermordet wurden. Es ist immer nur von Massen und Millionen die Rede, von einer Anonymität, die durch Exponate wie die 'Effekten' gesteigert und bestätigt wird.[18] Die Macht der Symbole ist so groß, daß sie für die Wirklichkeit gehalten werden. Indem man das Museum Auschwitz instandhält, erhält man also weiterhin auch die Symbole.

18. Zur von der SS gewollten Anonymität der Häftlinge in den Lagern, s. S. Kofman: Erstickte Worte, Wien 1988, passim.

Keeping up Symbols

One of the strongest impressions visitors to the permanent exhibition in Auschwitz-Birkenau take home is of the pile of women's hair. Taking this as an example the article discusses some aspects of conservation work in Holocaust museums. The article also shows how strong the impact of the museum's artefacts is on the process of symbolisation of concentration and death camps.

Konserwować symbole

Na zwiedzających wystawę Muzeum Oświęcim-Brzezinka najsilniejsze wrażenie zdaje się wywierać góra kobiecych włosów. Dlatego właśnie z powodu siły oddziaływania poobozowych reliktów zamierza się ustalić zasady konserwacji w miejscach pamięci na terenie byłych obozów koncentracyjnych. Prowadzone badania mają wskazać w jakiej mierze związane z historią KL Auschwitz eksponaty oddziałują na proces symbolizowania obozu koncentracyjnego i obozu zagłady.

Jonathan Webber

Jewish Martyrdom in the Holocaust: A Representative Category?

* I should like to thank my friend and colleague Detlef Hoffmann for suggesting I write a paper on this topic and for inviting me to present some preliminary ideas on this theme at a conference he organized in Loccum in March 1995.

1. Introduction

We know very little about the one million Jews who died in Auschwitz. There is not even a complete record listing all their names, with their dates and place of birth. Relatively speaking, we know much more about why Auschwitz was located where it was, how it was constructed, how it was managed, how much it cost to run — although, to be sure, none of these things are without controversy. As far as the victims are concerned, less is known and less is remembered. What is commonly taken as the representation of Auschwitz, as far as Jewish victimhood is concerned, is the numbers involved, the impossibility of grasping the vast scale it encompassed.[1]

The implication of this, at the ordinary human level, is that Jews have come to be content with a knowledge of the Holocaust in general, and of Auschwitz in particular, which at best rests on the symbolism of the numbers themselves — 'six million', of whom perhaps eighty thousand came from France, half a million from Hungary, one hundred and twenty thousand from Holland, and so on. Such figures are so totally immense that they have perforce come to be used as the standard form of description of the identity of the Jews who were murdered: even a list of the places that those Jews came from would be too long for the ordinary person to remember, too long for the ordinary synagogue to inscribe on its walls or embed in its liturgy. Inevitably, numbers have come to represent the Holocaust, a representation that in turn rests on the recollection of the names of a handful of the main death–camps — Auschwitz, Treblinka, Majdanek, Sobibór — where it supposedly 'all happened'. In the ordinary public Jewish memory today, vast elements of the Holocaust have disappeared from view: not only the names of the death–camps from where there were very few survivors — most notably Bełżec, from where only three persons are said to have survived, out of total Jewish losses there of six hundred thousand; not only the hundreds of place-names of the small towns and villages in eastern Europe where Jews were murdered by shooting; but also the names of the individual Jews themselves. With this immense scale of

1. The total figure for the number of Jews who died in Auschwitz is a subject of disagreement among historians; the figure of one million here quoted represents the most recent view of the historical research department of the Auschwitz State Museum (Piper 1991).

human catastrophe, how could the names of these people be remembered? In practice, different forms of representation have established themselves as the basis for commemorative activity; there is no other way. Certainly the ordinary Jewish schoolboy in London or New York would be hard–pressed to name even ten Jewish victims of Auschwitz (outside his own family circle), and might well see no particularly good reason for doing so.

Under these circumstances, then, ordinary Jewish attempts at representing Auschwitz and the Holocaust have taken on several forms. Apart from visual representations, which is the theme of this exhibition, one of the most commonly encountered is the use of memoirs and diaries, and the oral accounts of survivors. Whether in films, books, or commemorative synagogue liturgies, excerpts from such diaries or survivor testimonies have come to form a particularly poignant mode of the attempt to recapture the essence of the Holocaust past. But by definition they can be no more than isolated details and fragments — the part standing for the whole — and even the totality of these diaries and testimonies are themselves no more than a very partial representation of the realities they describe. 'Everything I am telling you now', as one survivor from Prague told her interviewer in 1955, 'is like a grain of sand by the sea — absolutely nothing compared to what happened' (Trunk 1982: 72). We are thus today at least at a double remove, relying on fragments of fragments.

What I wish to discuss in this essay — the issue of Jewish martyrdom in the Holocaust — is in one sense no more than another such isolated detail. But like so many details of the Holocaust, it is important in helping us to understand the totality. The use of the term 'martyrs' to describe the six million Jews who were murdered in the Holocaust is very common. But in what sense were they martyrs? Were those Jews who did consciously go to their deaths as martyrs somehow 'typical' of all Holocaust victims? Did all the Jews who died see themselves as martyrs? Or is Jewish martyrdom yet another representation, a contemporary category that is merely presumed to do justice to the totality of the catastrophe?

2. Where does the notion of Jewish martyrdom in the Holocaust come from?

The English word 'martyr' has been used for a long time as a term to represent Jewish Holocaust victims, and indeed it was used during the war itself. A book published in 1943 by the American Federation for Polish Jews that gave a series of detailed reports about the murder of Jews in Poland, including the camps at Chełmno, Treblinka, and Bełżec, appeared under the title *The Black Book of Polish Jewry: An Account of the Martyrdom of Polish Jewry under the Nazi Occupation.* Despite this reference in the title to the 'martyrdom' of Polish Jews, the book does not contain any discussion of theological matters which would justify the use of this term. It seems that the word entered English usage in this context without a significant declaration of principles; and indeed it is still the standard term used in English today. Thus for example the official English name for Yad Vashem in Jerusalem is 'The Holocaust Martyrs' and Heroes' Remembrance Authority'. This secular Israeli usage, referring to both 'martyrs' and 'heroes', is doubtless intended to draw attention to those 'heroic' Jews who fought the Germans or became involved in underground activities, of which the most famous example are those Jews who participated in the Warsaw Ghetto Uprising in 1943. It seems to suggest that all those Jews who died in the Holocaust were martyrs, but some were heroes as well. In this view, martyrdom was thus achieved by ordinary Jews simply for having passively accepted being murdered because of their identity as Jews — a passivity that was indeed later derided by many Zionists as characteristic of Holocaust victims having gone 'like sheep to the slaughter'. Is this adequate as a representation of the facts? Does the term 'martyrdom' in effect convey the idea of a non-heroic death and thereby conceal within it a very specific understanding of the nature of Jewish victimhood in the Holocaust? It is important to emphasize that there is no single Jewish view regarding the history and meaning of the Holocaust; different kinds of Jews, whether secular or religious, Zionist or non–Zionist, see the Holocaust according to different moral perspectives and therefore present the facts of the Holocaust differently. The case of Yad Vashem could thus be interpreted in different ways.[2] Here, however, I wish to pursue the specifically religious character of martyrdom in the Jewish tradition — not only because martyrdom has a long history in that tradition but also because religious Jewish accounts are relatively seldom represented in wider discussions of the problem, and to ignore them is to misrepresent the past.[3]

Only a handful of Holocaust memoirs and diaries from a traditionally Orthodox Jewish perspective have been published, but it is clear even from this small body of literature that it represents the Holocaust quite differently from ordinary secular accounts. Central to this Orthodox Jewish representation is the notion of martyrdom — or, to use the correct Hebrew term, *kiddush hashem*, which is not quite the same thing as martyrdom. Jews do not have martyr–saints as there are in Christian traditions, with the result that to use the term 'martyr' in respect of the Jewish victims of the Holocaust is something of a cultural distortion (or alternatively, for secular Jews, an attempt to fix Jewish victimhood within a broader category meaningful within the non–Jewish world). *Kiddush hashem* means the sanctification of the name of God — to bring God into the world, and thereby achieve the divine purpose for which humanity was created.

2. James Young, for example, notes that it links specifically with nationalist Israeli approaches to the Holocaust, mapping a dialectic relationship between martyrdom and heroism on to key aspects of Israeli identity (Young 1993: 209–82). It may also be, however, that Yad Vashem here drew on political ideas current during the wartime itself: Isaiah Trunk (1982: 34) refers to an underground pamphlet published in the Warsaw Ghetto (1940–April 1943) under the title 'Martyrdom and Heroism'.

3. The dominance of secularist accounts of Holocaust–related Jewish history is well described (although somewhat overstated) by N. M. Gelber: 'As a native of Lvov I was invited to participate in the writing of the Book of Lvov...[At] a meeting of the writers' panel for this volume, I met some thirty people: doctors, lawyers, poets, writers and journalists and among these were to be found only two observant Jews...During the discussions and arguments that followed, the nature and contents [of the proposed volume] became evident. I realized that they would falsify completely the traditional Jewish image of Lvov and would describe it as a secular–nationalist, proletarian and socialist city devoid of its most important source — that of authentic traditional Judaism. I have seen this time and again in the hundreds of memorial volumes which ignore the truth, that the great majority of Jews in the destroyed communities were believing Jews' (Schindler 1990: 140, n. 3).

Although the general duty to practise *kiddush hashem* is first mentioned in the Hebrew Bible (e.g. at Leviticus 18: 3–5, 22: 31–2), finding the most appropriate way to fulfil this in practice was only really developed in the Talmud and later commentaries, largely in the light of Jewish historical experience. The Bible indicates two basic concepts. First, Jews should consecrate their lives to God, and should indeed do everything they can to preserve their lives for this purpose; they should not put their lives in unnecessary danger in order to observe their religion. On the other hand, there comes a point beyond which it makes no moral or theological sense for Jews to preserve their lives if they are being forced to abandon their religion altogether — such as during a period of religious persecution. What the Talmud was concerned to establish was the definition of the latter situation: under precisely which circumstances should Jews choose to die for their religion?[4] What *kiddush hashem* came to mean in the Talmud was an injunction to make the right decision, taking into account all the relevant facts and circumstances. For example, under 'normal' circumstances it was felt to be morally and theologically wrong for Jews to allow themselves to be put to death rather than break the sabbath, but in 'abnormal' circumstances such a course of action was to be preferred. Of course, the Jewish authorities could not force a Jew to die for his or her religion, but the existence of these talmudic guidelines did make it possible for the ordinary pious Jew to develop a sense of the role models that he or she should try to follow, particularly in situations of religious persecution. Some of the relevant texts even slowly found their way into the liturgy, thereby reinforcing the common awareness and historical consciousness of Jews that death at the hands of non–Jews (a frequent enough occurrence, particularly in medieval Europe) was more than just a theoretical possibility. It could involve the individual, and it could involve the entire local Jewish community. It was a part of the love of God, an acceptance of God's justice even though man would never be able to really understand it. But it needs to be emphasized that *kiddush hashem* did not necessarily mean death: in some circumstances the duty of *kiddush hashem* — correct moral and ethical behaviour, undertaken in praise of God — could be better achieved by trying to stay alive.

4. The relevant references are scattered, and the arguments subtle, but Sanhedrin 74a–b is the locus classicus.

The rabbis of each generation of massacres had the unfortunate duty of having to interpret and apply these guidelines. Before the Holocaust, probably the most important shift in thinking took place after the massacre of whole Jewish communities in the Rhineland in the year 1096, at the hands of the Crusaders. Many Jews then committed suicide, rather than fall into the hands of the Christians who had threatened them with forced conversion. Suicide is clearly forbidden in Jewish law — but in recognition of the courage and devotion shown by these Jews, the rabbis in the following generations came to accept that what they had done was indeed *kiddush hashem*, an act of glorification rather than one of desperation. To cite the poetic imagery that subsequently found its way into the folktales and liturgical elegies: these Jews had somehow 'sacrificed' themselves to God.[5] It is worth recalling this medieval precedent in order to grasp that the rabbis who were responsible for their congregations during the Holocaust period similarly drew on ancient Jewish tradition in the way they expressed their leadership, but at the same time made innovations. Innovations were inevitable: although the rabbis who functioned in the major ghettos (Warsaw, Kaunas, Drohobycz, etc.) in the earlier part of the war could have had no idea that the Germans intended to murder every single Jew they could lay their hands on, without any exception, nevertheless they were aware that the Nazi persecution was without historical parallel in the Jewish memory — in terms of its ruthlessness of scale, brutality, and apparent absence of any viable mode of escape. How could Jews practise *kiddush hashem* under these circumstances? From the limited information that is available (i.e. from the memoirs of the handful of distinguished rabbinical scholars who happened to survive the war), we know that this question evidently absorbed the minds of Orthodox rabbis, particularly in eastern Europe, and, by extension, of the countless masses of Orthodox Jews who looked to these rabbis for leadership and spiritual encouragement at the time of their greatest need.

5. This sacrifice imagery, deriving biblically from the story of the binding of Isaac (Gen. 22), thereafter remained a dominant motif in Jewish allusions to losses incurred during pogroms. The Hebrew word *korban* (also used in Yiddish), meaning 'sacrifice', can be found in Holocaust memoirs written by pious Jews and on early Holocaust monuments erected shortly after the war in eastern Europe. It is likely that the adoption of the term 'Holocaust' (deriving from the Greek for a 'whole burnt offering') drew both on this imagery as well as on Christian notions of sacrifice, which by definition is something which is total, and where nothing is held back (I am grateful to Ivan Strenski for clarification of this point). The theological implications of this usage are today seen, especially by more secular Jews, as an unacceptable way of categorizing Jewish losses at the hands of the Nazis — hence the increasing popularity of the alternative term 'Shoah' ('total destruction'). In the effort, perhaps, to distance themselves from the secular Jewish world, Orthodox Jewish usage today is tending towards the term 'Churban' — a term also meaning 'total destruction', but self-consciously evoking earlier Jewish catastrophes of major significance as this is the classical term used to refer to the destruction of the Temple in Jerusalem by the Romans in AD 70.

3. *Kiddush hashem* during the Holocaust

The character of Holocaust literature written from this kind of Orthodox Jewish perspective is thus not 'history' in the usual sense. Rather the Holocaust is seen as a set of human problems that should be studied and contemplated as morally instructive, within the framework of Jewish law. It is a Holocaust representation in which the names of the chief German actors and the details of their respective careers fade into the background, and where instead the names of pious Jews and the details of their moral traumas emerge prominently into light. In this approach, problems of ritual and other enquiries about the demands of Jewish law form the true representation of the Holocaust, and accordingly I should like now to give a few examples — or isolated fragments, as they should perhaps be called.

Perhaps the most important question that was raised, and one which constitutes the best way in to this complicated subject, was whether the Nazi persecution was a religious persecution or not. Once again, with the benefit of the hindsight that we possess today, it seems an absurd question; but during the time before Jews actually found themselves in front of the firing squad or inside the gas chamber, the question was very real. If the Nazi persecution was to be understood as a situation where Jews were being forced to give up their religion, then according to talmudic law (and as later restated by Maimonides) Jews should not obey any Nazi order that conflicted with their religion; if they were then shot for disobeying such orders they would automatically be said to have died as martyrs for *kiddush hashem.*

It seems that the situation in Germany was rather different, in this perspective, from how things looked in German–occupied eastern Europe (Zimmels 1977: 244–50). The German rabbis felt that the Nazis had no religious motive in their actions against Jews: they were not interested in Jews giving up their religion, and persecuted even those Jews who had converted to Christianity. The prohibition introduced by the National Socialist government in 1933 on the kosher slaughtering of animals according to Jewish religious law was not expressed as part of an anti–religious campaign but was issued (so it was claimed) to avoid cruelty to animals; it applied to all inhabitants, not just to Jews. A synagogue functioned in Vienna throughout the war; there was a *mikva* (ritual bath) in Berlin and Hamburg during the war, and even in 1943 a new *mikva* was built in Hamburg after the existing one had been bombed. So most rabbis in Germany did not define what was happening as a *religious* persecution.

But in German–occupied eastern Europe the persecution was much more anti–religious in character. Perhaps one of the most detailed Orthodox memoirs to come out of the war was put together by Rabbi Ephraim Oshry, the responsible rabbi in the ghetto established by the Germans in Kaunas (the capital of prewar Lithuania, known in Yiddish as Kovno); one of the cases he cites makes this point clear. A German decree was issued in August 1942 in the Kaunas ghetto, stating that praying or studying Talmud was now a crime, punishable by death. Rabbi Oshry (whose community was famous before the war for its piety and talmudic learning) was immediately asked whether a Jew could be permitted to put his life in danger by praying or studying Talmud. His answer is interesting and important. Reviewing the evidence, he pointed out that the Germans deliberately wanted to undermine the teaching of children, took away Torah scrolls and holy books by force, closed down houses of learning and prayer, and often imposed special forced labour specifically on the sabbath and Jewish holidays so as to cause Jews to desecrate the holiness of those days. Rabbi Oshry concluded that the enemy's main intention was not merely to destroy the Jews but also to destroy their faith and religion. What the Germans were doing amounted in talmudic terms to the explicit denial of the perfection of the one God — and in such a situation the law of submitting to death for *kiddush hashem* unquestionably applied. What this meant was that Jews should disobey the German order, even if it meant putting their lives in danger. Oshry said he did not wish to force Jews to pray or learn Talmud, but that this would be his recommendation — they should do these things for *kiddush hashem* — and he personally conducted daily lectures on Talmud. In accordance with his wishes, a couple of weeks later, in September 1942, the Jews in the Kaunas ghetto gathered for prayer on the Jewish New Year and followed the New Year's Day ritual of blowing the *shofar* (ram's horn), even though the noise would undoubtedly have attracted the attention of the SS. Unfortunately we do not know from Oshry's account if the SS made any specific retaliation for this infringement of the order.[6]

6. For an account of this episode see Oshry 1983: 78–80; Zimmels 1977: 248–50; Rosenbaum 1976: 50–2 and 165, n. 11. Rabbi Oshry survived the war and was later appointed to a rabbinic post in New York City. He published a three-volume work in Hebrew (1949–69) describing his wartime decisions, under the title *Mima'amakim* ('Out of the depths [I cried out unto thee]', based on Ps. 130: 1); an abridged one-volume English edition appeared later (Oshry 1983). The latter is very terse, however, and does not reproduce the argumentation underlying the decisions reached. Readers without specialist knowledge of talmudic literature are therefore referred in this article to scholarly secondary sources which have analysed in detail both Oshry's work and the memoirs of other rabbinic scholars published after the war; these sources give full bibliographic references for cases cited.

I have cited Rabbi Oshry's decision in order to give a preliminary indication of the kinds of problems that Orthodox Jews faced during the Holocaust period (and the kinds of Holocaust histories, built up out of such representative problems, that are disseminated amongst Orthodox Jewish circles). It should be noted, however, that not all Orthodox rabbis would necessarily have shared his legal opinion, on this or any other issue. On the contrary, during the Holocaust there were substantial differences of opinion between rabbinic leaders about precisely how religious Jews ought to behave; the examples that follow are thus intended to illustrate these issues rather than offer generalizations on all rabbinic decisions reached during the war.

Oshry (1983: 34–5) records a case where he decided that under no circumstances may Jews commit suicide, whatever the suffering they had to endure[7], and the same subject was also discussed at length in other ghettos, especially by various rabbis in the Warsaw Ghetto. Rabbi Yitzhak Nissenbaum is recorded as having made an important speech there in which he explained that the suicides committed in the Middle Ages took place in a situation where the enemy wanted to convert Jews to Christianity — but that the Nazis were different, as they simply wanted to have the pleasure of killing Jews physically. Suicide, he explained, was an acceptable solution in the Middle Ages because that way the Jews frustrated the wishes of the enemy, and in so doing practised *kiddush hashem*. The only way for the Jews to frustrate the wishes of the *Nazi* enemy was for them to survive: thus the very act of *survival* would in these circumstances constitute *kiddush hashem*. Here, in this speech of Yitzhak Nissenbaum, one can see how the concept of *kiddush hashem* is rendered historical and consciously adapted to the circumstances. Rabbi Nissenbaum told his listeners that they must therefore do everything they could in order to survive — for example, by escape or by bribery. All this represents a clear movement away from the practice and the imagery of sacrifice that had largely dominated thinking about *kiddush hashem* since the Crusader massacres of 1096; and Nissenbaum coined the term *kiddush hachayim* (the sanctification of life) to convey the point. Other rabbis expressed similar opinions during the war, thereby clearly offering the evidence that *kiddush hashem* does not necessarily mean death, as I mentioned above. Rabbi

7. Rosenbaum (1976: 35–9) discusses the complex technicalities of this case at some length; what Oshry also took into account in reaching his decision was that suicide had to be avoided at all costs, since it would engender a spirit of despair and so play into the hands of the Nazis. In fact the suicide rate was surprisingly low in the east European ghettos (apart from certain famous cases such as the suicide of Adam Czerniaków, president of the Jewish Council of Warsaw), in contrast with its comparatively high incidence amongst assimilated Jews in Germany and Austria; but certainly there were no Masada–like mass suicides during the Holocaust (Zimmels 1977: 82–6; Trunk 1982: 15).

Menachem Ziemba of Warsaw, who also argued specifically that *kiddush hashem* expresses itself differently in different times, took the view that Jews ought physically to resist the Germans, and 'fight to the very end' (Zimmels 1977: 63–4; Schindler 1990: 61, 65; Trunk 1982: 15).[8]

8. Both Rabbi Nissenbaum and Rabbi Ziemba died in the Warsaw Ghetto in 1943.

If survival, according to these opinions, was now to take precedence in formulating an attitude to *kiddush hashem*, the question soon arose as to whether Jews could try to save their lives by escaping from the ghetto and disguising themselves as Christians. My impression is that this was one of the questions most commonly asked of rabbis during the Holocaust. The rabbis agonized over it: on the one hand, for a Jew actually to get himself or herself a certificate of baptism amounted to the very opposite of *kiddush hashem*, and therefore could not be encouraged; on the other hand, in the opinion of Jacob Avigdor, Chief Rabbi of Drohobycz and Borysław in southeastern Poland, how could a rabbi in effect support and strengthen the decrees of the Nazis, who regularly shot Jews for acquiring false papers or otherwise going into hiding? So, for this latter reason, which he justified on the grounds that Jews were in all these cases disobeying the enemy and thus in effect acting under duress — a talmudic principle that separates action from intention, thereby in effect acknowledging the appalling realities facing Jews during times of persecution, which during the Holocaust enabled many rabbis to be lenient on a variety of issues — Rabbi Avigdor decided to allow it (Zimmels 1977: 78–9).[9]

9. Rabbi Avigdor survived the war and later took up a rabbinic post in Mexico City.

A similarly lenient attitude was displayed by Rabbi Oshry following an order made by the Germans in the Kaunas ghetto in May 1942 that any Jewish woman found to be pregnant would be immediately put to death (such a decree was rare during the war, and in fact is known only from Kaunas and Theresienstadt). Given that the primary purpose of marriage, in Jewish tradition, is procreation, Rabbi Oshry was asked whether henceforth married women could use a contraceptive (normally forbidden), and whether a pregnant woman could or should undergo an abortion (also normally forbidden). His decision on both these questions was in the affirmative; and marriages continued to be consecrated (Oshry 1983: 71ff.; see also Zimmels 1977: 212–14; Rosenbaum 1976: 40–4).

A particularly moving case is reported from Auschwitz on the eve of the Jewish New Year in 1944: the SS made one of their routine 'selections' in the concentration camp, weeding out those 'surplus' labour–camp prisoners who were regarded as no longer *arbeitsfähig* (capable of work) to be sent to the gas chamber. One thousand four hundred male teenagers were thus 'selected' and confined to a barrack, to await execution the following day. In the meantime, relatives of these young men began to plead and bargain with the *kapos* guarding the barrack to release some of them. The *kapos* had to be bribed: since an exact count had been taken of the internees, the *kapos* would release someone only if somebody else would replace that person. To replace one life with another is expressly forbidden in the Talmud (who can say that one life is more precious to God than another?), but it so happened that a distinguished rabbi and Talmud scholar, Zvi Hirsch Meisels of Vac in Hungary, who was himself in Auschwitz at the time, was asked by a religious Jew whether he could under these circumstances try to save the life of his only son. Meisels writes in his memoirs that he found it difficult to give a straight answer, knowing that he could not in fact permit it, but that once this Jew had understood that the answer was no, he displayed a sense of great relief that the moral issue (as far as he was concerned) was settled, and also some spiritual satisfaction in the knowledge that according to Jewish values he could accept God's decree regarding the death of his son 'with love and joy' (Rosenbaum 1976: 3–5, 109–11; Zimmels 1977: 113).[10]

It should by now be clear from the theological and sociological background underlying the notion of *kiddush hashem* that pious Jews could draw on countless ritual contexts to express their faith at the last. Yet again it should be recalled that although the idea of Jews risking their lives during the Holocaust period in order to fulfil some religious precept may seem to us absurd, given our historical hindsight and our knowledge that all Jews within the Nazi domain had been condemned to death anyway, nevertheless both within the ghettos prior to deportation and also within the labour camps, even inside Auschwitz, Jews would often have felt that they had somehow been spared from immediate death; many perhaps believed that they would somehow survive the war altogether. For pious Jews to risk their lives in such situations was technically quite unnecessary and, in the opinions of the rabbis cited above, probably wrong. And yet Holocaust stories told by Orthodox Jewish survivors emphasize not only the divine 'miracles' they witnessed that kept them alive but also the utterly remarkable performance of Jewish ritual obligations in the most difficult circumstances. According to eyewitness accounts, the ceremonial lighting of a candle on the first night of the festival of Chanukah, the distribution of Hebrew prayer–books, the wearing of *tefilin* (phylacteries), even the construction of a *succah* (temporary ritual dwelling) on the festival of Succot (Tabernacles) in 1943 — all of these things, taking the form of snatched and hurried attempts to enact fragments of religious Jewish life, are recorded from Auschwitz.[11] Knowledge of the correct date in the Jewish calendar, regularly confirmed by newly arriving transports of deportees, constantly provided religious prisoners with an anchorage in their own cultural world.[12] On the festival of Succot in 1944 a *succah* was again erected in Auschwitz, this time by Rabbi Meisels, who encouraged the performance

10. Rabbi Meisels's memoirs significantly bear the title *Mekadeshei hashem* ('They who practise kiddush hashem'), published in 1955 in Chicago, where Meisels held a post after the war, after first having been chief rabbi of Bergen–Belsen and of the British sector in Germany.

11. For sources documenting the four examples cited see, respectively, Rosenbaum 1976: 118, 53, 78–9, 115–16; Schindler (1990:100) also cites a case of *tefilin* worn in Auschwitz. Sometimes these 'fragments of religious Jewish life' consisted only of representations of the fragments — as for instance the emotional humming by Jewish girls, in their barrack in Birkenau on the eve of the Day of Atonement, of the well–known solemn melody of Kol Nidrei (an account I heard *in situ* in 1995, at the fiftieth–anniversary commemoration of the liberation, from one of the women involved, now Mrs Miles Lerman). Trunk (1982: 24) cites a somewhat macabre version of something similar, when on the eve of the Day of Atonement a female Jewish *kapo* ordered a violinist in her block to play this melody and then suddenly interrupted her, shouting 'Enough! You've had enough pleasure!'

12. I am indebted to Rabbi Shlomo Zalman Lehrer, a former Auschwitz prisoner now living in Antwerp, for this observation.

of many religious Jewish customs in Auschwitz: for the same festival he managed to obtain a set of *arba minim* (Rosenbaum 1976: 113–15).[13] He also blew the ram's horn on New Year's Day on twenty different occasions, including a visit (at great personal risk) to the block where the 1,400 boys were incarcerated prior to being gassed later that day (Rosenbaum 1976: 110–11).

In all these cases — of which indeed many other similar examples are cited in the literature from Buchenwald, Płaszów, Stutthof, Mauthausen, and other camps — mention is routinely made of the enormous psychological consolation and encouragement that the practice of such rituals conveyed to the participants and onlookers. Given the substantial risks involved (being found out would normally have meant at least a flogging if not immediate death by shooting), such practice can at one level be regarded as a form of preparation prior to altruistic suicide, comparable perhaps to the stirring emotions engendered in modern times for the notion of dying for one's country; but what it certainly succeeded in doing was granting to many Jews the opportunity — under the most appalling conditions — to learn how to die as a Jew, and to face the end with dignity and probably also scorn towards the murderers:

> Rabbi Mendele Alter, the brother of the Gerer rebbe, was among a group of Jews in Treblinka during the [hot] summer of 1942 who were ordered to undress. Realizing that these were his last moments the Rebbe pleaded desperately for a glass of water. A Jewish guard, usually noted for his cruelty to fellow Jews, was touched by the plea. He provided the water under the impression that the Rebbe wished to quench his thirst before dying. Instead, the Rebbe used the water to cleanse his hands as an act of purification prior to *kiddush hashem*, urging, 'Fellow Jews, let us say the *viddui* [confession] before dying.'[14]

4. Jewish martyrdom in the Holocaust and the problem of generalization

Martyrdom in general, and *kiddush hashem* in particular, undoubtedly form a genre of historical reflection and glorification that is especially prone to mythologization. The story–telling is often dehistoricized, narratives of the heroes and their exploits merge anachronistically into each other, the isolated fragments become framed in a new representational setting. I have cited sources for the examples I have given, but these (I am sure) will be thought by some to be indeed of no more importance than as mere footnotes to the history: perhaps in fact there were many Jews, perhaps even a majority of Orthodox Jews, who cried out 'Shema Yisroel' or some other appropriate biblical verse as they were led out

13. The *arba minim* (which normally comprise a palm branch, a citron, and sprigs of myrtle and willow — an especially challenging combination to put together in Auschwitz) were in fact incomplete (no myrtle was to be found), and in the absence of any reference-books Rabbi Meisels had to rely on his memory of the talmudic commentaries to reach a decision whether this incomplete set could in fact be used to satisfy the ritual requirements.

14. As reported by an eyewitness (Schindler 1990: 62). There are many such stories in the literature, describing rabbis who encouraged their followers on the way to execution by singing, reciting psalms, even dancing, so as to prepare themselves spiritually for the great honour and privilege that God had given them — to die for *kiddush hashem*. Eliach (1988: 160–1) cites a case of pious Jewish women in the ghetto in Bochnia (southern Poland) who, having been 'selected' for execution, obtained the agreement of the SS to prepare themselves for death by taking a ritual bath in a *mikva*; the building had to be specially reopened, heated, and cleaned for the purpose — after the bath, the women were shot. Stories on these themes also include the idea that this type of devotion occasionally inspired non–observant or secular Jews to adopt Jewish ritual practices both to identify themselves with these Orthodox Jews and to learn from them how to die with dignity: see, for example, Zimmels 1977: 62–3 (an assimilated Jew who begged to be circumcised) or Eliach 1988: 155–9 (an assimilated Jewish *kapo* who in solidarity with a group of Hasidim in his barrack refused to eat on the fast of the Day of Atonement, and for this was shot in front of them by an SS officer). A good example of scorn towards the murderers is cited by Eliach (1988: 159–60): a Hasidic Jew about to be shot received permission from the German officer in charge to recite a short prayer. Quoting from the daily liturgy, what he recited (first in Hebrew, then in German) was: "Blessed are You, O Lord our God, King of the Universe, who has not made me a heathen."

to be shot or gassed. But would this entitle Jews today to characterize all Jewish losses during the Holocaust under the rubric of *kiddush hashem*, or gloss them in English as martyrs?

In brief, the emphasis on *kiddush hashem* in this kind of Holocaust representation simplifies the Holocaust by essentially reducing it down to two agendas: there was the German agenda (the 'unquenchable lust for Jewish blood', as it is described) and there was a Jewish agenda (a long history of a relationship with the divine, in which there is one unbroken tradition of giving up one's life according to God's will). 'Let them proceed with their business, and we shall proceed with ours', to cite a classic formulation of the idea, uttered by a young Hasidic Jew in a cellar in Cracow whilst the Germans paced overhead (Schindler 1990: 187, n. 29).[15]

15. Interestingly enough, a very similar remark is also reported from a town in Lithuania (cited in Trunk 1982: 57) and from another town in the Ukraine (Eliach 1988: 159–60).

In this perspective, the problem of isolated fragments disappears from view: individual events, whether adequately attested or not, become redefined as examples of predetermined categories; there is no longer any particular need to deliver a full account or full narration of the totality of the facts. It is, of course, this latter problem of an appropriate historical emplotment of the Holocaust that inevitably absorbs the energies of the professional secular historian — whence the questions surrounding its representation (see, for example, Friedländer 1992 and discussions cited there). Martyrdom, or *kiddush hashem*, is clearly far from 'typical' of Jewish responses during the Holocaust: the whole thing is infinitely more complicated. It is not only that some Jews chose to fast before their deportation, while other Jews lost their faith; there is a much wider range of issues. Economic life in the ghettos was to a large extent taken over by a new Jewish underworld, consisting of extortionists, blackmailers, informers, bribers of all kinds; the cruelty of many Jewish *kapos* in the concentration camps is well attested by countless survivors; most Orthodox Jewish males did follow German orders to cut off their beards and sidelocks (i.e. rather than try and preserve them as a form of resistance), and in general seemed to have followed those rabbinical rulings that enabled them to ignore standard forms of ritual on the grounds of preserving life — eating non–kosher meat, for example (Trunk 1982: 103–8).[16] For the person interested in a generalized historical picture — as opposed to a mythologized view of martyrdom and heroism — it is necessary to look far afield. A good example is provided by Isaiah Trunk (1982: 56) in his reference to the huge quantities of mail, mainly postcards, that were sent in from provincial towns to friends and relatives in the Warsaw Ghetto (and now preserved in the Ringelblum archive). They form an excellent source for gaining an insight into the state of mind of a good cross–section of the Jewish population:

16. There are, of course, attested cases of rabbis who refused to cut off their beards or wear other than Hasidic dress (Schindler 1990: 99), although Zimmels (1977: 40) implies that most rabbis did shave off their beards, specifically in order to conceal their status as leaders from the eyes of the Germans. This meant that once they were deported to a concentration camp none but their followers from their home town would necessarily know who they were (see for example Eliach 1988: 155).

> adults and children, men and women, simple people and educated people, religious and non–religious, people of different professions and political affiliations. These documents record resignation and desperate calls for help, faith in divine providence and utter atheism, apathy and feverish efforts to find some kind of rescue, natural optimism and unlimited despair, a clear sense of what was in store and completely unfounded illusions. The letters tell us how diversely different people reacted to the same events.

A similar diversity of reactions was noted by Rudolph Hoess, commandant of Auschwitz, in his autobiography: he describes a mother who managed to joke with her children despite the terror in her eyes; a young woman in front of a gas chamber who helped the small children and elderly women undress and keep calm; women who shrieked, tore their hair and became totally hysterical; children who refused to enter the gas chamber and had to be dragged in; a man who hissed at him 'Germany will pay a heavy penalty for the mass murder of the Jews'; and (curiously) a Dutch Jew who gave him a list of Dutch families hiding Jews (Trunk 1982: 56–7).

It needs to be recalled, moreover, that Jews were murdered in large numbers in eastern Europe by an array of local nationalists and fascists whose political programme, while coinciding in this respect with that of the Nazis, derived from sources substantially different from German state theories regarding the objective need for the genocide of the Jews. East European fascists, particularly in Lithuania and the Ukraine, often took the initiative in undertaking pogroms of Jews after the German attack on the Soviet Union in 1941 because of their anger at Jewish collaboration (both real and imagined) with the Soviet authorities prior to that date. In each country it was a different story: in Byelorussia, by contrast, the Germans found it comparatively difficult to find local recruits for their auxiliary police to undertake actions against Jews; and in Poland there were numerous shifts and adjustments of position among the various underground political parties, especially in their attitudes towards the German murder of Jews — although towards the end of the war, Polish fascists joined the Home Army and often murdered Jewish partisans hiding out in the woods. 'The Poles were worse than the Germans — or so many a Polish Holocaust survivor will today confidently recount.

Given the totality and complexity of all these circumstances (on which, of course, much more could be said), the very notion here of a 'Holocaust' as a unitary category — or at least a meaningful category supplied ex post facto — speaks clearly of the Jewish need for a retrospective simplification of the past. Technically, the 'Holocaust' as a single event or category can be faulted on many grounds, but the usage should alert us to the widespread apperception — largely, although not exclusively within the Jewish world alone — that there is indeed a single issue here. And it is in relation to that single issue that the reaching out for martyrdom, or *kiddush hashem*, as the all–embracing category to account for the totality of the victims, would seem ostensibly to be addressing itself. If 'Holocaust', then 'martyrs': these are the basic categories used, whatever the complexity of the 'facts' might otherwise have led us to believe.

5. Conclusions: Martyrdom as a representation of the Holocaust

'Every man and woman who died in the Holocaust is a holy martyr,' declared the Lubavitcher rebbe in a speech in 1990 (Boteach 1995: 190).[17] With this statement the rebbe echoed rabbinic opinions articulated in the Warsaw Ghetto, where for example Rabbi Shimon Huberband (in a work bearing the title *Kiddush Hashem*) applied the term *kiddush hashem* to every victim of the Holocaust: 'As Maimonides ruled [he wrote], "A Jew who is killed, though it may be for reasons other than conversion but simply because he is a Jew, is called *kadosh* [holy, i.e. a martyr]"' (Schindler 1990: 60).[18] From such a perspective there is no moral need to make the historical distinction between (say) Jews murdered in the gas chambers at Auschwitz and Jews murdered by Polish partisans in the forests — they are all martyrs. Nor does martyrdom in this sense involve self-sacrifice, a conscious decision to die specifically for *kiddush hashem*. It is this latter which appears to be an innovation within Jewish theological responses during the Holocaust (that is, despite Huberband's supposed reference to a classical source): the category has been extended to embrace all those who went to their deaths, regardless of their state of mind or religious belief — and it would presumably even include Jews (such as Edith Stein) who had converted to Christianity, as well as the children of such people, who were murdered by the Nazis because of their Jewish ancestry.

17. The Lubavitcher rebbe, who lived in Brooklyn and died in 1994, was a saintly figure with a substantial international following, who led a powerful Hasidic movement of Jewish outreach.

18. It is not clear, however, whether Maimonides in fact ever made such a statement (Schindler 1990: 164, n. 7).

This is clearly all rather different from the notion of *kiddush hashem* as it was developed by pious Jews in the early Middle Ages; this is necessarily so in the twentieth century, when as a reflection of the widespread assimilation and secularization in the Jewish world, much of the force of the classical Jewish concept of living a life and dying a death to sanctify God has ceased to have the socially accepted meaning it once had. Probably the majority of Jews who died in the Holocaust would have thought of themselves as secular rather than as religious (although the dividing–line is not self–evident), and to settle on a single category to account for them all might at first have seemed no easy task. But the extension, by leading rabbis, of *kiddush hashem* to cover all the Jewish victims has nicely coincided with the inclusive approach embedded in secular notions of Jewish martyrdom. Martyrdom, in today's Jewish world, thus comes as a sort of ecumenical compromise, especially in English–language usage: in addition to the implicit reference to the classical religious imagery, it evokes the innocence of the victims (best exemplified by the one million or so children who were murdered), and also links Jewish victimhood in the Holocaust with wider notions of national sacrifice (ironically secular in their usual connotations today) common in a variety of non–Jewish national European traditions.

This vagueness and sense of compromise surrounding the use of the term martyr is conveniently illustrated in the text of a Holocaust memorial service proposed by the Rabbinical Council of America (Rosenberg and Heuman 1992: 347–63). Six candles are lit (for 'the six million'), each dedicated liturgically to a particular sub–group of Holocaust victims, and as such offering an interesting insight into how these are to be characterized: (1) the helpless infants, children and teenagers; (2) mothers who died with their children in their arms; (3) mothers and fathers who were separated from their families; (4) scholars, teachers, and rabbis; (5) heroes of the resistance who fought the Nazis; (6) the martyrs who gave their lives to help their brothers. In this part of the service 'martyrs' thus appear here as a sub–group, defined by their particular form of behaviour. However, immediately after this candle–lighting comes the Memorial Prayer, which begins as follows: "We remember this day the nameless millions of martyrs of the children of Israel...offered up by the Nazis on altars of savagery and demonic brutality...". Note the shift: here the 'martyrs' represent the entire collectivity of victims; moreover, they have not sacrificed themselves (as the Jews of 1096 would have said about themselves), but rather are sacrificed by the enemy, i.e. according to the enemy's set of values. But nevertheless their deaths in some unknown (or at least unspecified) way add something to Jewish history and Jewish destiny. The Memorial Prayer continues "...We must sanctify the names of the *kedoshim* [martyrs, the plural of *kadosh*] whose deaths deepened the holiness of Your chosen people. We must dedicate ourselves to the perpetuation of Your saving remnant through greater devotion to Your holy Torah and through dedication to the creation of a holy land in the State of Israel...".

Just how Jewish deaths in the Holocaust can be deemed to have deepened the holiness of the Jewish people, though, the natural corollary to any theory of martyrdom, remains unclear; it is the subject of much controversy (and much misunderstanding), and also much passion. There is a long tradition in Judaism of arguing with God, and complaining that the death of the righteous is not the best way for God to achieve His purpose in the world (see for example Laytner 1990). One of the main founders of the United States Holocaust Memorial Museum in Washington, which opened in 1993, himself gave an impassioned impromptu performance in the last functioning synagogue in Cracow in 1979: "Where were You", he called out, "when all over Europe Your sons and daughters were burning...?" (Eliach 1988: 212–13). But not all rabbis agreed on the need to question God. We cannot 'explain' the Holocaust, the Lubavitcher rebbe said in his 1990 speech, for we are limited by the earthbound perspective of mortal understanding; as it is written in the book of the prophet Isaiah (55: 8), "For My thoughts are not your thoughts" (Boteach 1995: 190). Both during the Holocaust and also today, the proverb of the Chofetz Chaim (an outstanding Lithuanian Jewish scholar who died before the war) is often quoted: "For the believer there are no questions; for the unbeliever there are no answers."[19]

19. For the attribution of this widely quoted proverb to the Chofetz Chaim (Rabbi Israel Meir Hacohen), see Rosenbaum 1976: 5–6.

In short, theories of martyrdom and their associated ideas represent the Holocaust in different ways to different kinds of Jews today. Martyrdom seems to be a satisfactory symbol, a cover–term to conceal the shame, the nagging doubts and debates over Jewish passivity, and the complexity and sheer incomprehensibility of what happened — and, at the same time, it offers the opportunity for pious Jews to elaborate this discourse and elevate it through the allusion to the re–enactment of ancient Jewish styles of *kiddush hashem*. Although there are signs, particularly in the United States, that perpetuating Holocaust memory (in some representation or another) has itself become a focus of Jewish ethnic identity, there are those Jews who deeply object to the recurrent sound of its demonic voice and would rather leave the dead in peace — and in silence. Why should the dead serve the living as a pretext for their belief or unbelief in God? Why should they, in fact, be taken as 'representing' anything at all? Perhaps indeed, to paraphrase Jacob Neusner (1981: 80), 'Auschwitz', or any representation thereof, profanes Auschwitz.

Męczeństwo Żydów: klucz do recepcji Holocaustu?

Sześć milionów Żydów, którzy padli ofiarą Holocaustu określa się często jako męczenników — ale czy byli oni nimi rzeczywiście, we właściwym tego słowa znaczeniu? Czy wierzący Żydzi, którzy świadomie szli na śmierć jako męczennicy, byli typowymi przedstawicielami wszystkich ofiar Holocaustu? Czy też należy to stwierdzenie rozumieć raczej jako odizolowany szczegół lub fragment przeszłości, który zwyczajowo uważamy za istotę Holocaustu? Za punkt wyjścia próby znalezienia tymczasowej odpowiedzi na to pytanie posłużyły w tym artykule historyczne świadectwa żydowskiego męczeństwa w znaczeniu religijnym, określane w hebrajskim jako *kiddush hashem*. Pojęcie to, nie utożsamiane w żaden sposób z męczeństwem w sensie chrześcijańskiej albo europejsko–narodowej tradycji, oznacza w pierwszym rzędzie próbę znalezienia najlepszej drogi, aby Woli Boskiej przysporzyć na świecie właściwego znaczenia. Jednak w praktyce nabierało ono raczej znaczenia pewnej strategii przeżycia, aniżeli przyjęcia śmierci jako czegoś oczywistego. I tak, wierzący Żydzi wystawieni byli w czasach Holocaustu na ciągłe konflikty moralne, np. czy rozkazy nazistów należy lekceważyć, by pozostać wiernym swej religii, czy też powinno podawać się za chrześcijan itd... Praktyki rytualne dawały z pewnością, w obliczu nędznej i rozpaczliwej przyszłości, wielką siłę moralną. Jakkolwiek tego rodzaju zachowania nie były w żaden sposób typowe dla całości środowisk żydowskich, zdaniem czołowych rabinów, doświadczenia tych Żydów, niezależnie od tego czy wierzących czy też o poglądach laickich — złożyły się na poszerzenie i nowe zdefiniowanie pojęcia *kiddush hashem*, które w miarę dokładnie identyfikuje się z całokształtem światowej opinii o żydowskim męczeństwie. Tym samym męczeństwo stało się dalece akceptowanym symbolem Holocaustu, mimo że właśnie w wyniku takiego sposobu myślenia wiele innych problemów, pozwalających na zrozumienie tej katastrofy, pozostało we mgle.

Jüdisches Märtyrertum im Holocaust: Eine Schlüsselkategorie?

Die sechs Millionen Juden, die dem Holocaust zum Opfer fielen, werden oft als 'Märtyrer' bezeichnet — aber waren sie Märtyrer im eigentlichen Sinne? Waren die gläubigen Juden, die bewußt als Märtyrer in den Tod gingen, typisch für alle Opfer des Holocaust, oder ist diese Vorstellung eher als ein isoliertes Detail oder Fragment der Vergangenheit zu verstehen, das wir gewohnheitsmäßig als Inbegriff des Holocaust auffassen? Als Ausgangspunkt für den Versuch, eine vorläufige Antwort auf diese Frage anzubieten, dienen in diesem Artikel die historischen Zeugnisse zum religiösen jüdischen Märtyrertum im Holocaust, das im Hebräischen mit dem Terminus *kiddush hashem* bezeichnet wird. Dieser Begriff, in keiner Weise identisch mit dem Märtyrertum im Sinne christlicher oder europäisch-nationaler Traditionen, meint in erster Linie das Bemühen um den besten Weg, dem Willen Gottes in der Welt Geltung zu verschaffen. In der Praxis gewann er aber oft eher die Bedeutung einer Überlebensstrategie als einer Bereitschaft, den Tod als selbstverständlich hinzunehmen. So sahen sich gläubige Juden während des Holocaust oft moralischen Konflikten aller Arten gegenüber — zum Beispiel, ob sie Nazi–Befehle mißachten sollten, um ihre Religion zu praktizieren, oder ob sie versuchen sollten, sich als Christen zu tarnen usw. Die Praxis ritueller Bräuche gab ihnen mit Sicherheit große moralische Stärke angesichts einer im übrigen zutiefst elenden und verzweifelten Situation. Obwohl solche Verhaltensweisen in keiner Weise typisch für die Gesamtheit der jüdischen Reaktionen waren, haben nach Ansicht führender Rabbis alle Juden, ob überzeugte Anhänger ihres Glaubens oder eher weltlich eingestellt, eine derartige Erfahrung gemacht — eine Ausweitung und Neudefinition von *kiddush hashem*, die ziemlich genau mit dem umfassenden Charakter weltlicher Auffassungen von jüdischem Märtyrertum zusammenfällt. So ist Märtyrertum zu einer weithin akzeptierten Deutung des Holocaust geworden, auch wenn gerade durch diese Denkgewohnheit viele andere Schwierigkeiten verschleiert werden, die sich dem Verständnis der Katastrophe entgegenstellen.

①

②

Camptime / Czas obozu / Lagerzeit
Auschwitz I

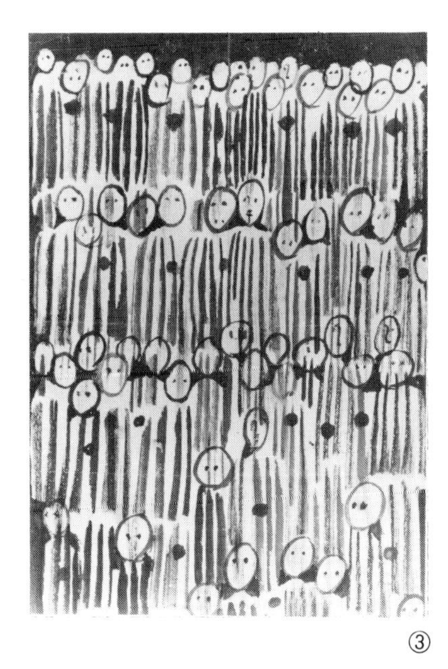

③

④

① W. Gawron, 1942: Roll–call, sketch / Apel, szkic / Appell, Skizze

② W. Siwek, 1943: Construction of the 'Werkhalle' / Budowa 'Werkhalle' / Bau der 'Werkhalle'

③ J. Szajna, 1944–45: The roll–call lasted a long time, my legs ached terribly

Apel trwał długo, bardzo bolały mnie nogi

Der Appell dauerte lange, meine Beine schmerzten sehr

④ D. Kamann, 1942–43: Album der Zentralbauleitung,

①

②

Camptime / Czas obozu / Lagerzeit
Auschwitz II

④

① Author unknown, 1942–44: Arrival of a Transport / Autor nieznany: Przybycie transportu, szkicownik / Autor unbekannt: Ankunft eines Transportes, Skizzenbuch

② B. Walter (?), 1944: Auschwitz–Album

③ Author unknown, 1940–45: Wrong — Right, lithographic stone / Autor nieznany: Nieprawidłowo — Prawidłowo, kamień litograficzny / Autor unbekannt: Falsch — Richtig, Lithostein

④ D. Kamann, 1942–43: Album der Zentralbauleitung

①

②

③

④

⑤

Gate / Brama / Tor
"Arbeit macht frei"

⑥

⑦

① Łuczko, 1945
② A. Bujak, 1974
③ "A Pictorial Record", 1985
④ W. M. Zieliński, 1986
⑤ "A Pictorial Record", 1985
⑥ P. Edel, 1944: Selfportrait / Autoportret / Selbstportrait
⑦ M. Kościelniak, 1972: Killed during Escape / Zabici w czasie ucieczki / Auf der Flucht getötet

①

②

③

④

⑤

⑥

Gate / Brama / Tor Birkenau
& Ramp / Rampa / Rampe

⑦

① S. Mucha, 1945

② S. Kolowca, 1945

③ A. Bujak, 1968

④ Author unknown, n. d. /
Autor nieznany, b. d. /
Autor unbekannt, o. J.

⑤ W. M. Zieliński, 1989

⑥ Oishi Yoshino, 1988

⑦ J. A. Brandhuber, 1949:
Arrival of a Transport at the Ramp /
Przybycie transportu na rampę /
Ankunft eines Transportes an der Rampe

①

②

③

④

Barbed Wire / Drut kolczasty / Stacheldraht

⑤

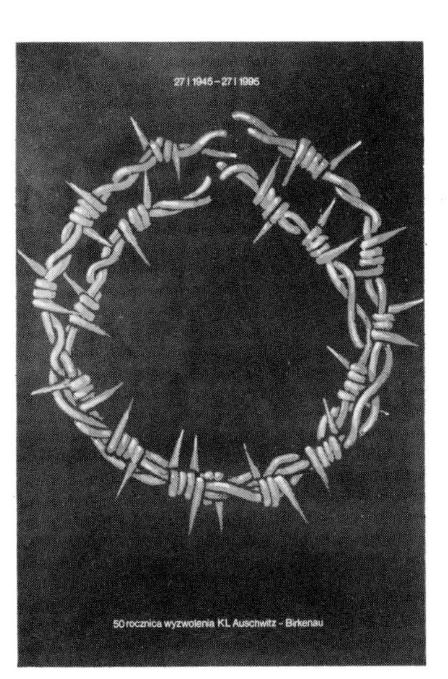

⑥

① Author unknown, n. d. /
Autor nieznany, b. d. / Autor unbekannt, o. J.

② J. A. Brandhuber, 1946:
Wires / Druty / Stacheldraht

③ A. Bujak, 1972

④ W. M. Zieliński, 1985

⑤ Z. Tołkaczew, 1945: Auschwitz Flowers /
Kwiaty Oświęcimia / Blumen von Auschwitz

⑥ W. Świerzy, 1994

①

②

③

④

Death Wall / Ściana Śmierci / Todeswand

⑤

① S. Łuczko, 1945
② A. Bujak, 1970
③ W. M. Zieliński, 1988
④ M. Kościelniak, 1972: Punishment–'Pillar' / Kara słupka / Gepfählt
⑤ Z. Łoboda, 1985

①

②

③

④

⑤

Gas Chambers — Crematoria / Komory gazowe — Krematoria / Gaskammern — Krematorien

⑥

⑦

① S. Mucha, 1945
② J. Frąckiewicz, n. d. / b. d. / o. J.
③ L. Grabowska, 1965
④ A. Bujak, 1971
⑤ W. M. Zieliński, 1987
⑥ Oishi Yoshino, 1988
⑦ J. Bacon, 1948:
Suicide / Samobójstwo / Selbstmord

①

②

③

④

Belongings / Rzeczy / Effekten

⑤

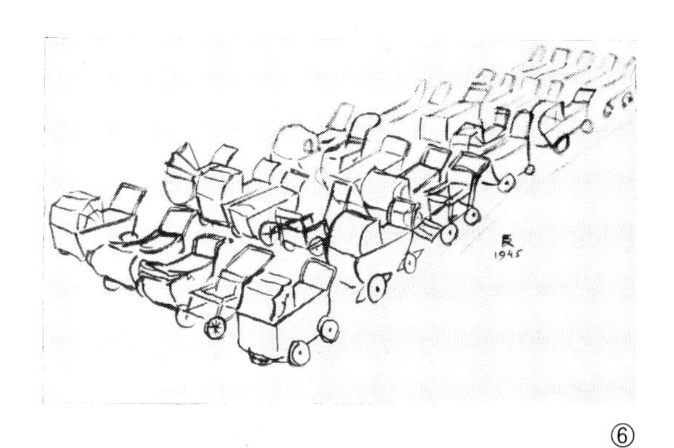

⑥

① Soviet Chronicle, 1945 /
Radziecka Kronika / Sowjetische Chronik

② Soviet Chronicle, 1945 /
Radziecka Kronika / Sowjetische Chronik

③ Author unknown, before 1955 / Autor nieznany, przed 1955 r. / Autor unbekannt, vor 1955

④ Author unknown, before 1955 / Autor nieznany, przed 1955 r. / Autor unbekannt, vor 1955

⑤ US Holocaust Memorial Museum, 1991

⑥ F. Reisz, 1945: Prams /
Wózki dziecięce / Kinderwagen

①

②

③

④

⑤

Symbols / Symbole

⑥

⑦

⑧

① L. Foryciarz, 1968

② A. Bujak, 1968

③ D. Laskawska, 1982:
Suffering / Cierpienie / Leid

④ S. Batruch, 1964:
Prisoners / Więźniownie / Häftlinge

⑤ Medal, 1989:
"Where is my Home?", Czechoslovakia /
"Gdzie mój dom?", Czechosłowacja /
"Wo ist mein zuhause?", Tschechoslowakei

⑥ Author unknown, n. d. /
Autor nieznany, b. d. / Autor unbekannt, o. J.

⑦ Postcard, Poland 1979 /
Karta pocztowa, Polska / Postkarte, Polen

⑧ E. Brzeski, 1980: Envelope /
Koperta / Briefumschlag

①

②

⑤

⑥

③

④

① "A Pictorial Record", 1985
② H. Hoffmann, 1937
③ A. Bujak, 1963
④ S. Mucha, 1945
⑤ Oishi Yoshino, 1988
⑥ Soviet Chronicle, 1945 /
Radziecka kronika / Sowjetische Chronik

AND EVERYBODY CROWDED INSIDE INTO THE SHOWER ROOM, THE DOOR CLOSED HERMETIC, AND THE LIGHTS TURNED DARK.
Zyklon B, a pesticide, dropped into hollow columns.
IT WAS BETWEEN 3 AND 30 MINUTES– IT DEPENDED HOW MUCH GAS THEY PUT– BUT SOON WAS NOBODY ANYMORE ALIVE.
THE BIGGEST PILE OF BODIES LAY RIGHT NEXT TO THE DOOR WHERE THEY TRIED TO GET OUT.
THIS GUY WHO WORKED THERE, HE TOLD ME...
WE PULLED THE BODIES APART WITH HOOKS. BIG PILES, WITH THE STRONGEST ON TOP, OLDER ONES AND BABIES CRUSHED BELOW... OFTEN THE SKULLS WERE SMASHED ...
THEIR FINGERS WERE BROKEN FROM TRYING TO CLIMB UP THE WALLS... AND SOMETIMES THEIR ARMS WERE AS LONG AS THEIR BODIES, PULLED FROM THE SOCKETS.
ENOUGH!
I DIDN'T WANT MORE TO HEAR, BUT ANYWAY HE TOLD ME.
THEY PULLED THE BODIES WITH AN ELEVATOR UP TO THE OVENS– MANY OVENS–AND TO EACH ONE THEY BURNED 2 OR 3 AT A TIME.
TO SUCH A PLACE FINISHED MY FATHER, MY SISTERS, MY BROTHERS, SO MANY
71

①

②

③

④

⑤

① A. Spiegelman, 1986–91: Maus II

② D. Kamann, 1942–43: Album der Zentralbauleitung

③ R. F. Stark, M. Stevens, 1991: Rain

④ Sonderkommando, 1944

⑤ F. Bedürftig, D. Kalenbach: Hitler, 1993

Detlef Hoffmann

Menschen hinter Stacheldraht

In seinen Werbekampagnen für eine Firma, die Kleidung herstellt, geht Oliviero Toscani bis an die Schmerzgrenze. Seine in diesem Jahr geplante Aktion soll unter dem Titel "Das Phantom der Freiheit" zu einer Diskussion über "reale und virtuale Gefängnisse" anregen, wie die Wochenzeitschrift "Die Zeit" am 19. Februar 1995 berichtete. Die Pulloverreklame soll diesmal nicht auf die großen Werbeflächen, die Bebilderung der Städte, beschränkt bleiben. Toscani möchte die weißen Straßenbahnwagen der Stadt Mailand mit (gemaltem) Stacheldraht umkleiden (Abb.1). Die Verkehrsbetrie-

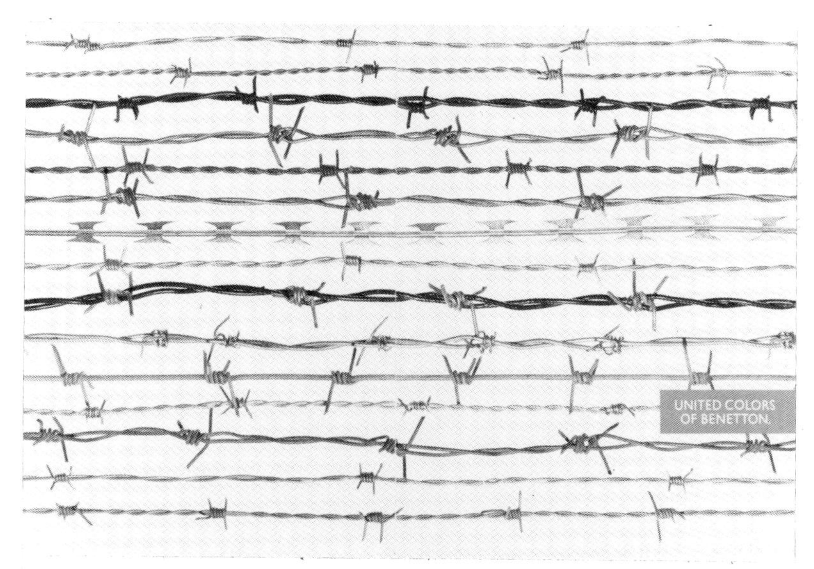

① Oliviero Toscani
Benetton advertisement / Reklama Benettona / Benetton Werbung
1994

be der Stadt zögern. Sie fürchten um ihr publikumsfreundliches Image. Denn könnte die Firma ihre Aktion realisieren, erschienen die Passagiere der Straßenbahn als Menschen, die hinter Stacheldraht gefangen gehalten würden.

Daß von dem Bild des Stacheldrahtes besonders agressive Signale ausgehen, verdeutlicht schon die Vorstellung, daß die Abbildung eines Lattenzaunes auf den Straßenbahnwagen zweifelsohne unproblematisch gewesen wäre. Stünde ein hölzerner Zaun für Idylle, Hausgarten und Privatheit, so steht der Stacheldraht für Absperrung, Lager oder Drahtverhau, für Öffentlichkeit und Staatsaktionen. Während Holz ein uraltes Material ist, produziert man Draht in größerer Länge erst zu Beginn der Neuzeit, in unendlicher Länge erst im 19. Jahrhundert. Draht in großen Mengen wird für die

Industrie benötigt, wie er selbst ein Produkt der Industrie ist. Er wird nicht nur in der Telegraphie verwandt, sondern auch für großräumige Zäune. Hierfür war der Stacheldraht eine erhebliche Verbesserung. 1873 hatte ihn William Donison Hunt in Illinois/USA zur Einfriedung großer Gebiete in der Land- und Forstwirtschaft erfunden. Nachdem Hunt 1878 die Stacheldrahtflechtmaschine entwickelt hatte, schnellte der Absatz in den USA und in Europa in die Höhe. In manchem Wildwestfilm steht der Stacheldrahtzaun für den Fortschritt, den alte Haudegen, deren Liebe dem freien Land gehört, nicht verstehen können.

Deuten schon diese Filme eine gewalttätige Verwendung des Stacheldrahtes an, so hat er seine Berühmtheit erst durch den Einsatz im Krieg erhalten. Es mag nur eine Legende sein, daß er zum ersten Mal im amerikanischen Sezessionskrieg bei der Verteidigung von Charleston 1863 eingesetzt wurde. Der Hinweis findet sich in Franz Maria Feldhaus' Lexikon zur Technikgeschichte.[1] Aber selbst wenn sich Feldhaus irrt, so signalisiert doch die Legende den engen Zusammenhang von Stacheldraht und modernem Krieg. Sowohl für Hindernisse als auch für Gefangenenlager wird der Draht eingesetzt, dessen amerikanischer Name "barbed wire" etwas freundlicher klingt als das deutsche Wort. Im Burenkrieg wurde er erstmals in großem Umfang verwandt, sowohl für strategische Zwecke als auch für Lagerzäune. Die Drahtverhaue des Ersten Weltkriegs verbinden ihn endgültig mit dem industrialisierten Krieg, sie lösen die spanischen Reiter ab. In der Antikriegspropaganda der Zwischenkriegszeit wird immer wieder das Bild des Toten im Drahtverhau verwandt, als Zeichnung, als Gemälde, als Foto, ja sogar als Installation auf der Straße: In einer Veranstaltung der ASSO-Gruppe Dresden hat Eugen Hoffmann 1928 — aus Anlaß des Antikriegstages — auf der Straße ein täuschend echtes Denkmal, einen Toten im Stacheldraht gezeigt.[2] Die Kriegspropaganda auf der anderen Seite belegt, daß der Stacheldraht überwunden werden kann. Der Film "Stoßtrupp 1917" nach dem Roman von Hans Zöberlein, mit dem die deutsche Propaganda auf die Verfilmung von Erich Maria Remarques "Im Westen nichts Neues" reagiert, führt die Dynamik der Kämpfer trotz der Drahtverhaue vor.[3] Noch 1944 sehen wir auf der Titelseite der Zeitschrift "Signal" einen Panzergrenadier, der den Stacheldraht zerschneidet (Abb. 2).[4]

Oliviero Toscanis Straßenbahnwagen sollen ein blutiges Gerät zitieren. Die Reaktion signalisiert, daß diese Bedeutung präsent ist. Die Stacheln saugen eine Vielfalt von Bedeutungen an. Immer geht es um Verletzung, Schmerz, Gefangensein. Toscanis Spürsinn für Bilder von symbolisierender Qualität mußte ihn eines Tages zum Stacheldraht führen. Bleibt zu fragen, wann der Kleiderhersteller mit Fotos des Lagers Auschwitz werben wird.

1. F. M. Feldhaus: Die Technik. Ein Lexikon, Wiesbaden, o.J., Spalte 1075/1076: "Bei Charleston verwendeten die Amerikaner 1863 zuerst Stacheldraht zur Errichtung von Hindernissen für die anstürmenden Feinde. William Donison Hunt führte diesen Draht 1873 als Einfriedungsmaterial von Tierweiden ein." Die zitierte Ausgabe ist ein Reprint der Auflage München 1970. Sein Techniklexikon hat der 1957 verstorbene Franz Maria Feldhaus 1914 in erster Auflage herausgegeben. Leider gibt er für seine Charleston-Information keine Quellen an. Ute Wrocklage hat in ihrer Magisterarbeit "Architektonische und skulpturale Gestaltung des Konzentrationslagers Neuengamme nach 1945", Oldenburg/Oldenburg 1992, S. 45 den Hinweis von Feldhaus überprüft, jedoch keine Belege finden können.

2. Vgl. D. Schubert: Das "harte Mal" der Waffen oder die Darstellung der Kriegsopfer, in: M. Diers (Hrsg.): Mo(nu)mente. Formen und Funktionen ephemerer Denkmäler, Berlin 1993, S. 137–152, Abb. S. 145.

3. Vgl. dazu D. Hoffmann: Der Mann mit dem Stahlhelm vor Verdun. Fritz Erlers Plakat zur sechsten Kriegsanleihe 1917, in: B. Hinz u.a. (Hrsg.): Die Dekoration der Gewalt. Kunst und Medien im Faschismus, Gießen 1979, S. 100–114, mit weiterführender Literatur. Vgl. auch D. Hoffmann/E. Riegel: Erst das Sichtbare macht Geschichte anschaulich, in: Kunst und Unterricht 58, 1979, S. 67–72, hier sind die Filme zusammengestellt. Das Buch von Zöberlein: Der Glaube an Deutschland, erschien 1931, die 44. Auflage 1944 (741.–770. Tausend).

4. Vgl. Signal. Eine kommentierte Auswahl abgeschlossener, völlig unveränderter Beiträge aus der Propaganda-Zeitschrift der Deutschen Wehrmacht, Hamburg 1977, Bd. 5, Schutzumschlag.

Zur Feier der 50. Wiederkehr der Befreiung der Häftlinge aus dem Konzentrationslager Auschwitz waren alle die Bilder in einer größeren Öffentlichkeit präsent, die Experten aus Büchern und Dokumentationen kennen. Anspruchsvollere Magazine, die wöchentlich oder gar monatlich erscheinen, zeigten Fotos des Geländes, meist von Fotografen aufgenommen, die auf eigentümliche Stilistik großen Wert legen. Die so ins Bild gesetzten Relikte werden als Zeugen für das Verbrechen zitiert, das Ende Januar 1945 beendet wurde. Die Annäherung an den bürokratisch geplanten Massenmord bleibt indirekt, Fakten liefert der Text, sich oft bewußt, daß auch die Fakten keinen Eindruck davon geben können, 'wie es eigentlich gewesen ist'.

② Title page from the Wehrmacht Propaganda Magazine "Signal" / Strona tytułowa pisma propagandowego Wehrmachtu "Signal" / Titelblatt der Propaganda–Zeitschrift der deutschen Wehrmacht "Signal".

Neben den fotografischen Aufnahmen des Geländes waren in den Zeitungen jene Bilder zu sehen, die aus der Zeit des Lagers stammen: Die Selektion auf der Rampe in Birkenau aus dem Lili–Jacob–Album; die vom Widerstand herausgeschmuggelten Fotos, auf denen wir sehen, wie Mitglieder des Sonderkommandos Leichen verbrennen und — sehr häufig — hinter dem Lagerzaun wartende oder nur stehende Menschen. Der Gestus, mit dem diese Dokumentarfotos präsentiert werden, unterstellt, daß uns hier vor Augen trete, 'wie es eigentlich gewesen sei'. Mit der gleichen Autorität wird dokumentarisches, also von damals stammendes, Material in den vielen Filmen vorgeführt, die über die Todesfabrik und ihr Ende berichten.[5]

Innerhalb der dokumentarischen Aufnahmen spielen die "Menschen hinter dem Stacheldraht" eine besondere Rolle. Hier wird kein Ereignis gezeigt wie die Selektion auf der Rampe, die Arbeit der Sonderkommandos, das Sortieren der Hinterlassenschaften der Ermordeten oder die Arbeit in Fabriken oder auf Baustellen. Auf diesen Fotos, die sich auf eigentümliche Art gleichen, sehen wir lediglich eine Gruppe von Menschen hinter dem Stacheldraht. Aus den eingefallenen Gesichtern schauen groß die Augen — sie stehen und blicken, das ist alles.

Wäre die Frage, 'wie es damals gewesen ist', ernst gemeint, wären diese Fotos kaum so berühmt geworden. Das Warten auf die Befreier — das diese Bilder signalisieren — hat es so nicht gegeben. Als sich die sowjetischen Truppen der 1. Ukrainischen Front Auschwitz näherten, befanden sich viele Häftlinge schon auf den Todesmärschen nach Westen. Die, die in den Lagern verblieben waren, lagen in den Baracken. Robert Antelme schildert in seinem 1957 erschienenen Buch "L'espèce humaine" (deutsch: Das Menschengeschlecht, 1987) die Befreiung des Lagers Dachau. Er berichtet, wie er neben einem alten Mann in der Baracke liegt, Maschinengewehrfeuer und Flugzeuge hört.

> "... Das Fieber kommt und geht. Die Läuse werden wieder wach. Hier hört man die Flugzeuge nicht mehr. Wieder die ineinander verschlungenen Beine,

5. Vgl. die vielen Abbildungen aus dem Film in T. Świebocka, J. Webber, C. Wilsack (Hrsg.): Auschwitz. A History in Photographs, Oświęcim, Bloomington und Indianapolis, Warschau, 1993, bes. S. 195 sowie S. 204f.

die Tritte mit den Fersen gegen die Wunden. Der Greis hat die Augen halb geschlossen. Mit meinem Fuß drücke ich auf den seinen:

"Wir sind bald frei!"

Er muß es mitkriegen, er muß leben. Selbst aus so weiter Ferne, dort, wo er jetzt ist, muß er es erfahren.

Er hebt die Augenlider an. Sie fallen sofort wieder zu. Mit dem Kopf macht er "nein".

"Sie sind da!"

Ich richte mich auf.

Ein runder Helm kommt auf dem Weg draußen, vor den Fenstern, vorüber.

In der Stube sind alle atemlos. Ich richte mich auf meinen Ellbogen auf.

Jetzt hört man es brüllen. Eine Art *Marseillaise*, angestimmt von Wahnsinnsstimmen, schwillt in der Baracke an. Im Barackengang schreit einer etwas. Er hält den Kopf in beiden Händen. Er sieht aus, als sei er verrückt.

"Ja habt ihr nicht begriffen! Wir sind frei, frei ..."

Er sagt es immer wieder, immer wieder. Er stampft mit den Füßen auf. Er brüllt.

Auf meinen Arm gestützt, folge ich mit den Augen den Stahlhelmen, die auf dem Weg vorübergehen. Ich drücke aus Leibeskräften, ich trete dem Greis auf die Füße.

"Wir sind frei, schauen Sie her! Schauen Sie her!"

Ich schlage aus Leibeskräften auf seinen Fuß. Er muß das sehen, er muß einfach. Er versucht sich aufzurichten. Er dreht sich nach dem Weg um, er reckt den Kopf. Die Stahlhelme sind schon vorüber. Es ist zu spät. Er fällt wieder zurück.

Ich falle ebenfalls wieder zurück. Ich habe nicht sofort hinunterspringen können, um zu den Soldaten zu gehen. Wir sind fast allein auf dem Bett, der Greis und ich. Die runden Helme sind vor meinen Augen vorbeigehuscht. Er hat nicht einmal etwas gesehen.

Die Befreiung ist vorbei."[6]

6. R. Antelme: Das Menschengeschlecht. Als Deportierter in Deutschland, München 1990, S. 403f.

Szenen wie diese sind kaum von symbolisierender Kraft, sie sind nicht fotografiert worden. Wie sollten sie auch fotografiert werden. Robert Antelmes Erzählung erfolgt aus dem Blick der Befreiten. Die Fotos jedoch werden von den Befreiern gemacht, den Befreiten war nicht nach Fotografieren zumute, sie hatten kaum die Kraft sich zu freuen.

Die Fotos von Menschen hinter Stacheldraht aus Auschwitz stammen alle aus dem Film "Chronik der Befreiung", der 1945 von vier sowjetischen Kameraleuten gedreht wurde: M. Oszwkow, N. Bykow, K. Kutub–Zade und A. Woroncow.[7] Die Kameraleute waren Filmberichterstatter der 1. Ukrainischen Front. Sie konnten erst einige Tage nach der Befreiung mit den Aufnahmen beginnen, anfangs gab es keinen Strom in den Baracken. Bis in den Herbst 1945, wahrscheinlich bis zum September, drehten die Kameramänner. Ihre letzten Aufnahmen zeigen die Menschen hinter dem Stacheldraht (Abb. 3).

7. Alle Angaben zu dem Film "Chronik der Befreiung" gehen auf Forschungen von Joachim Seinfeld zurück, die er mir freundlicherweise zur Verfügung gestellt hat.

③ Still from the film "The Chronicle" / Zdjęcie z filmu "Kronika" / Standfoto aus dem Film "Chronik"
1945

Das Filmmaterial wurde mehrfach unterschiedlich montiert. Eine erste Zusammenstellung von 20 Minuten fertigten die Sowjets, sie wurde über viele Jahre im Staatlichen Museum Auschwitz–Birkenau gezeigt. 1991 stellte das Museum aus dem Material einen 15 Minuten langen Film zusammen, keine neue Montage, vielmehr eine ideologische Reinigung. 1989 erarbeitete Irmgard von zur Mühlen eine weitere Montage, die alles erhaltene Material in der Abfolge der Entstehung zeigt, unterbrochen von Interviews mit dem noch lebenden Kameramann A. Woroncow. Hinzugenommen wurden Bilder aus dem Lili–Jacob–Album sowie Szenen von der Eroberung Krakaus und Kattowitzes.

Die Einstellungen, die ins Bildgedächtnis eingegangen sind, haben die Kameraleute spät gedreht, sie wurden — wie man sagt — gestellt. Im Mai 1945 machten sie den ersten Versuch, eindrucksvolle, bedeutungsvolle Ikonen der Befreiung zu erstellen. Am Tor des Stammlagers mit dem Motto "Arbeit macht frei" drängen sich gestikulierend und lachend die Gefangenen, sie jubeln den sowjetischen Soldaten zu, die sich dem Tor nähern. Sie brechen das Schloß auf, die Flügel springen vor, die Menschen sind frei. Eine Befreiung wie im Traum, wie 1989 im November. Doch die Szene fand keine Aufnahme in den endgültigen Film — sie wirkte wohl nicht authentisch. Das ist eben die Illusion des Dokumentarischen, daß es vorgibt, es sei gewesen, wie es dem späteren Augenschein gegenübertritt.

Die Menschen hinter dem Stacheldraht, aufgenommen im Herbst 1945, sind auch in dem im Museum gezeigten Film zu sehen. Anders als die Sequenz am Tor haben sich diese Bilder durchgesetzt, obwohl sie ebenso gestellt worden sind. Aber was heißt gestellt? Sicher, wäre das Lager noch in SS–Verwaltung gewesen, hätten sich Gefangene niemals dem Stacheldraht nähern können. Die SS versuchte auch die Selbstmorde, das In–den–Draht–gehen, zu verhindern — führte es doch zu einem Kurzschluß und entsprechendem Arbeitsaufwand. Und daß die Gefangenen die sowjetischen Soldaten nicht hinter dem Drahtzaun wartend empfangen haben, wurde schon erwähnt. In diesem Sinne fehlt den Bildern Authentizität, sie sind in den Augen eines knöchernen Positivismus 'falsch'. Auf der anderen Seite sehen wir hinter dem Stacheldraht jene Menschen, die bis zum 27. Januar 1945 Häftlinge des Lagers waren, sie stellen sich vor der Kamera auf, um zu bezeugen, was mit ihnen geschah. Gemeinsam mit den Kameraleuten fertigen sie ein Bild von großer symbolisierender zentripetaler Kraft. Dieses Bild saugt nicht nur die Bilder auf, die seit dem Beginn des Jahrhunderts von Gefangenen gemacht wurden, es prägt auch die zukünftigen Bilder (Abb. 4).

④ Roberto Innocenti
Illustration from the Children's Book "Rosa Weiss" / Ilustracja z książki dla dzieci "Rosa Weiss" / Illustration aus dem Kinderbuch "Rosa Weiss"
1985

Die Antwort auf die Frage nach der Authentizität, nach dem, wie es ohne Hinzufügen und ohne Wegnehmen gewesen ist, nach dem, was gerne 'dokumentarisch' genannt wird, ist komplex. Die Menschen präsentieren sich so, wie sie re–präsentiert werden wollen. Das, was nicht mehr sichtbar ist, hat sich in das Bild eingeschrieben. In seiner quälenden Bewegungslosigkeit sammelt sich die abwesende Erzählung der ihnen angetanen Gewalt, die abwesende Leidensgeschichte. Dieses Bild ist engstens mit den deutschen Konzentrationslagern verbunden. Wo immer und wann immer Menschen hinter dem Stacheldraht gezeigt werden — wie jenes

Farbfoto des Lagers Trnopolje in Bosnien–Herzegovina — sind die Szenen von 1945 latent präsent.[8]

Doch das Filmbild vom Herbst 1945 symbolisiert nicht nur Leid und Gewalt, es fixiert einen historischen Moment. Nicht nur der Stacheldraht ist — wie gezeigt — engstens mit der Moderne verbunden, auch das Lager, in dem — von einem undurchdringlichen Zaun umgeben — Menschen verwahrt werden, ist ein Produkt der Moderne, der Menschenrechte. Kriegsgefangene werden im 19. Jahrhundert nicht mehr erschlagen oder in die Sklaverei verkauft, sie werden in Lagern bis zum Kriegsende aufbewahrt. Zunehmend regeln internationale Abmachungen ihre Rechte. Doch auch neutrale Staaten waren nach dem Haager Vertrag von 1907 gezwungen, Truppen der kriegführenden Mächte auf ihrem Staatsgebiet in Haft zu nehmen.

So thematisiert der Stacheldrahtzaun Gefangenschaft in Zeiten der Gewalt. Die hier Festgesetzten warten auf das Ende des Krieges, auf die Freiheit. Die Bauten, die Anlagen dieser Lager sind ephemer, sie sind nicht auf Dauer gebaut wie Rathäuser und Schlösser. Wird das Lager nicht mehr gebraucht, trägt man es ab. Was hier geschah, geht in die Latenz des Bildgedächtnisses ein, das den Zustand schmerzhafter Gefangenschaft bewahrt. Die deutschen Konzentrationslager sind ebenfalls ephemere, zeitlich begrenzte Anlagen. Doch ihr Zweck ist es nicht, Menschen bis zum Ende gewaltsamer Auseinandersetzungen zu verwahren, ihr Zweck ist erfüllt, wenn alle Insassen ermordet sind. Am Anfang wurde der Tod bei der Zwangsarbeit billigend in Kauf genommen, dann wurde er zum Ziel alles Tuns. Am Ende dieser Entwicklung stehen die Todesfabriken auf polnischem Territorium.

Das Bild der Menschen hinter dem Stacheldraht, der Überlebenden, läßt auch die Abwesenheit der Ermordeten zum Thema werden. Der Zufall, der Glücksfall des Überlebens repräsentiert die Regelhaftigkeit des Todes. Die Ermordung von Juden war die Regel, das Überleben war die Ausnahme. Insofern symbolisiert das Bild der Menschen hinter Stacheldraht die manifesten destruktiven Strukturen der Moderne.

8. Vgl. dazu in einem größeren Zusammenhang D. Hoffmann: Fotografierte Lager. Überlegungen zu einer Fotogeschichte deutscher Konzentrationslager, in: Fotogeschichte 54, 1994, S. 3–20, bes. S. 13.

People Behind Barbed Wire

The film “Chronicle of the Liberation”, produced by a Soviet filmcrew between January and autumn 1945, shows some people standing behind barbed wire fences. Even though this was filmed in autumn 1945, they are by far the most famous images in the film. Although, or maybe because they are set up, they have especially come to symbolize imprisonment and liberation and have therefore become the representative image in people's minds. These images bring together several different branches of modernisation: barbed wire (invented in 1873) and the prison camp (from the start of the 19th century), both are associated with the bourgeois idea of property (fenced property), and the humanization of war (prisoners of war). Those who survived by chance also represent the victims who were murdered under the rules of the system, therefore this photo symbolizes modern destructive structures.

Więźniowie za kolczastym drutem

Nakręcona przez operatorów sowieckich od stycznia do jesieni 1945 roku "Kronika wyzwolenia", zawiera wiele ujęć z wyzwolonymi więźniami, patrzącymi obco na widzów zza drutu kolczastego. Ujęcia te kręcono dopiero jesienią 1945 r. Są jednak najbardziej znanymi obrazami tego filmu. Jakkolwiek, albo może właśnie dlatego, że są one upozowane, w sposób szczególny symbolizują niewolę i oswobodzenie, i z tego powodu utrwalone są w pamięci. Omawiane sekwencje łączą w sobie kilka przejawów nowoczesności: drut kolczasty (wynaleziony w 1873 r.) oraz obóz jeniecki (powstały z początkiem XIX wieku), definiując pojęcie własności (ogrodzona własność) oraz humanizację wojny (więźniowie). To, że kilka przypadkowo ocalałych osób reprezentuje również zamordowanych zgodnie z niepisanym prawem panującego systemu, sprawia, że także fotografie same w sobie symbolizują destrukcyjne przejawy moderny.

Yasmin Doosry

Vom Dokument zur Ikone: Zur Rezeption des Auschwitz–Albums

* J. Levin, die Leiterin des Fotoarchivs von Yad Vashem gewährte mir liebenswürdigerweise Einsicht in das vor kurzem restaurierte Auschwitz–Album. I. Salmon möchte ich für ihre Gastfreundschaft während meines Aufenthaltes in Jerusalem danken.

Frühjahr 1945. Soldaten der US–Streitkräfte befreien in Thüringen das Konzentrationslager Dora–Nordhausen. Im allgemeinen Durcheinander macht sich die frierende Lili Jacob, vorher in Auschwitz inhaftiert und dann nach Dora–Nordhausen transportiert, auf die Suche nach warmer Kleidung. In einer der SS–Unterkünfte öffnet sie die Schublade einer Kommode und entdeckt dort, eingeschlagen in einen Pyjama, ein Fotoalbum.[1] Damit hat Lili Jacob ein Dokument gefunden, das bis heute einzigartig geblieben ist.[2]

Das in Leinen gebundene Album enthält 29 Fotokartons (28,5 × 24,1 cm). Diese sind, mit Ausnahme der ersten und der letzten Seite, alle beidseitig mit jeweils zwei bis vier Fotos beklebt. Von den ursprünglich 197 Abzügen sind sieben entfernt worden, deren ursprüngliches Vorhandensein aber aus Lichträndern und Klebespuren zweifelsfrei zu erschließen ist.[3]

Die weißen Ränder der querformatigen, ca. 10,5 × 8 cm großen Fotos sind unterschiedlich breit und unregelmäßig beschnitten. Die Bilder wurden freihändig auf die Kartons aufgeklebt, so daß ihre Kanten nur ungefähr in einer Flucht liegen und nicht exakt parallel zu den Rändern der Kartons verlaufen. Die braun–weiß getönten, meist gestochen scharfen Abzüge sind nach Themen geordnet. Diese sind durch sorgfältige Beschriftung kenntlich gemacht, wobei die Schönschrift in einem merkwürdigen Kontrast zu der nachlässigen Montierung der Fotos steht. Auf der ersten Fotoseite erscheint unter zwei hochformatigen Männerporträts der Titel des Albums: "Umsiedlung der Juden aus Ungarn". Es folgen die Kapitel "Ankunft eines Transportzuges", "Aussortierung", "Männer bei der Ankunft" und "Frauen bei der Ankunft". Unter der zusammenfassenden Überschrift "Nach der Aussortierung" schließen sich vier weitere Kapitel an: "Noch einsatzfähige Männer", "Noch einsatzfähige Frauen", "Nicht mehr einsatzfähige Männer", "Nicht mehr einsatzfähige Frauen und Kinder". Die letzten drei Kapitel sind betitelt: "Nach der Entlausung", "Einweisung ins Arbeitslager" sowie "Effekten". Dem ganzen Album ist auf der ersten Seite eine mit Bleistift eingetragene Widmung vorangestellt: "Andenken von

1. Vgl. u. a. die Zeugenaussage von Lili Jacob (bzw. Zelmanovic) im Frankfurter Auschwitz–Prozeß, in H. Langbein: Der Auschwitz–Prozess. Eine Dokumentation, Wien, Frankfurt, Zürich 1965, Bd. 1, S. 149f.

2. Serge Klarsfeld hat das gesamte Album ediert, s. S. Klarsfeld (Hrsg.): The Auschwitz–Album. Lili Jacob's Album, New York 1980. Meine Verweise auf die Nummern der Fotos folgen der Zählung Yad Vashems, wo sich das Original–Album befindet. Die mit Bleistift unter den Fotos eingetragenen Ziffern sind in Klarsfelds Ausgabe erkennbar, wenn auch oft nur mit Mühe.

3. Die fehlenden Fotos hat Lili Jacob aus dem Album herausgelöst und sie Menschen geschenkt, die Verwandte oder Freunde darauf wiedererkannt hatten. In S. Klarsfelds Ausgabe des Albums (s. die vorige Anm.), die keine Seitenzählung hat, sind fünf der fehlenden Fotos in dem Abschnitt "Five photos, missing from the original album, which appear here thanks to the reproductions made in Prague 1946" reproduziert.

Deinem Lieben und Unvergesslicher und Treuliebender Heinz" (sic!).

Dieses 'Liebesgeschenk' erläutert kühl und sachlich die zeitliche Abfolge und die systematische Durchführung der Maßnahmen, die in der — im Album nicht dargestellten — Ermordung zahlloser Menschen in Auschwitz–Birkenau ihren Abschluß fanden. Art, Auswahl, Anordnung sowie Kommentierung der Fotos führen in aller Deutlichkeit vor, was unter dem harmlos klingenden Begriff "Umsiedlung" zu verstehen ist. 'Heinz' — sofern er es war, der das Album zusammengestellt hat — kommt gleich zur Sache, indem er auf die Gruppe von Menschen weist, die es (hauptsächlich) 'umzusiedeln' gilt: Die beiden ersten Fotos zeigen gläubige Juden mit Bärten und Hüten, aufgenommen im Halbprofil. Diese Ansicht war geeignet, die angeblich rassischen Merkmale von jüdischen Menschen hervorzuheben — war doch durch die Nazi–Propaganda auch dem letzten Dorfbewohner bewußt, was er unter einem 'Talmudgesicht' zu verstehen hatte.[4] Im Mittelpunkt des Interesses stehen jedoch nicht Juden schlechthin, sondern Juden aus Ungarn: Vom 16. Mai bis zum 8. Juli 1944 wurden in 53 Transporten Männer, Frauen und Kinder von Ungarn nach Auschwitz–Birkenau deportiert. Täglich trafen zwei bis fünf Güterzüge mit jeweils etwa 40–50 Waggons in Birkenau ein.[5]

4. Vgl. J. Streicher (Hrsg.): Der Stürmer. Deutsches Wochenblatt zum Kampfe um die Wahrheit, 17. Jg. (1939), Nr. 9, 1. März 1939 (Titelblatt).

5. Die Zahl der von Ungarn nach Auschwitz–Birkenau deportierten Juden ist umstritten, vgl. J.–C. Pressac: Die Krematorien von Auschwitz. Die Technik des Massenmordes, München, Zürich 1994, S. 197 ff.

Die den beiden Porträtaufnahmen folgenden 18 Fotos illustrieren die "Ankunft eines Transportzuges" in Birkenau. Auf dem ersten Bild (Foto 3) sind zwei Güterzüge mit noch geschlossenen Wagentüren zu sehen, zwischen denen, auf der noch leeren Ausladefläche, SS–Männer patroullieren. Auf allen weiteren Fotos dieser Serie entsteigen unübersehbare Massen von Menschen den Waggons und füllen die Entladefläche. Zwischen diesen meist ungeordneten Menschenmengen sind, neben Mitgliedern des "Arbeitskommandos Rampe" in Häftlingskleidung, nur vereinzelte SS–Männer zu sehen (Foto 16, 18). In dem Kapitel "Aussortierung" hingegen erscheinen sie mit einer Ausnahme (Foto 24) auf jedem der 16 Fotos. Bereits die ersten beiden Aufnahmen dieses Kapitels (Fotos 21, 22) machen ihre Funktion deutlich: Sie haben die Deportierten zu zwei langen Kolonnen geordnet, die eine aus Frauen und Kindern, die andere aus Männern bestehend. Diese rücken, weiterhin von SS–Männern dirigiert und in Schach gehalten, bis zur großen Kreuzung des Lagers vor (Foto 23). Dort entscheiden SS–Ärzte, ob die neu eingetroffenen Menschen als 'Nicht–Einsatzfähige' gleich in den Gastod zu gehen haben oder als 'Einsatzfähige', eine Galgenfrist bei schwerer Zwangsarbeit erhalten.[6]

6. Vgl. Pressac (s. die vorige Anm.), S. 198 f.

Schauplatz der Ankunft und der Aussortierung ist die 'Rampe', eine dreigleisige Schienenanlage mit breiter Entladefläche, die zwischen den Abschnitten BI und BII das Lager vom 'Todestor' bis zu den Krematorien II und III von Osten nach Westen durchläuft. Ihr Ausbau war in Erwartung der Ungarn–

Transporte beschleunigt vorangetrieben worden. Ort der Selektion ist der Schnittpunkt der Rampe mit der großen Querstraße, die in Nord–Südrichtung das Lager zwischen den Sektionen B II c (Lager der ungarischen Juden) und B II d (Männerlager) durchschneidet (Abb. 1).

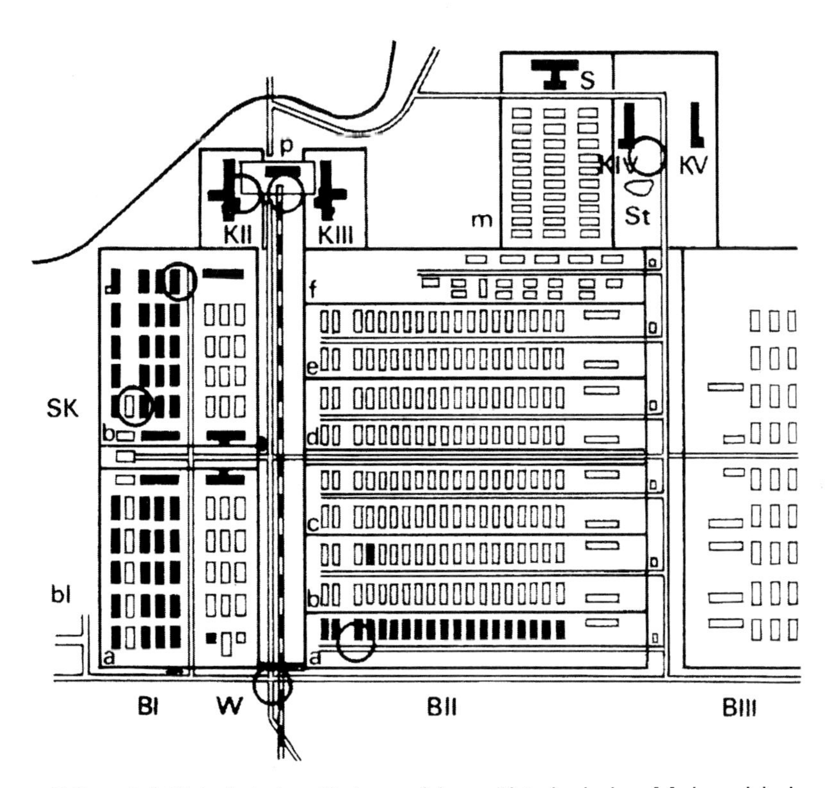

① Layout map of the former Concentration Camp Auschwitz–Birkenau / Mapa byłego obozu Auschwitz–Birkenau / Lageplan des ehemaligen Konzentrations– und Vernichtungslagers Auschwitz–Birkenau

Offensichtlich ist der Fotograf bemüht, bei der Mehrzahl der Ankunfts– und Selektionsszenen so viele Menschen wie möglich auf die Platte zu bannen und wiederholt die enorme Länge der Rampe zu zeigen. Aus diesem Grund wählt er für mehrere Aufnahmen einen erhöhten Standort, wahrscheinlich das Dach eines Waggons (z. B. Foto 4, 16, 21, 26). Für die beiden Kapitel "Männer (Frauen) bei der Ankunft" entscheidet er sich hingegen in erster Linie für Gruppenporträts, die er oft frontal aufnimmt (Foto 37, 42–46, 57–60). Dasselbe Prinzip ist auch bei den Kapiteln mit den Themen "Noch einsatzfähige Männer (Frauen)" zu erkennen (Foto 61, 63, 75; 76–79). Die Menschen, die einem Aussonderungsprozeß unterzogen werden sollen oder die 'Qualitätskontrolle' bereits passiert haben, werden aus der Nähe aufgenommen, quasi mit einem Vergrößerungsglas betrachtet.

Deutlich wird dies auch in dem Abschnitt "Nicht mehr einsatzfähige Männer". Er wird auf zwei sich gegenüberliegenden Seiten mit jeweils drei Fotos eingeleitet: Auf der linken Seite ein verwachsener, in einem Korbstuhl sitzender junger Mann, ein alter Jude im Profil und eine Gruppe alter Männer und Frauen (Foto 88–90); auf der rechten Seite ein im Gras hockender Greis, ein Jude mit einem Krückstock neben sich sowie ein Gruppenbild mit alten und jungen Männern (Foto 91–93). Es fällt auf, daß dem Betrachter des Albums als Beispiele für die — zum Tod bestimmten —

'Nicht–Einsatzfähigen' in dieser Serie meist orthodoxe Juden vorgeführt werden (z. B. Foto 96, 97, 100–103).

Am Anfang des Kapitels "Nicht mehr einsatzfähige Frauen und Kinder" stehen ebenfalls Fotos einzelner Frauen, die alt oder behindert sind (Foto 115–117). Es folgen wie im vorangegangenen Abschnitt Gruppenaufnahmen alter und junger Frauen, unter denen sich auch eine Schwangere befindet (Foto 122). Sie halten durchweg Kinder auf dem Arm oder an der Hand, während man bei den Fotos der "Noch einsatzfähigen Frauen" bis auf eine Ausnahme (Foto 77) vergebens nach Kindern sucht.[7] Wie die männlichen Todeskandidaten sind auch die für die Gaskammer selektierten Frauen und Kinder teilweise noch innerhalb der Lagerbegrenzung (Foto 120, 125), aber auch im Birkenwald von Birkenau aufgenommen (z. B. Foto 130–140). Dort mußten sie warten, bis sie in das Krematorium V geführt wurden. Hier löst sich die seit dem Kapitel "Aussortierung" herrschende Ordnung wieder auf.

7. Dieses Foto findet sich im Album ein zweites Mal (Foto 56) in dem Kapitel "Frauen bei der Ankunft".

In den Abschnitten "Nach der Entlausung" und "Einweisung ins Arbeitslager" werden kahlgeschorene, teilweise Häftlingskleidung tragende Männer und Frauen vorgeführt, die nun vollends der Lagerordnung unterworfen sind. Zeigen die vorangegangenen Fotos noch Menschen mit individuellen Merkmalen, so verlieren sich diese bei ihrer Eingliederung in das Lagersystem. Dies bringt 'Heinz' auch dadurch zum Ausdruck, daß er den Aufnahmen kleiner Gruppen zu Beginn der 'Entlausungs–Serie' (bes. Foto 149–151) Bilder folgen läßt, die von immer mehr Menschen bevölkert werden: Auf den letzten Fotos des Kapitels "Einweisung ins Arbeitslager" sehen wir ebenso wie im Anfangskapitel "Ankunft eines Transportes" kaum zu überblickende Menschenmassen, zu Kolonnen formiert oder aufgestellt zum Appell (z. B. Foto 161, 166).

Das Album schließt mit dem Kapitel "Effekten": Auf der Rampe türmt sich das Gepäck der Deportierten; es wird von einem Häftlingskommando in die Effektenlager, im Lagerjargon kurz 'Kanada' genannt, einsortiert.

Liest man das Album als fortlaufenden Bericht, so offenbart sich in seinem Aufbau und seiner Struktur das Bemühen, ein bestimmtes Bild des Lagersystems in Birkenau und der dort agierenden SS zu entwerfen: Das Album will Ordnungssinn, Leistungsfähigkeit und Effektivität dokumentieren sowie den 'unerschütterlichen' Willen, dies alles durchzusetzen.

Doch wer konnte ein derartiges Dokument erstellen? Sowohl das Verbot, im Lager zu fotografieren[8] als auch die schiere Menge und die Motivwahl der Fotos ließen die Vermutung aufkommen, daß sie nur im Auftrag der Lagerleitung entstanden sein konnten. Die Professionalität der Aufnahmen, aber auch Zeugenaussagen führten zu Bernhard Walter, der in Auschwitz I, dem Stammlager, den Erkennungsdienst aufge-

8. s. APMO, Syg. D–Aul–1/99: Kommandanturbefehl Nr. 4/43 vom 2.2.1943.

baut und geleitet hatte. Nur er und sein Mitarbeiter Heinz Hofmann durften im Lager Fotoapparate mit sich führen. Jahrelang leugnete Bernhard Walter jede Verbindung mit dem Album und verwies statt dessen auf Hofmann, der spurlos verschwunden war. Erst im Frankfurter Auschwitz–Prozeß gab er zu, der Urheber einiger Fotos zu sein. Damit war aber noch nicht geklärt, von wem die Widmung stammt und wie das Album nach Dora–Nordhausen gelangt war.[9]

9. Vgl. Klarsfeld (s.o. Anm. 2) in der Einleitung sowie Frankfurter Staatsanwaltschaft, AZ. 4 Js 444/59, Bd. 17; Bl. 2783 ff.; Bd. 39, Bl. 6738ff.; Bd. 73, Bl. 1378ff.

1946 bietet Lili Jacob das Album dem Staatlichen Jüdischen Museum in Prag zur Reproduktion an. Erst drei Jahre später werden in dem Buch "The Tragedy of Slovak Jewry" über 30 der aus dem Album abfotografierten Aufnahmen veröffentlicht.[10] Weitere sechs Jahre vergehen, bis die Fotos erneut ins Bewußtsein einer begrenzten Öffentlichkeit treten: 1955 entdeckt Erich Kulka im Prager Jüdischen Museum zwei Schachteln mit der Aufschrift "Fotografien aus Auschwitz". Als ehemaliger Häftling von Auschwitz–Birkenau erkennt er sofort die Bedeutung der Glasnegative. Noch im selben Jahr fährt er zusammen mit Ota Kraus nach Polen. Die beiden versuchen vor Ort die Fotos zu verifizieren. Bei dieser Gelegenheit erhält das Staatliche Museum Auschwitz–Birkenau einen kompletten Satz der Aufnahmen.[11]

10. Documentation Center of CUJCR, Bratislawa (Hrsg.): The Tragedy of Slowak Jewry, Prag 1949, S. 97 ff.

11. APMO, Syg. D–F, Tom 1a; fol. 54 ff.: Schreiben E. Kulkas an R. L. Braham vom 9. 10. 1980.

Die Ergebnisse ihrer Reise publizieren Kulka und Kraus in der vierten Auflage ihres 1946 zum ersten Mal erschienenen Buches "Továrna na smrt" ("Factory of Death", "Die Todesfabrik"), indem sie dort 42 der Fotos abbilden und mit Erläuterungen versehen.[12] 1957 übergibt Kulka mit Zustimmung der tschechischen Behörden Arie Segal, der im Auftrag von Yad Vashem, The Holocaust Martyrs' and Heroes' Remembrance Authority, Jerusalem, in Prag recherchiert, einen Satz der SS–Aufnahmen. Im Juli 1958 berichtet Kulka im Yad Vashem Bulletin von den Fotos und bemerkt dazu: "The collection of the copies of the photographs has also been acquired by Yad Vashem".[13] Auf Initiative von Serge Klarsfeld erhält Yad Vashem am 24. 8. 1980 das Originalalbum von Lili Jacob. Bereits 1961 hatte sie dem Staatlichen Museum Auschwitz–Birkenau sowie 1979, auf Anregung von Erich Kulka, dem "Public Committee of Auschwitz Survivors in Israel" angeboten, ihnen das Album zu übergeben.[14]

12. O. Kraus, F. Kulka: Továrna na smrt. Dokument o Osvětimi, Prag 1957, S. 51ff.

13. E. Kulka: 200 hitherto unknown Photos of Auschwitz, in: Yad Vashem Bulletin 3 (1958), S. 22 Anm. 3.

14. APMO, Syg. D–F, Tom 1a: Schreiben von Lili Zelmanovic an Kazimierz Smoleń vom 2. 4. 1961 (fol. 81) und vom 28. 6. 1961 (fol. 84); Schreiben ders. an E. Kulka vom 28.(?). 1979. Vgl. auch S. Klarsfeld (s.o. Anm.2), Einleitung.

Nachdem Yad Vashem die Auschwitz–Fotos 1957/58 archiviert und katalogisiert hatte, waren sie weltweit zugänglich. Sie wurden seitdem tausendfach in Büchern, Zeitschriften und in den Massenmedien reproduziert. Gilt es, den von Deutschen begangenen Massenmord ins Bild zu setzen, so bedienen sich Autoren, Verlage, Ausstellungs– und oft auch Filmemacher bevorzugt der Fotos aus dem Auschwitz–Album. Bis etwa Mitte der sechziger Jahre stand ihr dokumentarischer Charakter im Vordergrund des Interesses. Erich Kulka, der neben Mitarbeitern des Staatlichen Museums Auschwitz–Birkenau als erster den Versuch unternahm, einzelne Szenen und deren Schauplätze in Auschwitz–Birkenau sowie einzelne

Personen zu identifizieren, hat immer wieder auf den Quellenwert der Fotos verwiesen. Noch im Oktober 1980 schrieb er: "Mrs Meier–Zelmonovic (Lili Jacob. - d. Verf.) is to be praised for having found and kept the album of photos copies (sic!) of which she probably sold several times over [...] But the real significance lies in the precise identification of every picture documenting the extermination of the Jews in Auschwitz. This important work should be accomplished as a priority, as long as Auschwitz survivors are able to wear witness. Without this achievement, the photos – in which the SS photographers purposely avoided any harsh and suspicious scene of armed SS–men accompanied usually by blood–hounds — these pictures could be presented by some Holocaust–denying author as a document about the peaceful "Umsiedlung der Juden aus Ungarn", the title picture of the album".[15] Hintergrund dieser Warnung vom 9. Oktober 1980 dürfte die Übergabe des Auschwitz–Albums an Yad Vashem im August 1980 und die sie begleitende öffentliche Aufmerksamkeit gewesen sein, die durchweg die Singularität des Albums betont, aber nicht seine Bedeutung als historisches Zeugnis, sondern seinen emotionalen Gehalt in den Vordergrund stellt.

15. s. Kulka (s.o. Anm. 11), fol. 57.

Ebenfalls im Zusammenhang mit der Übergabe der Fotos an Yad Vashem veröffentlicht Serge Klarsfeld 1980 das ganze "Auschwitz–Album" und gibt ihm den Untertitel "Lili Jacob's Album".[16] Diese Bezeichnung, die den Blick von der unendlichen Vielzahl der mit den Ungarn-Transporten nach Auschwitz–Birkenau deportierten Juden auf eine einzige Person verengt, prägt sich dem Bewußtsein der Öffentlichkeit ein. Vielfach ist nur noch von "Lilis Album" die Rede. Mit Klarsfelds Edition erhalten breite Kreise Zugang zu den SS–Fotos, doch die Praxis ihrer Verwertung ändert sich kaum: Die Entstehung, die Absichten der Urheber des Albums, die Funktion der Fotos und ihre Zusammenhänge untereinander spielen kaum je eine Rolle. Statt dessen werden einzelne Bilder aus dem Gesamtkomplex herausgerissen, ihre Beschriftung im Album oft unterschlagen. Sie werden neu geordnet, 'antik' eingefärbt, beschnitten, überdimensional vergrößert und sogar spiegelverkehrt reproduziert.

16. s. Klarsfeld (s.o. Anm. 2).

Für letzteres findet sich sowohl in der historischen Ausstellung von Yad Vashem als auch in der Dauerausstellung (Raum 1 von Block 4) des Staatlichen Museums Auschwitz–Birkenau je ein Beispiel. Hier wie dort handelt es sich um Bilder, die im Album dem Kapitel "Nicht mehr einsatzfähige Frauen und Kinder" zugeordnet sind. Die Aufnahme in Yad Vashem gibt eine alte, gebeugt gehende Frau wieder, die von kleinen Kindern umgeben ist (Abb. 2). Auf dem Foto im Staatlichen Museum Auschwitz–Birkenau ist ein Zug von Frauen festgehalten, von denen die meisten Kinder verschiedener Altersgruppen auf dem Arm tragen oder an der Hand führen (Abb. 3). Durch die seitenverkehrte und zugleich um ein Vielfaches vergrößerte Reproduktion (vgl. Foto 143), aber

② In the historical exhibition at Yad Vashem the photo 119 from the 1944 Auschwitz–Album can be seen reproduced in mirror image and partly cut (see markings) /
Wystawa historyczna Yad Vashem, 119 zdjcie z Auschwitz–Album z 1944 r. skadrowane z oryginau (por. markery) w lustrzanym odbiciu /
In der historischen Ausstellung Yad Vashem ist das Foto 119 aus dem Auschwitz–Album von 1944 spiegelverkehrt reproduziert und beschnitten zu sehen (siehe Markierungen).

auch dadurch, daß nicht stehende oder wartende, sondern sich vorwärtsbewegende Menschen abgebildet sind, werden jene beiden Aufnahmen dem Rundgang in der Ausstellung angepaßt: Die Besucher laufen scheinbar in dieselbe Richtung wie die Menschen auf den Fotos. So wird ihnen die Empfindung suggeriert, die Opfer auf ihrem Weg in die Gaskammer zu begleiten. Dementsprechend lautet in Yad Vashem der Kommentar zu der Fotosequenz, in die das Bild der alten Frau mit den kleinen Kindern eingefügt ist: “On the way to death”. Indem der Eindruck vermittelt wird, daß Besucher und Opfer denselben Weg gehen, wird zwischen beiden ein emotionales Band geknüpft.

③ Room 1 in Block 4 of the Auschwitz Museum with the partly cut and mirror–imaged photo (143 in the 1944 Auschwitz–Album) / Muzeum Oświęcim–Brzezinka, sala wystawowa 1 w bloku 4 ze skadrowanym z oryginału zdjęciem w lustrzanym odbiciu / Raum 1 in Block 4 des Museums Auschwitz–Birkenau mit dem spiegelverkehrt reproduzierten und beschnittenen Foto 143 aus dem Auschwitz–Album von 1944.
J. Seinfeld

Eine ähnliche Wirkung ruft das Beschneiden der aus dem Album reproduzierten Fotos bis hin zur Präsentation bloßer Ausschnitte hervor. So ist etwa die Reproduktion der eben erwähnten Aufnahme kindertragender und –führender Frauen in Auschwitz unten und rechts beschnitten, in Yad Vashem rechts und links (Abb. 2, 3). In zahlreichen Ausstellungen, Publikationen und Filmen hat diese Praxis Schule gemacht.[17] Zunächst hat es den Anschein, als wolle man hierdurch lediglich die Aufmerksamkeit des Betrachters auf das 'Wesentliche' konzentrieren. Dennoch ist Skepsis gegenüber einem solchen Vorgehen angebracht. Oft werden dadurch für ein richtiges Verständnis notwendige Hinweise auf die Schauplätze einzelner Szenen ausgeblendet. Auch wird nicht selten der Blick des Betrachters auf einzelne aus der 'Masse der Opfer' herausgegriffene Menschen gelenkt. Anscheinend glaubt man, die Ungeheuerlichkeit des Massenmordes sei dem heutigen Betrachter der Fotos, der als Angehöriger der westlichen Zivilisation von der hohen Bewertung alles Individuellen geprägt ist, am besten über die Einfühlung in das Leid aus der Menge der übrigen Betroffenen ausgewählter Einzelpersonen vermittelbar, das er sich als mögliches eigenes Leid vorstellen kann (Abb. 4). Mit einer solchen Einstellung, die sich an besonders anrührenden, in Museen und Medien herausgestellten Häftlingsschicksalen orientiert, mag es im übrigen auch zusammenhängen, daß die von Serge Klarsfeld eingeführte Bezeichnung "Lili Jacob's Album" so bereitwillig aufgenommen wurde: Das Album ist in der Ikonographie der Medien gewissermaßen zu einem persönlichen Attribut der Finderin der SS–Fotos geworden, die wie durch ein Wunder der Lagerhölle entronnen ist (Abb. 5).

17. So sind z. B. in Yad Vashem u.a. die Fotos 21, 25, 28, 35, im Museum Auschwitz–Birkenau die Fotos 53, 128 in beschnittener Form zu sehen. Das Magazin "Der Spiegel", Nr. 4 vom 23. 1. 1995 bildete für seine Titelgeschichte "Auschwitz. Die letzten Tage" das Foto 10 in reduzierter Form auf seinem Titelblatt ab und weckte damit Zweifel an seinem (ebd. S. 3) erhobenen Anspruch auf "historische Genauigkeit".

④ A. Bujak, 1973

Da nur eine kleine Auswahl dieser, noch dazu oft verstümmelt wiedergegebenen Aufnahmen breite und dauerhafte Publizität erlangt hat, wurden viele Menschen, von denen zum großen Teil wohl nur noch die Bildzeugnisse aus dem Album existieren, unbewußt und unvermerkt zum zweiten Mal "aussortiert" — nun aufgrund ihrer vermeintlich geringeren 'Medienwirksamkeit'. Das ganze Ausmaß der Realität des Massenmordes mag man den Nachgeborenen anscheinend nicht zumuten. Informationen, die ihnen erlauben würden, sich ein eigenes Urteil zu bilden, werden ihnen vorenthalten.[18] Man verändert die Bedeutung des einzelnen Bildes, indem man es aus dem Gesamtkontext des Albums, aus dem Zusammenhang mit vorangehenden und nachfolgenden Bildern herauslöst. Auch wird, worauf bereits Kulka hinwies, nicht mitgeteilt, was auf den Fotos nicht erscheint. Ebenso fehlen Erklärungen, warum die Deportierten von der SS gerade in dieser und nicht in einer anderen Form aufgenommen wurden. Die SS–Männer sahen sich selber gewiß nicht als "Täter". Noch weniger war es ihre Absicht, ihre Opfer als Individuen abzubilden, um einen Gleichklang zwischen Abgebildeten und mitfühlenden Betrachtern herzustellen. Das Album ist vielmehr als ein Selbstlob der SS für ihre Fähigkeit zu werten, ein funktionsfähiges Lager für Hunderttausende aufzubauen und den amorphen Massen von "Untermenschen" Ordnung aufzuzwingen. Sie sieht sich als Wächterin eines effizienten gesellschaftlichen Subsystems, in dem die Stellung und das Lebensrecht des Einzelnen von einer 'wissenschaft-

18. So könnte man am Beipiel des Fotos 122 aufzeigen, was es bedeutete, als Schwangere nach Auschwitz deportiert zu werden. Die Fotos 96 und 97 veranschaulichen die Praxis der Deutschen, orthodoxe Juden durch das öffentlich durchgeführte Abschneiden ihrer Bärte zu demütigen. Anhand der Fotos 93ff. ließe sich verdeutlichen, daß man sich bei der Deportation ungarischer Juden anfangs auf die in der Mehrzahl orthodoxen und chassidischen Gemeinden Transkarpathiens und Nordostungarns konzentrierte.

lichen' Überprüfung seiner biologischen Substanz und einer daraus abgeleiteten Beurteilung seiner "Einsatzfähigkeit", d.h. der wirtschaftlichen Rentabilität seines Überlebens abhängt. Um den zuletzt genannten Aspekt zu veranschaulichen, verläßt der Fotograf seine Überblicksposition und nähert sich einzelnen Menschen oder Gruppen. Er ordnet, sortiert und katalogisiert sie mittels Porträt–, Gruppen– und Nahaufnahmen. Dabei legt er die Grundlagen seines ideologischen Denkrasters offen, indem er "rassische" Merkmale und körperliche Behinderungen durch Krankheit, Alter oder Geburtsfehler stigmatisiert.

Offenbar gibt es menschlich nur allzu verständliche emotionale Hemmungen, diesen kalten, rechnerischen, unmenschlichen Blick der SS zum Ausgangspunkt einer aufklärenden Sachdiskussion über das Auschwitz–Album zu machen. Man behandelt die Fotos nicht als zu entschlüsselnde Bildzeugnisse, sondern als Ikonen, deren Anblick, wie eine antike Tragödie, Furcht und Mitleid erzeugt, die man aber nicht unbedingt zu verstehen braucht. Es geht um das persönliche Gefühlserlebnis, nicht um eine genauere Bestimmung des Verhältnisses zur Vergangenheit. Doch gerade bei diesem Album, dessen Fotos so oft reproduziert werden, sollte man sich Rechenschaft ablegen: Wer hat diese Aufnahmen für welche Zwecke gemacht, welche Prämissen und Zielsetzungen stehen hinter den mannigfachen Erscheinungsformen, in denen sie uns heute dargeboten werden?

⑤ Photo from the English magazine "Hello" from January 21. Lili Jacob at Yad Vashem holding the Auschwitz–Album / Zdjęcie z angielskiego czasopisma "Hello" z 21 stycznia 1995 r. Lili Jacob w muzeum Yad Vashem, w jej ręku Auschwitz–Album / Foto aus dem englishen Magazin "Hello" vom 21. Januar, 1995, auf dem Lili Jacob im Museum von Yad Vashem das Auschitz–Album in ihren Händen hält.
Gamma / FSP

From Document to Icon: On the Reception of the Auschwitz Album

In attempting to visualize the Holocaust, the Auschwitz Album is often referred to. The album is the sole surviving document that can enable the next generation to picture the selection of the Jews prior to their death in the gas chambers of Auschwitz–Birkenau. The range and variety of forms in which these photographs are presented by different media is determined by a number of different aims. Because these photos have been used so repeatedly the world over they have become impressed upon the memory of many people as the image of the Holocaust. However, very few people actually know the circumstances under which these photos were taken. To fully comprehend the individual photographs and the album as a whole one must also consider the historical context.

Od dokumentu do ikony: uwagi do recepcji Auschwitz-Album

Celem przedstawienia Holocaustu sięga się często do tzw. Auschwitz-Album. Ta, wykonana na zlecenie SS kolekcja zdjęć, stanowi bowiem jedyny dokument, który może unaocznić potomnym selekcję Żydów, skazanych na śmierć w komorach gazowych Auschwitz-Birkenau. Wybór i wielorakość form prezentowania tych zdjęć przez różne środki przekazu zależy od celów jakim ma służyć prezentacja. Część tych zdjęć, poprzez upowszechnienie ich na skalę światową, utrwaliła się w umysłach szerokiej rzeszy ludzi jako obrazowy dokument Holocaustu. Jednak mało kto zna warunki, w których zdjęcia te powstały. Uwzględnienie historycznego kontekstu pozwala na objaśnienie i zrozumienie okoliczności powstania albumu, jak i utrwalonych na poszczególnych zdjęciach zdarzeń.

Katharina Engeln

Vom Tempus–Projekt zur Ausstellung 'Representations of Auschwitz'

Ein Projekt der Kommission der Europäischen Union setzt sich für drei Jahre ein ehrgeiziges Ziel: 134 Lehrer, Wissenschaftler und Studenten aus Polen, Großbritannien und Deutschland befinden sich in diesem Zeitraum im Austausch, um sich mit den das 20. Jahrhundert prägenden ethnischen Konflikten und Völkermorden in Europa zu befassen.[1] Neben den Universitäten von Krakau, Oldenburg und Oxford ist auch das Staatliche Museum Auschwitz–Birkenau in Oświęcim Partner des Projektes. Der Grund ist evident: Auschwitz ist zum Symbol für industriell organisierten Massenmord und Genozid geworden.

1. s. J. Webber, in: Der intellektuelle Rahmen des Projektes 'Civil Society and Social Change in Europe after Auschwitz', Oxford o. J.

Die Teilnehmer des Projektes, die aus den verschiedensten Fächern kommen, erkunden und erforschen seit August 1992 Gelände, Sammlungen und Archivmaterialien des Museums und interessieren sich auch für dessen pädagogische Arbeit. Diese Recherchen bilden darüber hinaus den Ausgangspunkt für das Ausstellungsprojekt 'Representations of Auschwitz'. Immer wieder stellte sich dabei die Frage, welche Bedeutungsveränderung die Baulichkeiten des ehemaligen Konzentrations– und Vernichtungslagers seit dessen Befreiung im Januar 1945 erfahren haben. Denn das Tor des Stammlagers mit der Inschrift "Arbeit macht frei", die Rampe, die Gaskammern und die Krematorien in Birkenau haben sich wie manche anderen Relikte auf dem Gelände nach und nach zu Zeichen und Erinnerungsmalen gewandelt, die über ihre einstige primäre Funktion innerhalb des Lagersystems hinausweisen.[2] Es ist ein Prozeß, der an Zeichnungen, vor allem aber an hunderten von Fotografien ablesbar ist, die seit 1945 entstanden sind.

2. Dem Versuch, Geschichte an den real verbliebenen Überresten dingfest zu machen, sind Grenzen gesetzt, vgl. die Diskussionsvorlage zum Symposion 'Vergegenständlichte Erinnerung' (veranstaltet vom Kulturwissenschaftlichen Institut in Essen 1991), Kap. II: Historische Referenz. Vom Überrest zum Relikt.

Einige davon sind in Krakau, dem Veranstaltungsort der Ausstellung zu sehen, das von dem Ort des Verbrechens ca. 70 km entfernt liegt. Sie führen vor Augen, wie Symbole sich in den Köpfen festsetzen, und verdeutlichen darüber hinaus die wiederholte Vereinnahmung von Auschwitz für religöse, politische und nationale Ziele. Die Bandbreite der Zeichnungen und Fotografien umfaßt alle Zwischenstufen vom Pathetischen bis zum Dokumentarischen. Sie zeigt weiterhin auf, in welchem Maße in einer von visuellen Medien beherrschten Welt Bildern eine zentrale Rolle bei der Auseinandersetzung mit dem Thema Holocaust zugewiesen wird. Doch können Bilder tatsächlich derartiges leisten, wo doch alle historischen, philosophischen und theologischen Erklärungsmuster sich bisher als unzureichend erwiesen haben, den bürokratisch organisierten und industriell durchgeführten Völkermord zu erklären?

Von einer ganz eigenen Wahrnehmung des Holocaust zeugen in der Ausstellung die künstlerischen Arbeiten von Naomi Tereza Salmon (Abb. 1, 2). In ihren 'Tableaus' zeigt sie Überreste aus

① Naomi T. Salmon
Object from the Yad Vashem Museum / Przedmiot z muzeum Yad Vashem / Objekt aus dem Yad Vashem Museum
1993

den Magazinen von Auschwitz, Yad Vashem und Buchenwald, die sie in Anlehnung an die Kriminologie 'Asservatenkammern' nennt. Jedes 'Tableau' besteht aus mehreren Fotos mit jeweils einem einzigen Gegenstand. In jedem 'Tableau' sind von der Künstlerin als 'Porträts' bezeichnete Abbildungen in mehreren Reihen untereinander angeordnet. Zu sehen sind gewöhnliche Gegenstände aus dem Lageralltag der Inhaftierten wie auch der SS. Gebrauchs–, Alterungs– und Verfallsspuren sind deutlich zu erkennen. Zwischen diesen eher harmlos wirkenden Objekten sind Motive eingestreut, die für Terror und Tod im Lager stehen. So finden sich auf einem 'Tableau', das sich aus Beständen des Magazins von Yad Vashem zusammensetzt, zwischen einer selbstgeschnitzten Pfeife, einer Schreibmaschine, einer Tabakschachtel und einer Mütze menschliche Knochensplitter, eine Dose mit dem schlampig aufgeklebten Etikett 'Zyklon B' und Patronen. Was beim ersten Hinsehen kühl und sachlich, gar distanziert erscheint, wie etwa das Bild einer zerfransten Zahnbürste, fängt plötzlich an, sich im Bewußtsein des Betrachters auf bestürzende Weise zu verlebendigen. Es ist, als ob er durch die Nähe zu den scheinbar vertrauten Alltagsdingen unversehens in die Reichweite von Tod und Gewalt geraten wäre. Zugleich gewinnen die immer gleich ausgeleuchteten und konturenscharfen Relikte eine eigentümliche Würde und geben Zeugnis von den 'Zuständen'[3] eines lebendigen Körpers, der einmal einer bestimmten Person gehört hat.

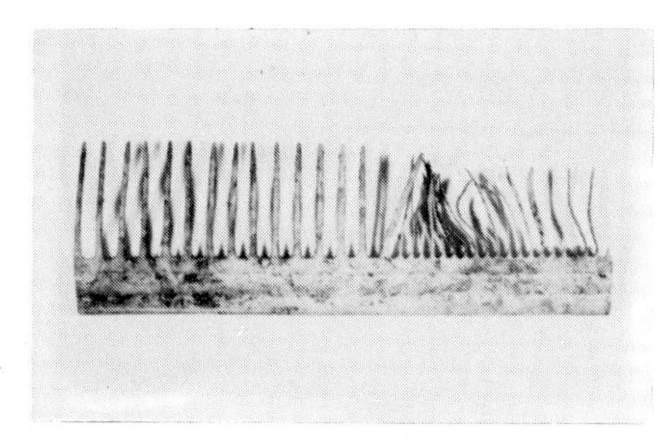

② Naomi T. Salmon
Object from the former Concentration Camp Buchenwald / Przedmiot z byłego KL Buchenwald / Objekt aus dem ehemaligen KL Buchenwald
1993

3. So N. T. Salmon 1994 in einem Text zu ihrer Ausstellung 'Asservate' in der Friedenskapelle Oldenburg.

Durch das künstlerische Arrangement gelingt es Naomi Tereza Salmon, Fragmente, an denen Erinnerung einen Halt findet, zu Impulsen einer durch die Persönlichkeit des jeweiligen Betrachters geprägten Reflexion zu machen. Ihre Fotos lösen Empfindungen und Assoziationen aus, die es ermöglichen, ein Stückchen von dem, was in Auschwitz geschah, auch jenseits von Sprache zu erahnen.[4]

4. Zum Problem der Verstehbarkeit des Völkermordes s. M. Brumlik: Trauerrituale und politische Kultur nach der Shoah in der Bundesrepublik, in: H. Loewy (Hrsg.): Holocaust: Die Grenzen des Verstehens. Eine Debatte über die Besetzung der Geschichte, Reinbek bei Hamburg, 1992, S. 204: "Wenn aber das Leiden und der Tod der Abermillionen in den Vernichtungslagern Ermordeten affektiv nicht darstellbar und daher in herkömmlichen Formen des Rituals nicht gestaltbar ist, wie — so ist endlich zu fragen — kann dann die Massenvernichtung im kollektiven Bewußtsein nicht nur der Deutschen, sondern der ganzen Menschheit bewußt gehalten werden?"

From the Tempus Project to the Exhibition 'Representations of Auschwitz'

Since summer 1992, participants in the Tempus project 'Civil Society and Social Change after Auschwitz' have been conducting fieldwork in the grounds of the museum, and carrying out research in its collections and archives. These research works constitute the starting–point of the exhibition 'Representations of Auschwitz'. The question of how the relics on the ground of the former concentration– and deathcamp have become symbols, and how these are represented in photographs, drawings and other artistic works are of special interest. As an example of an individual perception of the Holocaust, photographs by Naomi Tereza Salmon are to be seen in the exhibition, which show objects from Auschwitz, Yad Vashem and Buchenwald.

Od projektu Tempus do wystawy 'Representations of Auschwitz'

Tereny byłego obozu Auschwitz, archiwalia i muzealia Państwowego Muzeum Oświęcim–Brzezinka stały się od sierpnia 1992 roku przedmiotem badań uczestników projektu Tempus 'Civil Society and Social Change in Europe after Auschwitz'. Rezultaty dociekań tworzą punkt wyjścia dla projektu wystawy 'Representations of Auschwitz'. Realizacji wystawy towarzyszy pytanie, w jaki sposób relikty i tereny byłego obozu koncentracyjnego — obozu zagłady — mogły stać się symbolami i jak przedstawiane są w fotografiach, rysunkach i innych dokonaniach artystycznych. Przykładem subiektywnego postrzegania Holocaustu są prezentowane na wystawie fotografie Noami T. Salmon, przedstawiające przedmioty z magazynów KL Auschwitz, Yad Vashem i Buchenwaldu.

Bärbel Schmidt

Fotografische Erinnerungsbilder der Besucher von Auschwitz

Seit dem Ende des Zweiten Weltkrieges haben rund 21 Millionen Menschen das Staatliche Museum Auschwitz–Birkenau besucht. Auf ihrem Weg über das Gelände des ehemaligen Konzentrations– und Vernichtungslagers werden sie von bestimmten Vorstellungen und Erwartungen gelenkt, die auch die Wahl ihrer Fotomotive beeinflussen.

Wissenschaftler, die ihre Schreibtischarbeiten durch Studien vor Ort ergänzen und vertiefen wollen, haben bereits vor ihrem Besuch ihre Problemstellung definiert und damit die Kriterien für das von ihnen benötigte Bildmaterial festgelegt. Der Blick von *Künstlern,* die den Ort betreten, ist ebenfalls vorgeprägt, und zwar sowohl durch ihre eigenen als auch in durch fremde Kunstwerke. Im Gegensatz zu den Wissenschaftlern verfolgen sie jedoch nicht das Ziel, Erkenntnisse zu verifizieren, sondern nähern sich dem Phänomen Auschwitz mit ihren spezifischen visuellen Gestaltungsmitteln und –möglichkeiten. Ihre jeweilige Wahrnehmung der symbolträchtigen Einzelmotive — Tore, Zäune, Baracken, Gebäude — kann sich sowohl in malerisch–stimmungsvollen als auch nüchtern–distanzierten Bildern niederschlagen. So zeigen Fotobände, wie das Tor des Stammlagers sich dunkel von dem Abendhimmel abhebt, Blumen vor Stacheldrahtzäunen wachsen oder Bahnschwellen von Unkraut überwuchert werden; sie können aber auch das Gelände von Auschwitz–Birkenau wie einen aus der Funktion genommenen Industriebetrieb erscheinen lassen. Wie Wissenschaftler und Künstler fahren auch *Pädagogen* — Erzieher, Sozialpädagogen, Lehrer, Dozenten — mit bestimmten Zielvorstellungen nach Auschwitz und wählen dort Motive aus, die ihre Arbeit unterstützen sollen: Aus dieser Interessenlage heraus können dokumentarische Fotografien entstehen, die ihren Vortrag oder ihre Erzählungen begleiten können.

Die Beweggründe der größten Besuchergruppe, der *Touristen,* sind uns dagegen weitgehend unbekannt. Es sind Menschen verschiedener Generationen, Religionen, Nationalitäten. Für jeden einzelnen von ihnen hat der Holocaust eine andere Bedeutung; sie alle leben in unterschiedlicher emotionaler Nähe zu dieser historischen Katastrophe. Ehemals inhaftierte Juden und sonstige Lagerinsassen, die den

Holocaust überlebten, sowie Menschen, deren Familienangehörige in Auschwitz ermordet wurden, werden viel stärker von der Atmosphäre dieses Ortes berührt als jene, die weder durch eigene Erfahrung noch durch die Erzählungen von Verwandten und Freunden von dem Terror der Nazis erfahren haben. Menschen aus Ländern, die nicht unter der Besatzung durch die Deutschen leiden mußten, werden mit diesem Ort anders umgehen als Menschen damals okkupierter Gebiete. Wer aus Polen, der Ukraine, aus Weißrußland oder Rußland kommt, weiß um die von Deutschen in seinem Land begangenen Verbrechen. Das Verhältnis, das die Bürger ost- und westeuropäischer Staaten zu ihren jüdischen Mitbürgern vor oder nach dem Krieg hatten, bestimmt sicher ebenfalls ihre Sehweise. Weiterhin beeinflußt auch Biographisches die Motivwahl in Auschwitz: Beeindruckende Seh- und Leseerfahrungen, Erzählungen und sonstige Erlebnisse, die mit dem historischen Ereignis nichts zu tun haben, die aber an diesem Ort wieder an die Oberfläche des Bewußtseins treten. Über die familiäre und gesellschaftliche Sozialisation der Besucher hinaus spielen schließlich auch persönliche und spontane Gefühle eine wesentliche, manchmal vielleicht die ausschlaggebende Rolle.

Doch zu welchen fotografischen Resultaten die genannten gesellschaftlichen und privaten Bedingungen führen, ist bisher nicht geklärt. Dominieren einzelne Motive, wie etwa das Tor mit der Inschrift "Arbeit macht frei" oder die Reste der Gaskammern, in der Bildproduktion der Besucher? Gibt es unter den Fotos Aufnahmen — die Ruinen von Birkenau in der Abendsonne, umgeben von Wiesenblumen oder eingebettet in Schnee —, die sich mit normalen Urlaubsfotos vergleichen lassen? Vor welchen Relikten des ehemaligen Konzentrations- und Vernichtungslagers und in welchen Posen lassen sich die Besucher fotografieren? Und vor allem: Unterliegen die Amateuraufnahmen ebenso wie die professionellen Fotografien zeitbedingten Moden, Strömungen und Geschmacksrichtungen?

Nicht um diese Fragen zu beantworten, sondern um sie genauer zu stellen, wird in der Ausstellung eine Abteilung mit Fotos eingerichtet, die Touristen aus ihren in Auschwitz-Birkenau gemachten Aufnahmen selbst ausgewählt haben. Sie sollten sich entscheiden, welche Aufnahmen ihnen am wichtigsten sind. Vielen wird diese Hierarchisierung ihrer Bilder, die auch eine Hierarchisierung ihrer Eindrücke in Auschwitz bedeutet, nicht leicht gefallen sein. In dem Ergebnis ihrer Bemühungen werden Betrachtungsweisen und Wertungen sichtbar, die in einer Ausstellung mit dem Titel 'Representations of Auschwitz' nicht fehlen sollten.

The Personal Photographic Records of Visitors to Auschwitz

Since the end of World War Two more than 21 million people have visited the former concentration and death camp Auschwitz–Birkenau. Many have documented their visit with the camera. A range of these privately taken photos will be shown in the exhibition 'Representations of Auschwitz'. The aim is to show a survey of the many perspectives and the varying emotional distance that different generations, religions and nations bring to the subject of the Holocaust. These perspectives will have influenced the visitor, through the lense of the camera, to make a particular choice of motif and mode of reproduction for their pictures.

Wspomnienia odwiedzających Auschwitz w fotografii

Od zakończenia drugiej wojny światowej ok. 21 milionów osób odwiedziło były obóz koncentracyjny — obóz zagłady Auschwitz–Birkenau. Wielu z nich uwieczniło swoje odwiedziny na fotografiach. Wybór tych prywatnych zdjęć można zobaczyć na wystawie 'Representations of Auschwitz', która oddawać ma różnorodność aspektów i postrzegania tego miejsca, w zależności od przynależności pokoleniowej, religijnej, i narodowościowej, jak i uczuciowej bliskości tematu Holocaustu. Własne i przekazane doświadczenia kierowały spojrzeniem turysty patrzącego przez kamerę, określając wybór motywów i formę reprodukcji.

Jolanta Kupiec

Zdobione listy więźniów KL Auschwitz–Birkenau ze zbiorów Państwowego Muzeum w Oświęcimiu

Prawo do korespondencji było jednym z niewielu przywilejów więźniów obozu oświęcimskiego. Przywilej ten można było bardzo szybko stracić, jeśli więzień naraził się ważniejszemu kapo lub któremuś z SS–manów. Oddział polityczny zawiadamiał Poststelle bezpośrednio lub pośrednio poprzez biuro Lagerführera o tym, który więzień czasowo (karnie) został pozbawiony prawa pisania i otrzymywania listów i którzy więźniowie mieli raz na zawsze zakaz kontaktowania się ze swymi rodzinami. Żydzi w zasadzie w ogóle listów nie pisali i nie mieli prawa otrzymywania przesyłek. Wyjątek stanowiła tzw. "Briefaktion" — jednorazowa akcja pisania listów zorganizowana w 1943 r. w obozie rodzinnym dla Żydów z Theresienstadt.

Jeden z więźniów, Rafał Kocik wspomina: "Były pewne kategorie więźniów, którym nie zezwalano na korespondencję z rodziną. Do takich należeli np. więźniowie noszący oznaczenie IL (Im Lager) oraz więźniowie z karnej kompanii."

"Listy w lagrze pisało się co cztery albo pięć tygodni, w zależności jak odliczano bloki do pisania listów. Po przybyciu do lagru pisało się dopiero po miesiącu. Z kwarantanny listów nie pisano" — wspomina w 1981 r. więźniarka Brzezinki i Oświęcimia, Maria Ślisz–Oyrzyńska.

Listy pisano tylko po niemiecku, kopiowym ołówkiem, na specjalnych drukach. Wysyłany list musiał być opatrzony imieniem i nazwiskiem nadawcy — więźnia, jego datą urodzenia, numerem obozowym i numerem bloku, w którym aktualnie przebywał. Formularze więźniowie najczęściej musieli "organizować" sobie sami. Maria Ślisz–Oyrzyńska pisze w swojej relacji: "... blankietów listowych — urzędowych nie rozdawano nam. Każda we własnym zakresie musiała sobie nie tylko taki blankiet zorganizować, ale i znaczek pocztowy za 12 pfenigów". Wspomina dalej, jak z jedną z współwięźniarek całe popołudnie i wieczór starały się zdobyć potrzebny blankiet, znaczek, ołówek, aby napisać pierwszy list i dać znak życia rodzinie. "(...) nasza Nachtwacha rewirowa (...) twardo za blankiet żądała całą porcję lagrowego chleba, zaś za znaczek z Führerem porcję margaryny.

Z wielkim żalem, rozpaczając, musiałyśmy każda oddać swój chleb i porcję margaryny."

W ten lub podobny sposób więzień mógł przesłać do rodziny minimalne informacje. Jednak, według wspomnień M. Ślisz–Oyrzyńskiej, "... nie wolno było pisać o tym, że jest źle, że jesteśmy głodne, brudne, że ciężko pracujemy, że chorujemy, że nas biją, że nas okradają, jednym słowem nie wolno było pisać PRAWDY! bo list nie przeszedł przez cenzurę, a nawet przez napisanie takiego listu można było zostać ukaranym przez zakaz pisania listów."

Więźniowie czy więźniarki starali się przesyłać, oprócz tych oficjalnych, listy nielegalne, bardziej osobiste. Wspomina po wojnie więźniarka Brzezinki, Anna Tytoniak: "Mnie też udało się wysłać list z pominięciem cenzury pocztowej. Czasem przy takiej nielegalnej wysyłce listów korzystałyśmy z pomocy kolegów, inne przesyłały przez "cywili", a zdarzało się nawet, choć rzadko, że wysłania listu podejmował się któryś ze "znośniejszych" SS–manów."

Więźniowi Ernestowi Kowalskiemu koledzy wcześniej osadzeni w obozie pomogli zdobyć formularze listów obozowych: "... Franciszek Targosz (...) niejednokrotnie przejmował ode mnie listy pisane do rodziny na formularzach obozowych i przekazywał je do ocenzurowania poza ustaloną kolejnością i częściej niż to mógł wysłać inny więzień. Targosz zjednał sobie przychylność SS–manów cenzorów m.in. przez to, że dawał im drobne prezenty w formie ręcznie malowanych obrazków, kartek pocztowych itp."

Więzień Franciszek Targosz odegrał dużą i specyficzną rolę w organizowaniu i patronowaniu obozowej twórczości plastycznej więźniów. Legalnie, lub nielegalnie ściągał do tzw. Lagermuseum uzdolnionych plastycznie kolegów, aby mogli tworzyć na potrzeby władz obozowych obrazy, portrety rodzin SS–manów, rzeźby i inne ozdobne przedmioty. Pomagał też w przesyłaniu poza obóz nadprogramowych, a zwłaszcza zdobionych listów więźniarskich. Pojawiły się i takie w pewnym czasie w obozie, "...ozdobne listy, na których malowano piękne widoczki, odbijano drzeworyty czy miedzioryty, które wychodziły poza obóz legalnie 'za przymrużeniem oka' cenzora."

"Czasem darowany obrazek czy malowana kartka świąteczna wręczona cenzorowi w odpowiedniej chwili, przełamywała jego ostatnie opory" — pisze sam F. Targosz w relacji z 1974 r. Pracując początkowo w różnych komandach obozowych, od czerwca 1941 r. Targosz zaczął pracę w głównej izbie pisarskiej więźniów, gdzie załatwiał również sprawę obiegu korespondencji, notując w kartotece wpływ listów do więźniów i ich wysyłkę do rodzin. Listy wpływające i wszelkie przesyłki kontrolowała Poststelle, skąd Targosz je zabierał, rejestrował i rozprowadzał do bloków. Poznał przy tej pracy cały tok postępowania z listami oraz wielu cenzorów. Wśród cenzorów niektórzy byli względnie dostępni, wysyłali listy bez skreśleń czy wycinań. Inni bywali "gorliwi", listy przez nich "...były pokrojone, pokreślone, wycinali z nich wiele zdań, a często cały list był niedoręczony" — wspomina Targosz.

Pracujący w Schreibstube przed Targoszem więzień Leon Mateja wspomina: "Praca w Schreibstube stwarzała warunki lepszego usytuowania się w społeczności więźniarskiej i niesienia pomocy innym. Posiadane możliwości wykorzystywałem udzielając jej artystom plastykom. (...) W czasie rozmów z nimi narodził się pomysł zdobienia formularzy listów obozowych. Z prośbą tą udałem się do Lagerführera Fritzscha. Fritzsch wyraził na to zgodę, oczywiście zastrzegając, że na tych rysunkach nie mogą znajdować się żadne elementy, które charakteryzowały życie obozowe". Mieczysław Kościelniak pisze w swojej relacji, iż "(...) nie bezinteresownie cenzorzy SS zgadzali się na wysyłanie listów ozdobnych, które nie stały w kolizji z jakimiś wymaganiami cenzorów, a na zewnątrz mogły być uznawane za dowód, że więźniom wiedzie się dobrze. Tematem ozdobnika na liście nie mógł być rysunek mówiący cokolwiek o obozie". Toteż w zbiorach Państwowego Muzeum w Oświęcimiu, obejmujących również poobozowe pamiątki artystyczne wykonywane przez więźniów, znajduje się osobliwa kolekcja ok. 200 oryginalnych listów, zdobionych barwnymi malowidłami, ale brak wśród nich zupełnie jakiejkolwiek scenki obozowej. Ten unikalny zbiór zawiera ocalałe listy ponad 20 więźniów, zdobione przez niektórych osobiście lub przez kolegów obozowych. Ozdobniki najczęściej znajdują się na pierwszej stronie formularza, innym razem umieszczone są w górnym rogu drugiej strony i mają formę prostokąta, owalu lub luźnego rysunku. Wykonane są wieloma technikami rysunkowymi i malarskimi: akwarelą, temperą, kredkami, tuszem — a także graficznymi, w formie drzeworytów czy miedziorytów. W swojej miniaturyzacji stanowią swoiste dzieła sztuki, nie tylko pod względem artystycznym. Ich wartość wzbogaca miejsce wykonania, miejsce urągające człowieczeństwu, urągające sztuce, która kieruje się pięknem i służy odczuciom estetyki. Swoją treścią wyrażają największe tęsknoty ludzi sterroryzowanych, ludzi odciętych brutalnie od należnych im praw. Wielobarwne ozdobniki to zminiaturyzowane przepiękne pejzaże w różnych porach roku, to kwiaty pojedyncze, w pękach czy bukietach, to sceny z dziecięcych bajek, dedykacje imieninowe, urodzinowe czy noworoczne, sceny Świąt Wielkanocnych i Bożego Narodzenia. Są też ozdobne inicjały, piękne konie F. Targosza i niezwykle liryczne sceny symboliczne, wyrażające tęsknotę za rodziną, żoną, dziećmi, narzeczoną. Wykonywali je najczęściej tacy więźniowie artyści jak: Mieczysław Kościelniak, Bronisław Czech, Franciszek Targosz, Czesław Lenczowski, Adam Bowbelski, Jan Komski, Czesław Kaczmarczyk i inni, znani lub nieznani. Zdobili listy wieczorami, po pracy lub w wolne niedziele.

Największą ilość zachowanych listów, ponad 80, zdobił Mieczysław Kościelniak, jak również zachowało się najwięcej pejzażowych ozdobników jego autorstwa. Wśród tych widoków i miniaturowych krajobrazów są wszystkie pory roku. Z wielu drobiazgowo odtworzonych górskich krajobrazów widać, iż Kościelniak przed wojną bywał często w polskich górach i chętnie przywoływał z pamięci konkretne widoki: Morskie Oko, Dolinę Strążyską, Czarny Staw, krokusy na hali czy góry w zimowej szacie. Te precyzyjnie odtworzone, maleńkie arcydzieła doskonale oddają atmosferę górskich lasów i majestatyczną powagę polskich Tatr, jak też mieniący się barwami śnieżny krajobraz w zimowym oświetleniu, czy rozbłyskujący wesołymi barwami letni pejzaż.

Konzentrationslager Auschwitz

Meine Anschrift:

Name:

geboren am:

Gef.-Nr.

Der Lagerkommandant

① Bronisław Czech
Illustrated letter / Ozdobnik na liście / Briefillustration
1942

Podobne bogactwo artystyczne i malarskie cechuje pejzażowe ozdobniki autorstwa Bronisława Czecha z Zakopanego, uzdolnionego plastycznie górala, świetnego narciarza. Ukochał ponad wszystko polskie Tatry, a tęsknota za nimi, za wiatrem, wolnością, górskimi zboczami, doprowadziła w obozowym zamknięciu i poniżeniu do przedwczesnej śmierci, mimo niezwykle ofiarnej pomocy kolegów obozowej niedoli. Barwy śniegu u Czecha są jeszcze bardziej intensywne i mocniej naświetlone, gdy maluje ciężkie śnieżne czapy przyginające zasypaną choinkę. Urzekają ozdobniki z owieczkami spokojnie pasącymi się nad górskim stawem (zdj. 1). Jest też majestatyczna limba, dostojnie górująca nad krajobrazem. Charakterystyczną cechą ozdobników B. Czecha jest sygnowanie ich u dołu maleńkim czerwonym trójkątem z literą "P" w środku, jego numerem obozowym "349" oraz imieniem "Bronek". Czasami sygnował miniaturowe obrazki na listach samym trójkątem i numerem.

Z krajobrazami łączą się też w wielu przypadkach ozdobniki pejzażowe o treściach symbolicznych, zawierające duże ładunki emocjonalne i ekspresyjne. I tutaj w ilości wykonanych ozdobników dominuje M. Kościelniak. Na ozdobniku listu Ernesta Kowalskiego przedstawił scenkę "Spotkanie" — nieoczekiwanie wraca do domu mąż, brat, ojciec (?), który z dala macha na powitanie ręką do biegnącej kobiety (zdj. 2).

Konzentrationslager Auschwitz

Folgende Anordnungen sind beim Schriftverkehr mit Gefangenen zu beachten:

1.) Jeder Schutzhaftgefangene darf im Monat zwei Briefe oder zwei Karten von seinen Angehörigen empfangen und an sie absenden. Die Briefe an die Gefangenen müssen gut lesbar mit Tinte geschrieben sein und dürfen nur 15 Zeilen auf einer Seite enthalten. Gestattet ist nur ein Briefbogen normaler Größe. Briefumschläge müssen ungefüttert sein. In einem Briefe dürfen nur 5 Briefmarken à 12 Pfg. beigelegt werden. Alles andere ist verboten und unterliegt der Beschlagnahme. Postkarten haben 10 Zeilen. Lichtbilder dürfen als Postkarten nicht verwendet werden.

2.) Geldsendungen sind gestattet.

3.) Es ist darauf zu achten, daß bei Geld- oder Postsendungen die genaue Adresse, bestehend aus: Name, Geburtsdatum, und Gefangenen-Nummer, auf die Sendungen zu schreiben ist. Ist die Adresse fehlerhaft, geht die Post an den Absender zurück oder wird vernichtet.

4.) Zeitungen sind gestattet, dürfen aber nur durch die Poststelle des K. L. Auschwitz bestellt werden.

5.) Pakete dürfen nicht geschickt werden, da die Gefangenen im Lager alles kaufen können.

6.) Entlassungsgesuche aus der Schutzhaft an die Lagerleitung sind zwecklos.

7.) Sprecherlaubnis und Besuche von Gefangenen im Konzentrations-Lager sind grundsätzlich nicht gestattet.

Der Lagerkommandant

Absender:

Meine Anschrift:

Name:

geboren am:

Gef.-Nr.

② Mieczysław Kościelniak
Illustrated letter / Ozdobnik na liście / Briefillustration
1943

Podobną wymowę posiada ozdobnik na liście Leona Mateji "Wizja powrotu do domu". Przy oknie siedzi młoda kobieta z maleńkim dzieckiem na kolanach. Za oknem w dali widać idącego w stronę domu mężczyznę. Sceny te symbolizują głęboką nadzieję, niewymowną tęsknotę, wiarę w powrót do wolności i radosne spotkanie z najbliższymi. Podobne odczucia wzbudzają scenki "Macierzyństwo" czy "Matka i dziecko" — precyzyjny, miniaturowy miedzioryt.

Wzruszającą dedykację dla żony z okazji Dnia Matki posiada drzeworyt Kościelniaka na liście F. Targosza: "Meiner Louise zum Muttertag 1943".

I znowu widok górskiego łańcucha, nad którym szybuje majestatycznie orzeł, władca przestworzy — symbol absolutnej wolności. Inny krajobraz, nizinny, w zimowej szacie: gdzieś na wolności, jakby w bajkowej śnieżnej przestrzeni, pędzi z nieznanej dali pociąg. Z kolei letni pejzaż z doskonale znaną postacią Don Kichota jadącego na koniu, symbolem niezłomnego wojownika, walczącego wytrwale, co prawda z wiatrakami, ale w obronie słusznej i szlachetnej sprawy. Wielu było w czasie wojny i wśród więźniów takich właśnie Don Kichotów, walczących czasem beznadziejnie, ale wytrwale, z hitlerowskimi potworami. Trudno natomiast uściślić symbolikę ozdobnika "Zawieja", gdzie w zimowym krajobrazie, wokół omrożonego drzewa wiruje w zamieci ogromny śnieżny starzec. Może być symbolem złego czasu, mrożącego świat lodową zawieją, ale może też oznaczać nadzieję, że po każdej, nawet najsroższej zimie, nadchodzi ciepła wiosna.

Z nadzieją na powrót do ukochanej rodziny wiążą się ozdobniki M. Kościelniaka na listach B. Pendzińskiego z 1943 r. Na czterech rysunkach tuszem widnieją pojedyncze portrety: żony Anny, córki Marylki i synka Eugeniusza. Piąty ozdobnik przedstawia żonę z dwójką dzieci na tle świątecznie ubranej choinki (zdj. 3). Wszystkie te portretowe ujęcia artysta wykonał z przemyconych przez Pendzińskiego zdjęć od rodziny. F. Targosz wspomina w relacji z 1959 r. o przysyłanych więźniom fotografiach: "Jeżeli w liście do więźnia znajdowała się fotografia, których w zasadzie nie wolno było posyłać, to w latach 1943 i 44 więzień fotografię wraz z listem otrzymywał, lecz fotografia miała być następnego dnia zwrócona do Poststelle, a stąd przekazana do depozytu rzeczy prywatnych więźnia. Zdarzało się, że więzień oddawał inną fotografię, a foto rodziny, jako drogocenny skarb, zachowywał."

Głęboką tęsknotą tchną też rodzajowe ozdobniki, jak np. "Wigilijny wieczór" — nastrojowa akwarelka z piękną świąteczną choinką, nakrytym do uroczystej kolacji stołem i konikiem na biegunach, zabawką — upominkiem dla ukochanego dziecka.

"Samotny żagiel" wyraża tęsknotę więźnia Antoniego Suchanka za ukochanym morzem. Sceny związane z życiem górali przywołuje na swoich miniaturach wspomniany już B. Czech. Więzień Czesław Lenczowski ze Starego Sącza ozdabiał często listy kwiatami a zwłaszcza scenami z bajek. Są tam wesołe krasnale, Jaś i Małgosia, Śpiąca Królewna z pięknym królewiczem itp.

Władysław Nowakowski malował na listach sceny z bajki Czerwony Kapturek, które więzień B. Pendziński adresował do dzieci: "An Genius Pendziński" lub "Meine Allerliebste Aniu, Genius u. Marylka".

Pełne uroku są ozdobniki ze świątecznymi scenkami, wykonywanymi na Boże Narodzenie, Wielkanoc lub z okazji imienin czy urodzin kogoś w rodzinie: w wieńcu z kwiatów widać dwie dłonie w uścisku — przy męskiej ręce widać

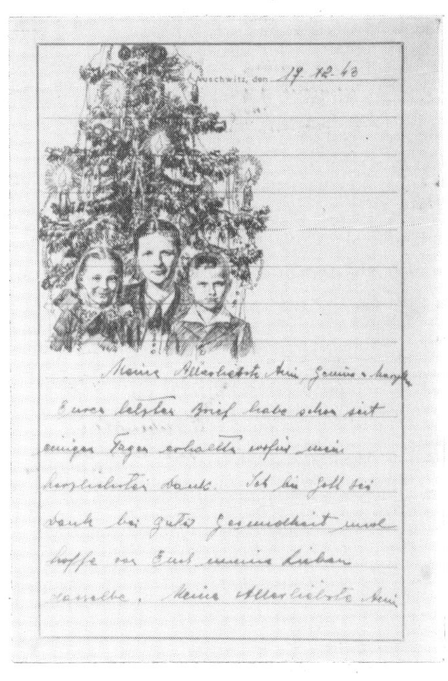

...uschwitz, den [illegible] 12. 43

Meine Allerliebste Aniu, Genius u. Maryl[illegible]

Euer letzter Brief habe schon seit einigen Tagen erhalten wofür mein herzlichsten Dank. Ich bin Gott sei dank bei guter Gesundheit und hoffe von Euch meine lieben [illegible]. Meine Allerliebste Aniu

③ Mieczysław Kościelniak
Illustrated letter / Ozdobnik na liście / Briefillustration
1943

fragment pasiastego rękawa. Nad wieńcem radośnie skacze dziewczynka, a pod spodem wypisana jest ozdobna dedykacja "Jeny Ich gratuliere zum Geburtstag"

Mieczysław Wiatr wysłał do domu list, malując na nim Mikołaja z workiem prezentów na tle domu, z bałwankiem śniegowym obok. Kazimierz Obal przesłał rodzinie listem z dn. 9.IV.1944 r. malowane pisanki, bazie i przebiśniegi. Lenczowski znowu namalował bajkowe krasnale, wesoło wychodzące z pisanek. Natomiast nieznany Węgier namalował więźniowi Franciszkowi Krzysteczko na liście do rodziny z dn. 25.XII.1944 r. dwie złączone dłonie w wieńcu wawrzynu i datę "1945". Jest tu też symbolika — wawrzyn to gałązki zwycięstwa, a data sugeruje czas zbliżającej się wolności i powitania z ukochaną osobą. Bardzo częstym motywem zdobniczym obozowych listów były kwiaty. Barwne, urocze bukiety polnych kwiatów z polskich łąk, niezapominajki, konwalie, bzy. Mogą być wyrazem miłości, pamięci, szacunku, są też wyrazem ukochania życia. Urzekają realizmem oddania barw i kształtów róże M. Kościelniaka, którymi zdobił listy kolegów, a także różnorodne, piękne kwiaty B. Czecha. Niezwykle uzdolniony plastycznie zakopiańczyk prócz umiłowania sportu narciarskiego, pięknie rzeźbił w drewnie, rysował, a także malował akwarelą i farbami olejnymi nie tylko na papierze i płótnie, ale też na szkle. Jego kwiaty mają właśnie cechy malarstwa na szkle. Chryzantemy, róże, bzy, rumianki malowane obrysowanymi konturem plamami barwnymi mogą być gotowym wzorem do przeniesienia na szkło.

Wszystkie przytoczone przykłady ozdabiania listów obozowych były reakcją psychiki na koszmar obozu, były próbą ratowania resztek piękna świata, którego brutalnie więźniów pozbawiono. Malowane obrazki wyrażały tęsknotę za utraconymi widokami, były ucieczką w zapamiętane z wolności miejsca. Były uzupełnieniem treści listów, w których niewiele można było napisać, były uzupełnieniem tego wszystkiego, czego słowa nie były w stanie wyrazić. Umęczona pamięć więźniów przywoływała z wolności polskie Tatry, piękno polskiego krajobrazu, barwne kwiaty z łąk i ogródków, aby w pewnym stopniu stały się maleńką namiastką wolnego świata, metafizycznym sposobem kontaktu z najbliższymi.

Listy przekazywane były po wojnie do zbiorów Muzeum w Oświęcimiu przede wszystkim przez ocalałych więźniów lub przez ich rodziny. Uważali oni, że jest to jedyne miejsce nierozerwalnie związane z tymi specyficznymi dziełami. Nie wszyscy jednak byli w stanie rozstać się ze swymi niezwykłymi pamiątkami. Mieczysław Kościelniak wspomina po wojnie: "Moje listy obozowe z wykonanymi przeze mnie ozdobnikami są dla mej żony i dzieci bezcennym skarbem". Przekazał jednak wraz z rodziną duży zbiór zdobionych listów do Muzeum, podobnie jak Leon Mateja, Bronisław Pendziński, Franciszek Targosz i wielu innych.

Motifs on Letters from Prisoners of Auschwitz–Birkenau Concentration Camp taken from the Collection at the Auschwitz State Museum

Officially prisoners of the camp were allowed to write a letter once a month to their families containing only a meagre amount of information. However, some managed to evade the censors and smuggled additional letters out of the camp decorated with pictures. They were made by artistically talented prisoners. Sketches were done with pencils and Indian ink, and paintings in watercolours and tempera paints. They painted landscapes, flowers, domestic scenes and fantasies. In these illustrations — one can even find some such examples on letters that were permitted by camp officials — the prisoners' longings to see their families and close friends are reflected. In this way prisoners created a means of mentally escaping from the camp to a place of freedom in their minds. These miniature works of art by the camp prisoners form a distinctive and separate group.

Bildmotive in Briefen von Gefangenen des KL Auschwitz–Birkenau aus den Sammlungen des Staatlichen Museums Auschwitz

Offiziell durften die Gefangenen des Konzentrationslagers Auschwitz–Birkenau durchschnittlich einmal im Monat einen Brief an ihre Familie schreiben, der nur spärliche Informationen enthalten durfte. Einige von ihnen umgingen die Zensur und schmuggelten zusätzliche Sendungen aus dem Lager heraus, die mit Bildern verziert waren. Sie wurden von inhaftierten Künstlern und von künstlerisch begabten Gefangenen angefertigt. Sie zeichneten mit Tusche und Buntstiften, malten mit Wasserfarbe und Tempera Landschaften, Blumen, Genre– und Märchenbilder. In diesen Illustrationen — sie finden sich auch auf den von der Lagerleitung genehmigten Briefen — spiegelt sich die Sehnsucht der Gefangenen nach ihrer Familie und ihnen nahestehenden Personen. Auf diese Weise schufen sich die Gefangenen einen mentalen Fluchtweg zu den im Gedächtnis verbliebenen Orten der Freiheit. In der Kunst der Lagerhäftlinge bilden diese Miniaturwerke eine Gruppe von ausgeprägter Eigenart.

Jeffrey D. Feldman

An Etymology of Opinion: Yad Vashem, Authority, and the Shifting Aesthetic of Holocaust Museums

> In the case of the social world, speaking with authority is as good as doing
> (Bourdieu 1994:53)

In August 1993, during a seminar in Cracow, an American woman in her early sixties offered what I perceived at the time to be a new and puzzling representation of Auschwitz. Her comment was made in the context of a conversation about a small, Holocaust memorial museum at a Jewish community centre near my home in the United States.[1] With an air of frustration and amazement she commented, "I felt more there [at the museum in the United States] than I did in Auschwitz." Six months later in Israel I overheard an American teenager complain as she left the Historical Museum at Yad Vashem, The Holocaust Martyrs' and Heroes' Remembrance Authority in West Jerusalem, "In [the United States Holocaust Memorial Museum in] Washington they have four floors of authentic objects. Here: *nothing* ".

Voiced distinctions between the quality of Holocaust museums — whether in reference to the emotional efficacy of the museum and memorial at Auschwitz–Birkenau or the artefact holdings of the historical exhibition at Yad Vashem — are powerful expressions of authority masked in the familiar concepts of taste. For most people, the physical place of Auschwitz–Birkenau lies beyond the lived space in which they have encountered representations of the Holocaust. Yet, there are ever–expanding avenues in which these images, narratives, and objects travel. Auschwitz in this reading, is a polysemic metonym or sign that signifies not only a Nazi death camp, but also the social world of individuals, museums, memorials, libraries, universities, and even governments, all of which produce, regulate, and circulate representations. The word *'Auschwitz'* itself thus embodies a linguistic conflict that ultimately engenders an epistemological confusion between place and representation of place.[2] The same is true of Holocaust museums, such as Yad Vashem: individuals come to associate one word or name with the infinite past experiences described in the place.

1. I wish to thank the people responsible for the Tempus Project. For a critique of this Museum in West Bloomfield, Michigan, see Mais (1988).

2. Dean MacCannell (1976:111) notes that all tourist encounters are confrontations between site and sign.

Judgements about Holocaust museums constitute the domination of one aesthetic over another. Even in situ, we do not see Auschwitz with a pure, undifferentiated gaze, but rather through the cognitive frames engendered by museum visits, historical discourse, and communal practice, all of which constitute a lived social world (Bourdieu 1979:4–5). Furthermore, a visit to a Holocaust memorial such as Yad Vashem is not a simple commemorative ritual, but rather a journey through the variegated landscape of historical and cultural dispositions that necessarily results in a new perspective on the whole.[3]

3. Although I think it is overstated to suggest that this condition is new, Arjun Appadurai (1990:4) suggests that the past is now not a land to return to in a simple politics of memory. It has become a synchronic warehouse of cultural scenarios, a kind of temporal central casting, to which recourse can be had as appropriate, depending on the movie to be made, the scene to be enacted, the hostages to be rescued.

Since the opening of the United States Holocaust Memorial Museum in Washington, DC., both the Auschwitz Museum and Yad Vashem have struggled to keep pace with the technological and epistemological innovations of the American museum. Things from Auschwitz–Birkenau and other extermination camps have always played central roles in exhibitions directed towards the commemoration of Jews murdered under Nazi rule. In recent years, however, a renewed interest in 'authentic artefacts' has found wide audience through the proliferation of post–modern museology as a contemporary idiom for Holocaust commemoration and education. This emergent emphasis on artefacts has catalysed a crisis of authority at Yad Vashem, which had cultivated previously an archival–documentation model of historical evidence.

1. Yad Vashem: Mountain of Memory, Grammar of Commemoration

Almost a decade after the liberation of Auschwitz, in 1953, the Israeli government passed the Martyrs and Heroes Remembrance Law (or 'Yad Vashem Law'[4]) and initiated the process whereby it sought to establish in the Jewish state the authoritative centre for Holocaust commemoration. Ben–Zion Dinur, a prominent Jewish historian and the education minister in 1953, was charged with translating the text of the new law into practice.

4. The name, "Yad Vashem", meaning literally "a hand and a name" is taken from Isa. 66:5. For a detailed history of the social politics leading to the passing of this law see Segev (1993); for the full text of the Law in English, see Dafni (1990:4–6).

Dinur's interpretation was consistent with the paradigms of a Zionist historian, wherein the central function of Yad Vashem would be "to gather into the homeland all commemoratory material regarding members of the Jewish people who fell, fought and rebelled against the Nazi enemy and German satellites, to establish a memorial for them and for the communities, organisations and institutions, which were destroyed because they belonged to the Jewish people" (Dinur 1957:8). The collection and possession of material was to be the founding act on which three subsequent categories of action would be predicated, namely: research, publication, and "inculcation of the lesson to be learned from this testimony." The subsections of Yad Vashem's collection were thus conceived in five categories, describing the range of possible information to be gathered: documentary material, testimony, memoirs, literary material, and museum material (Dinur 1957:10). Dinur was appointed founding chairman of Yad Vashem, and thus his research taxonomy came to provide the scientific basis for all historiography based on the collection of over fifty million documents stored at the Jewish national 'Mountain of Memory'.[5] Within this context, the massive archive at Yad Vashem grew to symbolize the authority of accurate research in the emergent world of Holocaust commemoration.

5. Yad Vashem is located in the hills of West Jerusalem in a complex known as Har Hazikaron, literally, 'Mount Memory', which also contains the national military cemetery.

Since 1957, Yad Vashem has become a reified landscape of Dinur's Yad Vashem research model. A monumental 'campus'[6] of museums, libraries, sculptures, memorials, gardens, and tourist facilities, Yad Vashem has hosted millions of Israelis and foreigners, thereby fulfilling its mission to inculcate the lessons of the Holocaust.[7] Three structures contain the massive archives of documents, testimonies, and artefacts through which Yad Vashem became known as the centre of Holocaust research. The photographs and documents selected from these archives for publication have institutionalised a visual and linguistic grammar of Holocaust imagery. Thus, the historical research model constructed at Yad Vashem has been responsible for organizing how one reads and creates knowledge of the Holocaust.

6. Yad Vashem employees refer to the site as a campus, an allusion to university life which draws attention to Yad Vashem as a research centre rather than a memorial.

7. For a discussion of the role of Yad Vashem as a holy site in Israeli civil Judaism, see Liebman and Don-Yehiya (1983).

2. A Portable Aesthetic

All visitors to Yad Vashem walk through the historical museum, where they are not only taught a Zionist chronology of the Nazi genocide against Europe's Jews, but are also taught how to see representations of the Holocaust.[8] The historical exhibition, which begins with an account of Hitler's rise to power in 1933 and ends with the trial of Adolf Eichmann in Jerusalem in 1961 contains large photographs accompanied by panels of text that explain the imagery, together with several cases containing objects such as bricks, badges, weapons, and human remains. The exhibition space is windowless; this, coupled with the dark floor and grey walls, shuttles the visitor from the bright Jerusalem daylight into the dark night of Jewish history.

8. The following observations are based on observations and interviews collected during ten months of continuous fieldwork at Yad Vashem in the period 1993/94.

Within the Historical Museum at Yad Vashem, the moral authority of the history presented is not determined solely by the size and content of the imagery, the details of the text, or the atmosphere of the space. Rather, authority is a product of the total structural relations between image, text, and object, which in turn have meaning relative to the landscape that both contains and is constituted by the museum. But although rooted physically in the specific context of Jerusalem, the Holocaust museum aesthetic created at Yad Vashem is highly mobile in that it is easily reproduced.

The exhibition on Jewish martyrdom (Block 27) in the contemporary museum at Auschwitz I, for example, re–enacts the dark–light, up–down dichotomy found at Yad Vashem. Visitors enter the exhibit at ground level, but from the upper level they descend a dark staircase to view an exhibition which documents gas chambers as well as Jewish resistance to the Holocaust. When they emerge from the Block they encounter a large piece of Jerusalem limestone, emblematic of Yad Vashem and the geography of Jerusalem. Similarly, visitors to the Holocaust Memorial Museum in West Bloomfield, Michigan, must descend a dark corridor to reach the start of the exhibition. Upon leaving the museum, they emerge in front of the towering structure of the largest community centre in the United States. In both cases, the museum experience is consistent with the norms established at Yad Vashem.

3. Washington: Objects, People, and a New Industry Standard

Although relics from Nazi Europe were included in the original definition of materials to be gathered by Yad Vashem, their importance was always considered secondary to that of the document archive. Today, however, the curators and administrative staff at Yad Vashem are particularly concerned to restructure the museum exhibition so as to give authentic artefacts a more prominent position. The new concern for objects is the direct impact of a new, American museum aesthetic propagated by the United States Holocaust Memorial Museum.

Since 1979, the museum in Washington has acquired over 30,000 artefacts germane to the Nazi period. These objects have been integrated into the museum together with photographs and texts. Holocaust survivors have been integrated into the exhibition as living witnesses, both through videos and as museum guides. But despite these new directions, the museum in Washington has re–invented the Yad Vashem museum aesthetic: an elevator takes visitors up into the darkness of Holocaust history and later returns them to the austere cityscape of America's capital's monuments.

The popularity of the Washington museum (as attested by the high attendance numbers), has threatened the monopoly of Yad Vashem as a source of Holocaust knowledge; its nationalistic subtext is seen as irrelevant outside Israel. Furthermore, the financial resources of the Washington museum have enabled it to build new technological, political, and social networks on a national and transnational level, including links with both Yad Vashem and the Auschwitz–Birkenau Museum. By mastery of the principles of success defined by the museum industry that it embodies and exemplifies, it has thus established itself as an authoritative centre of Holocaust commemoration.

4. From Testimony to Authenticity

With the great care and devotion that befits this sacred task, we have treated, preserved and stored them in our archives. (Salmon–Levine et al. 1986:1)

The great irony of Yad Vashem as an institution lay in the fact that Dinur's epistemology of Holocaust research created an opposition between material evidence and surviving individuals. The most compelling evidence of the Nazi crimes, however, was the thousands of survivors who entered Israel after the war, each carrying his or her own history based on experience rather than documentary evidence. The historian's solution to this profound contradiction between people and paper was to translate experience into textual narratives. Thus emerged the concept of survivor testimonies: textual representations from living survivors that could be collated with descriptions of the deceased by surviving relatives. Together with the bureaucratic records left by the Nazis, these testimonies would provide individual case–studies around which documentary history could be reconstructed accurately. Oral histories from survivors were transcribed, and survivors could then be trained by the historical staff to integrate the tropes of Yad Vashem into their stories.[9] In this way, survivors became historical footnotes within the numerical and chronological discourse of Holocaust history.

9. The training of Holocaust survivors is a controversial subject for several reasons: the narrative homogeneity it produces opens survivors to intense criticism from revisionists; it is likely that the training process is reciprocal, and the metaphor of training — which is rarely overtly voiced — signifies the subordination of individuals within the hierarchy of the institution; such subordination, it can be argued, is consistent with the negative reception of survivors (referred to in slang as *sabon* or "soap") by the Israeli public up to the period following the Eichmann trial; by contrast, testimony classes can be a highly redeeming experience for survivors who learn a powerful vocabulary which enables many to bring a discursive order to the chaos of their past experience.

Material relics, by contrast, could be included directly in the museum's exhibition cases. The shocking nature of these material goods, Dinur believed, would be the most powerful medium for "conveying something of the terrors and suffering of the period" (Dinur 1957:16).[10] Artefacts were subsequently taken out of the historical museum and returned to the storerooms as Yad Vashem attempted to de–emphasize the terror in its exhibition and add depth to the museum's ability to relay the spiritual and creative humanity of individual and collective Nazi victims. The redeployment of artefacts at Yad Vashem resulted in the restructuring of the landscape. A new art museum, dedicated in memory of the French resistance, opened as a contiguous expansion of the historical museum. Unlike the historical museum, the art museum introduced a standard, modern art gallery aesthetic into the Yad Vashem model, including white walls and an even lighting (with the exception of a low–light gallery designed to hold fragile drawings from the ghetto in Terezin).[11]

10. For Dinur, material survivors included music and films, as well as objects and human remains.

11. For a retrospective of drawings from Terezin see Shomer-Zeichik (1994).

This new architectural and ideological expansion of the Yad Vashem museum arose in response to criticisms from Jewish leaders outside Israel that Yad Vashem portrayed a nationalist message that was inappropriate in the political context after the 1967 Six–Day War between Israel and the surrounding Arab states. These criticisms were part of a broad reappraisal of Jewish history and philosophy that subsequently came to be reflected in the theory and praxis of the United States Holocaust Memorial Museum.[12] As enthusiasm for the museum in Washington grew, Yad Vashem once again saw the need to reinvent its museum. In June 1993, the foundation pit for a monumental expansion to the historical museum was opened. By January 1994, an experimental exhibition was planned by the Yad Vashem museum curators which was to inaugurate the latest expansion of the historical museum. The goal of the exhibition was to integrate authentic artefacts from the Lodz ghetto with the latest museum technology. Ultimately, the exhibition opened in the main gallery of the art museum since financial crisis and planning delays had impeded the construction the new historical wing.[13]

12. The first and most comprehensive re–reading of Jewish history was David Biale's Power and Powerlessness in Jewish History (1986). Michael Berenbaum's After Tragedy and Triumph: Essays in Modern Jewish Thought and the American Experience (1990) was more significant, however, in that Berenbaum was to become the first director of the Holocaust museum in Washington.

13. This chronology is based on my involvement in the organizational work of the Łódź exhibition, January — July 1994.

5. Negotiating a New Landscape of Authority

In June 1994, as a research assistant for the curator of Yad Vashem's historical museum, I helped to co–ordinate the loan of sewing machines and tables from the Lodz ghetto that now resided in the collection storehouses of the United States Holocaust Memorial Museum. In addition to a team of museum researchers and historians, my work peers included a staff of over thirty museum volunteers, most of them women. About a third of them were survivors.

The co–opting of survivors and authentic artefacts constitutes two of the most prominent acts through which Yad Vashem as an institution has recently attempted to maintain its own symbolic status within the culture of Holocaust commemoration. Yet, beyond the redeployment of people and objects within Yad Vashem, the overall shifting aesthetic of Holocaust museums has engendered a new symbolic relation between Yad Vashem and Auschwitz. Unlike Auschwitz, which since its liberation has always been forced to negotiate a dual identity of place and representation of place (being simultaneously a former death camp and a representation of a death camp) Yad Vashem has never had to negotiate the consequences of its own representation. The post–modern, cognitive framework of Holocaust representations, however, is predicated on an awareness of past models, of which Yad Vashem was the most prominent. Due to the culture which it helped create, therefore, Yad Vashem, like Auschwitz, has become an object of the past which it seeks to describe.

It is unsettling to consider that the crisis of authority at Yad Vashem might signify the displacement of ideological capital with financial capital as the shaping force of Holocaust commemoration. In such a model, a myth of democracy would mystify the agenda of possessive individualism manifest in the collection practices of Western museums. It is important to understand, however, that the shifting balance of authority, which has registered such profound effects at Yad Vashem, is due in part to the inevitable passing of the present generation of Holocaust survivors. Without human survivors only objects will remain to maintain the tangible, three–dimensionality of Holocaust history. Yet, even as objects maintain their continuous vigil, they cannot perpetuate the voices of individual people. As Bourdieu suggests, however, the voice of authority is often more significant than the voice of experience. The shifting contours of Holocaust museum aesthetics must therefore be met with complex readings of Holocaust exhibitions and historiography. These efforts begin with the basic recognition that judgements of taste regarding memorials cannot be dismissed as mere statements of opinion. Rather, they are key expressions of a social world wherein the conflicting subjects and objects of Holocaust representation are negotiated by individuals.

Etymologia opinii: Instytut Pamięci Yad Vashem, w poszukiwaniu nowoczesnych form wystawiennictwa w muzeach Holocaustu

Instytut Pamięci Yad Vashem, założony w 1953 r. w Izraelu, był pierwszym muzeum poświęconym wyłącznie pamięci Holocaustu. Do momentu otwarcia w 1992 r. "United States Holocaust Memorial Museum" w Waszyngtonie, zarówno ze względu na swoją architekturę, jak i pełnioną funkcję, było wzorem przekazywania wiedzy o Holocauście. Imponujące archiwum ucieleśniało jego autorytet i za pomocą posiadanej dokumentacji oraz naukowych badań wspierało wiedzę o przeszłości. Muzeum potwierdzało również rolę Izraela jako miarodajnego zródła wiedzy o Holocauście, określając jasno, że pierwszą lekcją, jakiej należy się nauczyć jest syjonizm.

Osoby, które przeżyły Holocaust postrzegano jako mało znaczącą Diasporę. Ich rola sprowadzała się do tego, by zaświadczyć o Holocauście przyszłym pokoleniom uczonych, a zaraz potem zapomnieć o przeszłości i stać się Izraelczykami. Muzeum Holocaustu w Waszyngtonie łączy dzieje Żydów w USA, znaczenie i posłannictwo historii Holocaustu z potrzebami amerykańskiej publiczności. Kilka podstawowych cech przejęto z estetyki Instytutu Yad Vashem. Nowością było jednak wyeksponowanie oryginalnych artefaktów, będących wymownym i dostrzegalnym świadectwem przeszłości. Nadmiernie uwypukloną syjonistyczną programatykę Yad Vashem zastąpiono bliższą Ameryce problematyką roli Amerykanina jako niezaangażowanego widza. Tych, którzy przeżyli Holocaust uważa się w pierwszym rzędzie za cennych świadków. Są przewodnikami, a ich relacje przekazywane są również za pomocą środków audiowizualnych. Muzeum dzięki swoim ogromnym środkom finansowym dostarcza informacji zwiedzającym, stosując najnowocześniejszą technikę, znaną publiczności na codzień. Bezpośredniość tej, zakrojonej na amerykańską publiczność, estetyki muzealnej podważyła monopol Yad Vashem jako zródła wiedzy o Holocauście, głównie dlatego, że gwarantuje dostęp do tej wiedzy bez konieczności odwiedzania Izraela. Ponieważ Muzeum to w coraz większym stopniu zyskuje uznanie jako centrum pamięci o Holocauście, stanowi dla Yad Vashem wyzwanie. Swój autorytet, jako centrum wiedzy o Holocauście, Yad Vashem usiłuje odzyskać poprzez wzbogacenie sal wystawowych o większą ilość oryginalnych przedmiotów, zaangażowanie osób, które przeżyły Holocaust oraz stworzenie nowego muzeum sztuki.

Meinungsetymologie: Yad Vashem, Wandel der Vorbilder und der Ästhetik der Holocaust Museen

Yad Vashem, gegründet 1953 in Israel, war das erste Museum, das sich ausschließlich der Erinnerung an den Holocaust widmete. Bis zur Einweihung des 'United States Holocaust Memorial Museum' in Washington im Jahre 1992 war es, sowohl was seine Architektur als auch was seine Funktion als Instrument der Wissensvermittlung über den Holocaust betraf, das Vorbild aller übrigen Holocaust–Museen. Sein beeindruckendes Archiv verkörperte die Autorität, die es in bezug auf die Erinnerung an die Vergangenheit mittels Dokumentation und wissenschaftlicher Untersuchungen ausübte. Es begründete auch die zentrale Stellung Israels als maßgebliche Quelle des Wissens über den Holocaust und stellte klar, das die Hauptlektion, die es zu lernen galt, der Zionismus war. Überlebende wurden lediglich als Überbleibsel der gering geachteten Diaspora wahrgenommen. Ihre Rolle bestand darin, zukünftigen Generationen von Wissenschaftlern als Zeugen zu dienen, danach aber sollten sie die Vergangenheit alsbald vergessen und Israelis werden.

Das Holocaust–Museum in Washington, Produkt einer auf breiter Grundlage vorgenommenen Neubewertung der jüdischen Geschichte in den USA, paßte sowohl die Gewichtung als auch die Botschaft der Erinnerung an den Holocaust den Bedürfnissen eines amerikanischen Publikums an. Einige grundlegende Merkmale der Ästhetik von Yad Vashem wurden aufgegriffen. Neu war jedoch die Hervorhebung originaler Artefakte als aussagekräftige und sinnlich wahrnehmbare Zeugnisse vergangener Realitäten. Ebenso wurde die Überbetonung der zionistischen Programmatik von Yad Vashem ersetzt durch eine für Amerika näherliegende Botschaft, nämlich die problematische Rolle der Amerikaner als untätige Zuschauer. Überlebende werden vor allem als wertvolle Augenzeugen und nicht als menschliche Wracks wahrgenommen, und sie können ihre Rolle als Museumsführer und auf Bildschirmen voll ausspielen: Dank seiner gewaltigen finanziellen Ressourcen ist das Museum in der Lage, seine Besucher durch ihnen vertraute moderne Technologie zu informieren.

Die Unmittelbarkeit dieser auf ein amerikanisches Publikum zugeschnittenen Museumsästhetik hat das Monopol von Yad Vashem als Quelle des Wissens über den Holocaust in Frage gestellt, vor allem insofern, als es, auch ohne Israel zu besuchen, Zugang zu diesem Wissen gewährt. Da das Museum mehr und mehr als ein führendes Zentrum der Erinnerung an den Holocaust anerkannt wird und damit Yad Vashems Autorität auf diesem Gebiet herausfordert, hat Yad Vashem versucht, durch Weiterentwicklung seiner eigenen Museumsästhetik seine Geltung wiederzugewinnen: Durch mehr originale Gegenstände in den Ausstellungsräumen, ein verstärktes Heranziehen von Überlebenden und den Aufbau eines neuen Kunstmuseums.

BIBLIOGRAPHY / BIBLIOGRAFIA / BIBLIOGRAPHIE

Amishai-Maisels, Ziva. 1993. *Depiction and Interpretation: The Influence of the Holocaust on the Visual Arts*. Oxford: Pergamon Press.

Ankersmit, F.R. 1988. "Historical Representation", *History and Theory*, XXVII, 3, 205-228.

Ankersmit, F.R. 1989. *The Reality Effect in the Writing of History. The Dynamics of Historiographical Topology*. Amsterdam: Koninklijke Nederlandse Akademie van Wetenschappen.

Ankersmit, F.R. 1990. "Reply to Professor Zagorin", *History and Theory*, XXIX, 3, 275-296.

Antelme, Robert. 1990. *Das Menschengeschlecht. Als Deportierter in Deutschland*. München: Deutscher Taschenbuch-Verlag.

Apenszlak, Jacob, ed. 1943. *The Black Book of Polish Jewry: An Account of the Martyrdom of Polish Jewry under the Nazi Occupation*. N.p.: American Federation for Polish Jews, with Association of Jewish Refugees and Immigrants from Poland.

Appadurai, Arjun. 1990. "Disjuncture and Difference in the Global Cultural Economy", *Public Culture*, 2/2, 1-23.

Batchelor, David. 1991. "Abstraction, Modernism, Representation", in Andrew Benjamin and Peter Osborne, eds., *Thinking Art: Beyond Traditional Aesthetics*, 45-57. London: Institute of Contemporary Arts.

Benjamin, Andrew. 1991. *Art, Mimesis and the Avant-Garde*. London: Routledge.

Berenbaum, Michael. 1990. *After Tragedy and Triumph: Essays in Jewish Thought and the American Experience*. Cambridge: Cambridge University Press.

Biale, David. 1986. *Power and Powerlessness in Jewish History*. New York: Schocken Books.

Boteach, Shmuel. 1995. *Wrestling with the Divine: A Jewish Response to Suffering*. Northvale, NJ: Jason Aronson.

Bourdieu, Pierre. 1979. *Distinction. A Social Critique of the Judgement of Taste*. London: Routledge and Kegan Paul.

Bourdieu, Pierre. 1994. *In Other Words*. Oxford: Blackwell.

Braun, Robert. 1994. "The Holocaust and Problems of Historical Representation", *History and Theory*, XXXIII, 2, 172-197.

Brumlik, Micha. 1992. "Trauerrituale und politische Kultur nach der Shoah in der Bundesrepublik", in Hanno Loewy, ed., *Holocaust: Die Grenzen des Verstehens. Eine Debatte über die Besetzung der Geschichte*, 191-212. Reinbek: Rowohlt.

Cargas, Harry James. 1990. *Shadows of Auschwitz: A Christian Response to the Holocaust*. New York: Crossroad.

Certeau, Michel de. 1988. *The Writing of History*, trans. Tom Conley. New York: Columbia University Press.

Cioran, E.M. 1990. *A Short History of Decay*, trans. Richard Howard. London: Quartet.

Czarnecki, Joseph P. 1989. *Last Traces. The Lost Art of Auschwitz*. New York: Atheneum.

Dafni, Reuven, ed. 1990. *Yad Vashem: The Holocaust Martyrs' and Heroes' Remembrance Authority, Jerusalem*. Jerusalem: Yad Vashem.

Dałek, Jerzy and Teresa Świebocka. 1989. *Cierpienie i nadzieja. Twórczość plastyczna więźniów obozu Oświęcimskiego.* Katowice: Państwowe Muzeum Oświęcim–Brzezinka; Krajowa Agencja Wydawnicza.

Davis, Colin. 1991. "Understanding the Concentration Camps: Elie Wiesel's *La Nuit* and Jorge Semprun's *Quel Beau Dimanche!*", *Australian Journal of French Studies*, 28/3, 291-303.

Diner, Dan. 1990. "Between Aporia and Apology", in Peter Baldwin, ed., *Reworking the Past: Hitler, the Holocaust and the Historians' Debate*, 135-45. Boston: Beacon Press.

Dinur, Ben-Zion. 1957. "Problems Confronting 'Yad Vashem' in its Work of Research", *Yad Vashem Studies*, 1, 7-30.

Documentation Centre of CUJCR, Bratislava, ed. 1949. *The Tragedy of Slovak Jewry.* Prague: V. Naubert and Sons.

Dunin–Wąsowicz, Krzysztof. 1979. *Ruch oporu w hitlerowskich obozach koncentracyjnych 1933–1945.* Warszawa: Państwowe Wydawnictwo Naukowe.

Eliach, Yaffa. 1988. *Hasidic Tales of the Holocaust.* New York: Vintage Books.

Feldhaus, Franz. N.d. *Ein Lexicon*, col. 1075/76. Wiesbaden: Lönith.

Friedländer, Saul. 1989. "On the Representation of the Shoah in Present-Day Western Culture", in Yehuda Bauer, ed., *Remembering for the Future*, vol.III, 3092-101. Oxford: Pergamon Press.

Friedländer, Saul, ed. 1992. *Probing the Limits of Representation: Nazism and the 'Final Solution'.* Cambridge: Harvard University Press.

Friedländer, Saul. 1992. "Introduction", in Saul Friedländer, ed., *Probing the Limits of Representation: Nazism and the 'Final Solution'*, 1-21. Cambridge: Harvard University Press.

Gossman, Lionel. 1990. *Between History and Literature.* Cambridge: Harvard University Press.

Gradowski, Załmen. 1978. *In hare fin gehinom. A dokument fin Ojszwicer Zonderkommando 1944.* Jerusalem: Chaim Wolnerman. [*W sercu piekła. Dokument oświęcimskiego Sonderkommando 1944.* Archiwum Państwowego Muzeum w Oświęcimiu, Zespół Wspomnienia, t. 135.]

Grassen, Richard W., and Bernhard Holecyek, eds. 1985. *Apokalypse - Ein Prinzip Hoffnung? Ernst Bloch zum 100. Geburtstag.* Heidelberg: Edition Braus.

Hoffmann, Detlef. 1979. "Der Mann mit dem Stahlhelm vor Verdun: Fritz Erlers Plakat zur sechsten Kriegsanleihe 1917", in Berthold Hinz, ed. al., *Die Dekoration der Gewalt: Kunst und Medien in Faschismus*, 100-114. Gießen: anabas.

Hoffmann, Detlef, and Enja Riegel. 1979. "Erst das Sichtbare macht Geschichte anschaulich", *Kunst und Unterricht*, 58, 67-72.

Hoffmann, Detlef. 1994. "Fotografierte Lager. Überlegungen zu einer Fotogeschichte deutscher Konzentrationslager", *Fotogeschichte*, 54: 3-20.

Iggers, Georg. 1993. *Geschichtswissenschaft im 20. Jahrhundert. Ein kritischer Überblick im internationalen Zusammenhang.* Göttingen: Vandenhoeck und Ruprecht.

Kellner, Hans. 1989. *Language and Historical Representation: Getting the Story Crooked.* Madison: University of Wisconsin Press.

Kellner, Hans. 1994. " 'Never Again' is Now", *History and Theory*, XXXIII, 2, 127-44.

Klarsfeld, Serge, ed. 1980. *The Auschwitz Album. Lili Jacob's Album.* New York: The Beate Klarsfeld Foundation.

Kofman, Sarah. 1988. *Erstickte Worte.* Vienna: Passagen Verlag.

Kraus, Ota, and Erich Kulka. 1957 (5th ed.). *Továrna na Smrt. Dokument o Osvětimi.* Prague: Nase Vojsko SPB.

Kulka, Erich. 1958. "200 Hitherto Unknown Photos of Auschwitz", *Yad Vashem Bulletin*, 3, 22-23.

Langbein, Hermann. 1965. *Der Auschwitz-Prozess: Eine Dokumentation.* 2 vols. Vienna: Europa Verlag.

Langbein, Hermann. 1994. *Ludzie w Auschwitz.* Oświęcim: Państwowe Muzeum Oświęcim–Brzezinka.

Lanzmann, Claude. 1986. "Shoah as Counter-Myth", trans. Jonathan Davis. *Jewish Quarterly*, 33, (Spring), 11-12.

Laytner, Anson. 1990. *Arguing with God: A Jewish Tradition.* Northvale, NJ: Jason Aronson.

Levi, Primo. 1992. *Ist das ein Mensch.* München: Deutscher Taschenbuch-Verlag.

Liebman, Charles S., and Eliezer Don-Yehiya. 1983. *Civil Religion in Israel.* Berkeley: University of California Press.

Lyotard, Jean-Franois. 1988. *The Differend: Phrases in Dispute*, trans. Georges van den Abbeele. Manchester: Manchester University Press.

Lyotard, Jean-Franois. 1992. *The Postmodern Explained to Children: Correspondence 1982-1985*, trans. various. London: Turnaround.

MacCanell, Dean. 1976. *The Tourist: A New Theory of the Leisure Class.* London: Macmillan.

Mais, Yitzhak. 1988. "Institutionalizing the Holocaust", *Midstream*, 34/9, 16-20.

Nancy, Jean-Luc. 1993. *The Birth to Presence*, trans. Brian Holmes et al. Stanford: Stanford University Press.

Neusner, Jacob. 1981. *Stranger at Home: 'The Holocaust', Zionism, and American Judaism.* Chicago: University of Chicago Press.

Okely, Judith. 1994. "Vicarious and Sensory Knowledge of Chronology and Change: Ageing in Rural France", in Kirsten Hastrup, ed., *Social Experience and Anthropological Knowledge*, 45-64. London: Routledge.

Orzeszko, Tadeusz. 1971. "Przegląd Lekarski — Oświęcim" *Relacja chirurga oświęcimskiego.* Kraków: Państwowy Zakład Wydawnictw Lekarskich.

Oshry, Ephraim. 1983. *Responsa from the Holocaust*, trans. Y. Leiman. New York: Judaica Press.

Parcer, Jan. 1993. *Memorial Book. The Gypsies at Auschwitz–Birkenau. Księga Pamięci. Cyganie w obozie koncentracyjnym Auschwitz–Birkenau. Gedenkbuch. Die Sinti und Roma im Konzentrationslager Auschwitz–Birkenau.* München: Państwowe Muzeum Oświęcim–Brzezinka; K.G. Saur–Verlag.

Piper, Franciszek. 1991. "Estimating the Number of Deportees to and Victims of the Auschwitz-Birkenau Camp", *Yad Vashem Studies*, 21, 49-103.

Pressac, Jean-Claude. 1994. *Die Krematorien von Auschwitz. Die Technik des Massenmordes.* München: Piper.

Rogoff, Irit. 1993. "Von Ruinen zu Trümmern", in Silvia Baumgart, ed., *Denkräume zwischen Kunst und Wissenschaft. Kunsthistorikerinnen-tagung in Hamburg.* Berlin: Reimer.

Rosenbaum, Irving J. 1976. *The Holocaust and Halakhah.* N.p.: Ktav.

Rosenberg, Bernhard H., and Fred Heuman, eds. 1992. *Theological and Halakhic Reflections on the Holocaust.* Hoboken, NJ: Ktav, for the Rabbinical Council of America.

Russell, Lord, of Liverpool. 1976. *The Scourge of the Swastika.* London: Corgi.

Salmon-Levine, Irit, Ilana Furi, and Yitzhak Mais, eds. 1986. *Testimony: Art of the Holocaust.* Jerusalem: Yad Vashem.

Sanders, Keith P. 1980 (2nd ed.). "Photojournalism Research", in Clifton C. Edom, ed., *Photojournalism: Principles and Practices*, 164–183. Dubuque, Iowa: Wn. C. Brown.

Schindler, Pesach. 1990. *Hasidic Responses to the Holocaust in the Light of Hasidic Thought.* Hoboken, NJ: Ktav.

Schubert, Dietrich. 1993. "Das 'harte Mal' der Waffen oder die Darstellung der Kriegsopfer", in Michael Diers, ed., *Mo(nu)mente: Formen und Funktionen ephemerer Denkmäler*, 137–152. Berlin: Akademie.

Segev, Tom. 1993. *The Seventh Million: The Israelis and the Holocaust.* New York: Hill and Wang.

Shomer-Zeichik, Bella. 1994. *Max Placek: Double Signature. Portraits of Personalities from the Terezin Ghetto.* Jerusalem: Yad Vashem.

Signal: Eine kommentierte Auswahl völlig unveränderter Beiträge aus der Propoganda–Zeitschrift der deutschen Wehrmacht. 1977. Vol.5. Hamburg: Jahr–Verlag KG.

Smoleń, Kazimierz and Teresa Świebocka. 1990. *Auschwitz — zbrodnia przeciwko ludzkości.* Warszawa: Państwowe Muzeum Oświęcim–Brzezinka; Książka i Wiedza.

Świebocka, Teresa, Jonathan Webber, and Connie Wilsack, eds. 1993. *Auschwitz: A History in Photographs.* Oświęcim, Bloomington, Warsaw: The Auschwitz–Birkenau State Museum, Indiana University Press, Książka i Wiedza.

Trunk, Isaiah. 1982. *Jewish Responses to Nazi Persecution: Collective and Individual Behavior in Extremis.* New York: Stein and Day [1979].

Wrocklage, Ute. 1992. *Architektonische und skulpturale Gestaltung des Konzentrationslagers Neuengamme nach 1945.* Oldenburg: unpublished M.A. typescript.

Wśród koszmarnej zbrodni. Notatki więźniów Sonderkommando. 1975. Oświęcim: Państwowe Muzeum Oświęcim–Brzezinka.

Young, James E. 1992. *Beschreiben des Holocaust.* Frankfurt am Main: Jüdischer Verlag.

Young, James E. 1993. *The Texture of Memory: Holocaust Memorials and Meaning.* New Haven: Yale University Press.

Young, Robert. 1990. *White Mythologies: Writing History and the West.* London: Routledge.

Zimmels, H. J. 1977. *The Echo of the Nazi Holocaust in Rabbinic Literature.* N. p.: Ktav.

Zych, Adam, and Dorotea Müller–Ott. 1993. *Auschwitz-Gedichte.* Oświęcim: The Auschwitz–Birkenau State Museum.